Inside Capitalism

An Introduction to Political Economy

Paul Phillips

Fernwood Publishing • Halifax

Editing: Doug Smith and Karen McElrea
Cover design: Beverley Rach and Larissa Holman
Design and production: Beverley Rach and Brenda Conroy
Printed and bound in Canada by: Hignell Printing Limited

A publication of:
Fernwood Publishing
Site 2A, Box 5, 8422 St. Margaret's Bay Road
Black Point, Nova Scotia, B0J 1B0
and 324 Clare Avenue
Winnipeg, Manitoba, R3L 1S3
www.fernwoodbooks.ca

Fernwood Publishing Company Limited gratefully acknowledges the financial support of the Department of Canadian Heritage, the Nova Scotia Department of Tourism and Culture and the Canada Council for the Arts for our publishing program.

NOVA SCOTIA Tourism and Culture   Le Conseil des Arts du Canada | The Canada Council for the Arts

National Library of Canada Cataloguing in Publication

Phillips, Paul, 1938-
Inside capitalism: an introduction to political economy / Paul Phillips.

Includes bibliographical references and index.
ISBN 1-55266-104-0

1. Economics. 2. Capitalism. 3. Canada—Economic conditions—1991- I. Title.

HB171.P48 2003   330   C2003-900132-6

Contents

Preface and Acknowledgments

A number of years ago I taught Economics of the Labour Process and Labour Relations, one of the core courses in the Labour and Workplace Studies program at the University of Manitoba. It was a somewhat frustrating experience. It was not that the students were particularly bad or lazy or anything like that. It was just that the only prior economics they had was the standard "Economics 101" course on the "Principles of Economics." To put it frankly, such preparation proved more of a hindrance than a help in aiding students to understand how the real labour market worked or how production was organized and income distributed in contemporary Canadian society. They had little knowledge of prevailing economic institutions and virtually no understanding of the central role of political and economic power in determining the organization of the economy and the distribution of income and wealth.

It was, of course, not the fault of the students. Orthodox principles texts, by adopting the mainstream neoclassical methodology, abstract from the real world, its institutions and its power relations. In doing so, workers, managers, employers and consumers all become dehumanized—reduced to automatons, pre-programmed to be *homo economicus*.

This is not the real world of the Canadian worker or of labour and work place studies. Or perhaps I should say it is not the real world at all, certainly not the real world of Canadian society today.

To rectify this deficiency I began looking for alternative texts and sources. There were few. Mostly they were American, a few British. But those texts available were based on a different institutional base, with quite different social values and ideological bases. The power relationships were different, and yet similar. The rich and privileged prevailed over the poor and dispossessed in all societies—but the way they did was not the same. The effects of NAFTA, for instance, are quite different on Canada from what they are on the United States (or Mexico). Canadian labour laws are quite different from those in the U.S.—and the results are quite different. Social programs in Canada are very different from those in the United States, but also from those in Great Britain. One can go on but the unavoidable conclusion is that Canadian political economy is different from that in the U.S. or in the U.K. and should be analyzed as such.

Historically, Canadian political economy has been extensively analyzed. Unfortunately, little by comparison has been written on the contemporary Canadian political economy from a labour perspective, or perhaps one should say from a classical political-economy perspective, in recent years. This book is an attempt to remedy that void. Political economy is not like orthodox, neoclassical economics, which has not changed in any material sense in many decades. Political economy theory evolves with the changing of institutions, the economy and the ideas of people. This book is just a guide to the progress of Canadian society as compiled in the first decade of the twenty-first century.

This is the fourth, and most ambitious and complete, version of my "introduction" to Canadian political economy that I have produced over the last decade or so. The first three were little more than notebooks designed to introduce my students to some of the basic concepts of classical political economy as applied to Canadian society and, in particular, to Canadian labour markets and institutions.

The present edition is greatly expanded in an attempt to capture and convey in a manner accessible not only to students but also to workers and general readers an understanding of how capitalism really works. The capitalist economy is not the sterile, dehumanized world of mainstream economics; not the superficial, self-serving world of the financial newspapers and the major media; but rather a real world that operates in a way that ordinary people often have to try to adjust to the realities of contemporary labour markets and of contemporary society. But they don't have to— our globalized capitalist economy is not inevitable. I hope this book will show, for instance, that unions matter, not only to the welfare of union members, but also to the welfare of society generally and to the continuing functioning of democracy.

Explaining the particular structure of Canadian political economy is the purpose of this book. It would not have been possible, of course, without the help, encouragement and support of a host of people. First, let me recognize the contribution of unions and various union bodies and federations to my life and intellectual growth over the past almost forty years. Unions have their flaws and weaknesses but over my entire career, stretching back to the early 1960s, unions have been the bedrock of solid community values of equality, equity and decency. They have been one of the few institutions that have maintained solid commitment to the welfare of "the little guy," which in practice means the majority of Canadians. In this sense, this book is dedicated to the Canadian labour movement and the people who have sacrificed their personal lives to its advancement and to the welfare of society.

Though I may be indebted to the labour movement for my inspiration, I am also indebted to a number of individuals for this particular publication. Wayne Antony, editor and trouble-shooter for Fernwood deserves much credit because without his support, encouragement and editorial assistance, this book would never have materialized. Doug Smith took my usual turgid prose, complete with Germanic sentence structure, and turned it into understandable and readable English. Bruce Spencer and John Shields reviewed earlier drafts and made valuable suggestions for revisions. The participants at the Society for Socialist Studies workshop, "Teaching Political Economy," held at the "Learneds" in Edmonton, also provided very helpful suggestions for what a book like this should contain. Thanks also to Karen McElrea for her excellent copy editing, to Tara Whittchen for typing the final manuscript, Brenda Conroy for proofreading and Beverley Rach for design and production.

But there are two special people I must thank. The book benefited greatly from the help given me by Jesse Vorst, who personally produced several trial versions for use in labour studies classes and who supplied constant encouragement. But most credit is due to my wife and partner, Donna, who had to listen to my rants and raves over the years. Many have since found their way onto the pages of this book.

Introduction

Political Economy and Contemporary Canadian Capitalism

Winter 2001. The price that Canadian consumers pay for natural gas to heat their homes jumps dramatically. Canadians might wonder why this would happen, particularly since there is is no natural gas shortage in Canada.

And the answer that most economists would give is relatively straightforward. Canada is part of a continental energy market. And since there was a natural gas shortage in the United States, prices rose all across North America. It is simply the law of supply and demand at work.

But other economists, who believe that politics and economics are intertwined, would argue that supply and demand explains only half the story. In the past, government-appointed regulators set the price that Canadian consumers were charged for natural gas. They made sure the gas companies made a profit, but they were also supposed to make sure that consumers were not gouged. The gas companies were free to sell gas to Americans at whatever price they could get. But that changed with the coming of the North American Free Trade Agreement in the 1990s. Under that agreement, Canadian gas producers could not charge U.S. customers more for their gas than they charged Canadian consumers. Canada could no longer have a domestic and export price for natural gas—either Canadian industry would have to lose out on big export sales to the U.S., or Canadians would have to pay the higher prices being charged in the U.S. The interests of the Canadian gas producers were placed ahead of those of Canadian consumers. In other words, politics and power were just as involved in determining Canadian gas prices as the law of supply and demand. Those economists who provide the second sort of explanation are called political economists.

The eminent Yugoslav economist Branko Horvat defined **political economy** as "a fusion of economic and political theory into one single social theory." To political economists the economy cannot be studied or understood independent of the distribution of economic and political power and of the social and political institutions that shape its operations. This approach is not new—some of the earliest and most distinguished economists, including Adam Smith, were political economists.

Economics is often understood as pure market relations independent of political, social and economic power. In this book, economists who view the world in such a fashion are referred to as orthodox economists. While their views have come to dominate the profession, theirs is a narrow approach that minimizes our ability to understand the real world, including the central institution shaping our society, the labour market. By restricting their analysis of welfare and efficiency to

1

the market, they ignore such crucial issues as quality of life, income distribution, the environment and the distribution of political power.

Most people take the **political–economic** world we live in for granted, viewing it as some sort of natural evolution of a market economy. If we are fortunate, we go to work where we follow a learned routine or some supervisor's instructions until our shift is done. We return home, share meals and household chores with our partners. Later, we take our kids—if we have any—to soccer practice or music lessons, and then sit down for an hour or so to watch a TV show that is interspersed with advertising. If we are fortunate and are members of a union, our wages and working conditions will usually be decent and better than those of our non-unionized neighbours. Then, together with our partners, we will earn a comfortable living, own our own house, car and appliances, perhaps have a cottage or be able to travel to sunspots or ski hills during vacations.

On the other hand, if we are among the not so fortunate—if we are unemployed, employed part-time or in low wage, non-unionized jobs, or are a single parent mother—life is very likely to be uncomfortable. We will live in poor quality, frequently rental, housing. At the end of the month there is often not enough money to feed the family. We may then be forced to visit a food bank. We have to rely on a deteriorating and increasingly costly public transit system. Our kids may be able to take advantage of local community club recreation programs but, just as likely in many disadvantaged residential areas that lack such programs, they will find their recreation within the local street culture or watching advertisement-laden TV. Holidays and vacations will be few and far between and usually spent in public parks or in the local area.

A few of us are truly fortunate. We have really well-paying, flexible and enjoyable jobs or we have our own private businesses where our employees generate the surplus income we enjoy. Our houses are large and upscale, with multiple vehicles gracing our driveways. Foreign recreational travel is a regular part of our annual routine. We can afford the best restaurants and season tickets to hockey and football, theatre, opera and the symphony. Our kids get the best schooling and virtually unlimited access to sport, recreational and cultural programs and facilities.

One thing that all Canadians are supposed to have is universal access to health care and to quality primary and secondary education. Unfortunately, the last few government cutbacks to social programs have undermined the universality of access to these social programs, at least for the lower of these three strata of society. But that is getting ahead of our story.

Such is the world we live in—the political–economic world we inhabit. Few of us question it. We grouse about taxes without necessarily recognizing that taxes are the price we pay for health care, education, roads, public transit, snow clearing, recreation and cultural facilities—all the social infrastructure that we rely on to make life liveable and secure. Indeed, taxes are the price of civilization. We complain about low wages. But do we ask why the wages of some workers are below any decent level? Even if we do ask, do we have any answers? What can we do about it? We condemn high prices and inflation without ever asking what causes them.

Every four years or so, provincial and federal politicians bombard us with promises to deal with our grievances. The parties on the right say "cut taxes." What they neglect to add is that in order to cut taxes they will have to cut services. Moreover, most of the tax cuts will benefit our third group, the "truly fortunate." Cuts to services will fall disproportionately on the first two groups, particularly the "unfortunate," the poor. These same parties argue that we can't raise wages, for that will cause inflation and unemployment. We must remain competitive, they argue, and we can only do this by holding down wages, making labour markets "flexible," working longer hours or taking two jobs, and postponing retirement. There is no alternative (the TINA argument pioneered by former British Prime Minister Margaret Thatcher), they claim, because the *market* dictates that workers must work harder and longer for Canadian business to remain competitive. Because this world view is in reality an attempt to revive in extreme form the economic policies of nineteenth-century liberalism, which argued against government interference in the market, it has come to be known as neoliberalism. (Neoliberalism is an orthodox economics taken to its extremes.)

> ### 1.1 The Conflict between Democracy and Neoliberalism
>
> The author [John Gray] concludes that "the free market is not, as New Right thinkers have imagined or claimed, a gift of social evolution. It was an end product of social engineering and unyielding political will, feasible in nineteenth-century England only because, and for as long as, functional democratic institutions were lacking.... [T]he implications for the project of constructing a worldwide free market are... that the rules of the game of the market must be *insulated from democratic deliberation. Democracy and the free market are rivals, not allies.*" ...
>
> Gray knows whereof he speaks because he was, until recently, closely associated with Margaret Thatcher and the New Right. "Those who seek to design a free market on a world wide basis," he wrote, "always insisted that the legal framework which defines and entrenches it must be placed beyond the reach of any democratic legislature."
>
> –Kari Polanyi-Levitt, "Some Books Refuse to Go Away," *Signalling LEFT*, vol. 2, no. 2 (June 2000) p. 12

But are these neoliberal[1] arguments, which underpin our current political economy, really valid? Are we so bound by grim economic "laws" that have given a name to economics from its early years—*the dismal science?* Must we accept the economic order we see around us? Why are we denied the democratic right to use legislation to change the rules of the game so that the economy serves people rather than the other way around?

The neoliberal argument is based on a number of fundamental assumptions that are, at best, questionable. The first is that the market is an efficient and democratic institution, even though democracy in this instance is defined as "one dollar, one vote," not "one person, one vote." But we all should ask: what is efficient and democratic about a system that pays CEOs over one hundred times as much as the average worker at the same company, or pays huge bonuses to its executive officers even as the company is falling into bankruptcy?

The second assumption is that markets involve competition between equal individuals or companies. Each firm, it is assumed, will compete with all the others by lowering prices to the minimum required to cover its costs. Each employer will compete with other employers for the best workers with premium wages. But it also means that when jobs are scarce, non-unionized workers will have to compete among themselves for available work by taking lower wages.

1.2 Adam Smith on the Balance of Power between "Masters and their Workers"

What are the common wages of labour, depends every where upon the contract usually made between those two parties, whose interests are by no means the same. The workmen desire to get as much, the masters to give as little as possible. The former are disposed to combine in order to raise, the latter in order to lower the wages of labour.

It is not, however, difficult to foresee which of the two parties must, upon all ordinary occasions, have the advantage in the dispute, and force the other into a compliance with their terms. The masters, being fewer in number, can combine much more easily; and the law, besides, authorises, or at least does not prohibit their combinations, while it prohibits those of the workmen. We have no acts of parliament against combining to lower the price of work; but many against combining to raise it. In all such disputes the masters can hold out much longer. A landlord, a farmer, a master manufacture, or merchant, though they did not employ a single workman, could generally live a year or two upon the stocks which they have already acquired. Many workmen could not subsist a week, few could subsist a month, and scarce any a year without employment. In the long-run the workman may be as necessary to his master as his master is to him, but the necessity is not so immediate....

Masters are always and every where in a sort of tacit, but constant and uniform combination, not to raise the wages of labour above the actual rate. To violate this combination is every where a most unpopular action, and a sort of reproach to a master among his neighbours and equals.... Masters too sometimes enter into particular combinations to sink the wages of labour even below this rate.... [When the workers resist, they] very seldom derive any advantage from the violence of those tumultuous combinations, which, partly from the interposition of the civil magistrate, partly from the superior steadiness of the masters, partly from the necessity which the greater part of the workmen are under of submitting for the sake of present subsistence, generally end in nothing, but the punishment or ruin of the ring-leaders.

–Adam Smith, *The Wealth of Nations*, 1776

The third is, in the words of Margaret Thatcher, that "there is no such thing as society. There are only individuals and families." That means that people all act as individuals without concern for the wider society. We are not, as the Bible would have it, "our brother's keeper."

A fourth assumption is that information is equally available to everyone in the marketplace. This assumption is perhaps one of the hardest to accept. Were cigarette smokers aware of the health hazards of smoking before the 1990s? Were car-buyers knowledgeable about the dangers of exploding gas tanks or tires when they bought certain models of vehicles? Were workers aware of the dangers of asbestos or PCBs when they were instructed by their employers to work with these hazardous materials?

One can go on and on with the list of restrictive assumptions that have to be made about markets, corporations, consumers and workers to justify the neoliberal model of the economy and the policies that follow. But probably the greatest weakness in this analysis is the absence of any concept of the importance of power in the performance of the economy. It is true that **market power** is a concern of many orthodox economists. When Air Canada took advantage of its economic power and the lack of regulation of the Canadian airline industry to destroy its main competitor, Canadian Airlines, orthodox economists recognized that the development was not a positive one for Canadian travellers. However, even though market power and unfettered competition had delivered Canadians into the hands of one corporation, the only solution that orthodox economists could provide was to open up the Canadian market to competition from U.S. airlines. This solution would likely lead to a situation where a powerful U.S. airline destroyed Air Canada.

Such market power, however, is just the tip of the iceberg in structuring our capitalist economy. Political economists are also concerned about the central role played by the state in distributing power within society. Furthermore, there are many other sources of power—political, institutional and class—which determine the performance of the economy and the distribution of the spoils. One of the main things that distinguishes political economy from orthodox, mainstream economics is its inclusion of power in analyzing contemporary Canadian capitalism.

The Intellectual Roots of Political Economy

The Greek word "oikonomia," from which our word "economy" is derived, originally meant "household management." In early societies this was a natural association since the household was central to these economies. However, by the time Adam Smith (often referred to as the "father of modern economics"), published his famous treatise *The Wealth of Nations* in 1776, Western Europe had already experienced three centuries of expanding trade, organized not by households but by associations of merchant capitalists. The household, though still the single most important economic institution, was gradually giving way to business institutions organized specifically for the purpose of carrying out market activity.

By Smith's time, these business organizations were involved not only in trade but increasingly in the production of goods and services that had previously been produced in the home. To emphasize that he was concerned, not primarily with household management, but with the *public* economy and economic *policy*, Smith and his classical followers adopted the term "political economy"—or the management of the "public economy." While Smith practised political economy, he is often referred to as a classical economist because of the role he played in establishing the discipline.

To Smith, political economy also involved the application of the methods of scientific enquiry to the analysis of the emerging system of markets. His major analytic tool was the **labour theory of value,** which argued that commodities produced for the market had a value based on the amount of labour expended on their production. The labour theory of value was elaborated on by two economists who followed in the classical tradition, but with quite divergent results. David Ricardo, the stockbroker who used his formidable analytic skills to attack the protection afforded English landowners by the existing "corn laws" (tariffs on the import of wheat), emphasized abstract, deductive theorizing.

The third great classical economist was Karl Marx. He elaborated with great effect the labour theory of value and Smith's analysis of stages in economic development from feudal agriculture, through trade, to the emergence of industrial capitalism. Marx also shared with Smith a concern with the economic functions of the state. Smith railed against the state on the grounds that the merchant states became agents for the merchant class, enriching them at the expense of the rest of society. What was required, Smith argued, was the replacement of state regulation with the **"invisible hand"** of the market mechanism where, in theory, everyone's selfish pursuit of economic gain would turn to the benefit of all.

By the time Marx was writing (the first volume of his magnum opus, *Das Kapital*, was published in 1867), Smith's optimistic view of the salutary effects of unregulated markets had proven wrong. Private economic power had usurped the power of the state and, in combination with the state, turned the market from Smith's institution of opportunity into an institution of oppression. It was also an institution that was forced to rely on unemployment and periodic depressions to maintain itself.

Marx combined economic analysis of the **means of production** with social analysis of the **social relations of production,** employing the concepts of power and class. By means of production Marx meant the actual physical plant, buildings, equipment, machinery and resources used to produce output for the market. How business employed labour, organized the workplace, controlled, disciplined and paid the workers, and thus dominated the resulting class system, he referred to as the social relations of production. Marxian political economy, thus, was never confined by the narrow assumptions and abstractions that increasingly characterized orthodox neoclassical economics (though in the Stalinist period in Eastern Europe, it frequently became dogmatic and devoid of intellectual vitality, and ignored the rise to power of the administrative class).

But while Marx and Ricardo were working in the tradition of political economy, other economists were moving the discipline in a different direction. To them economics should focus on the market, not politics. In the hands of these neoclassical (or "new" classical) economists, the discipline became increasingly divorced from observation and analysis of the real world and more a discipline of deductive speculation, mere mathematical formulae without grounding in real time or space. It became focused on pure market relations independent of human agency or institutions, or of political, social and economic power. In the words of the American economist, Robert Heilbroner:

> [economics] ceased to be the proliferation of world views which, in the hands now of a philosopher, now a stockbroker, now a revolutionary, seemed to illuminate the whole avenue down which society was marching. It became instead the special province of professors, whose investigations threw out pin-point beams rather than the wide-searching beacons of the earlier economists.[2]

While this approach came to dominate the profession, eventually becoming the orthodox view, a variety of schools of political economy continued to survive. In Britain and Germany in the late nineteenth century, economic historians argued that neoclassical economics with its emphasis on the individual and on static, equilibrium analysis of quantifiable variables was an inappropriate theoretical framework for the analysis of long-term social and economic change. They began the evolution of **institutional economics**, an approach to political economy that stresses the institutional forces controlling the economy and its organizational structure; and the functions and importance of technology, the state, the law, property rights and social controls in determining economic performance. (Perhaps its two best-known practitioners, however, have been the Americans, John R. Commons and Thorstein Veblen.)

A third element in the evolution of modern political economy can be traced to John Maynard Keynes and Michael Kalecki in the 1920s and 1930s. From different points of view both argued that, at the total economy level, the market was not a stable, self-regulating mechanism as neoclassical theory postulated—and they had the evidence of the great depression of the 1930s to prove their views. In fact their views had much in common with the crisis theory of Marxian political economy. As a result, in this book I will draw from all these strands of political economy to present a model of the contemporary economy.

Canadian Political Economy

Political economy has had a long and honorable tradition in Canada and for many years represented the core of the economics discipline. The main reason was the importance given to economic history and, in particular, to the uniqueness of the Canadian pattern of economic development. Inspired by the work of the late Harold Innis, a dominant figure at the University of Toronto from the 1920s through the 1940s, Canadian economic historians developed a non-Marxist school of political economy. This was based on what Innis called **staples** (raw material exports) and the impact of staple dependence on other political, social and economic institutions. It has proved to be Canada's major international contribution to the field of economics.

In the last three decades, a new school of Canadian political economy has attempted to integrate much of this traditional institutional Canadian approach with elements of Marxist political economy and Keynesian/Kaleckian economics. As the editors of a recent collection in this new school point out there are still many issues to work out:

> [W]hile political economy is based on a tradition that investigates the relationship between economy and politics as they affect the social and cultural life of societies, within political economy there have been divergent tendencies. Broadly, the liberal political economy tradition has placed determinate weight on the political system and markets, while the Marxist tradition grants primacy to the economic system and classes. Such facile statements, however, underplay the complexity of positions within each tradition. Political economy at its strongest has focused on processes whereby social change is located in the historical interaction of the economic, political, cultural, and ideological moments of social life, with the dynamic rooted in socio-economic conflict.[3]

The intent of this book is to provide the tools to understand more fully the political economy of everyday life, of work and leisure, wages and prices, unemployment and consumption. It should help the reader to evaluate the pronouncements of governments, business and right-wing policy institutes supporting cuts to unemployment insurance, privatizing education and tax cuts for the wealthy. Our world is being constantly shaped and reshaped by conflict and change—the political economist looks for the causes of those changes and seeks to develop policies that can harness that change.

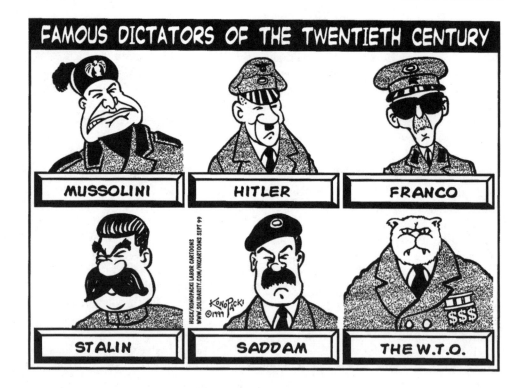

Notes

1. I use the term *neoliberal* throughout this book to describe the policies of privatization, deregulation and marketization associated with the right-wing and corporate political agenda that has come to dominate politics virtually world-wide in the last two decades. Earlier, in the 1980s, the term frequently used was *neoconservative* to describe this agenda, primarily because it was associated with the Conservative parties of Britain and Canada and the declared ultra-conservative, U.S. President Ronald Reagan. However, the term neoconservative included backward views of social policy—intolerance to gender equality, sexual diversity, civil rights, ethnic, racial and religious diversity— while the more pervasive neoliberalism was restricted to resurrecting the laissez-faire (in literal translation, "leave alone") economic policy of the nineteenth century that has come to dominate not only conservative parties, but increasingly, also liberal, communist and even social democratic governments. Thus, I shall use neoliberal to describe this right-wing political agenda throughout though it should be clear that this also incorporates what others refer to neoconservative.

2. Robert Heilbroner, *The Worldly Philosophers* (New York: Simon and Schuster, 1972), p. 166.

3. Wallace Clement and Glen Williams, "Introduction," in *The New Canadian Political Economy*, Wallace Clement and Glen Williams, eds. (Kingston: McGill-Queen's, 1989), pp. 6–7.

Chapter 1

Political Economy and Economics
The Issues

The Political Economy of What? How? and for Whom?

Any society needs to produce goods and services to fulfil basic human needs—food, clothing, shelter—but few societies today produce only these necessities. In economics what is produced beyond mere necessity (or subsistence) is called a surplus. It is necessary, therefore, for a society not only to decide how the necessities are to be produced, but also how, how much and what surplus goods and services are to be produced. Therefore, any society must have a mechanism for determining what is to be produced. Second, it needs a method for organizing production. Finally, of course, the goods and services produced must ultimately be distributed for consumption. Therefore, there must be a mechanism for deciding who will receive those goods and services and, in particular, who will receive the surplus. In short, the questions any society must determine are what, how and for whom the system will produce. The way those questions are answered determines the nature of that society's economic system. Within subsistence and traditional societies the most important mechanisms have been the family, custom and religious practice; within command economies (such as the former Union of Soviet Socialist Republics) it has been political decision-making; and within both market socialist societies (such as Yugoslavia) and market capitalist societies it is the market.

Subsistence and Traditional Societies

Subsistence and traditional, non-market societies[1] relied primarily on the family, often composed of many generations and related nuclear families, the tribe or clan and on custom to determine what and how to produce. In these societies, the surplus was often minimal and consumed communally. Little was ordinarily produced for trade with others inside or outside the family or clan. Within the family, the distribution of work was organized primarily around a sexual division of labour. The limited surplus that was produced usually would be shared through feasts and other social gatherings or used to support a religious and political leadership. Where, as in early Egyptian kingdoms, this leadership became a ruling elite over a larger body of peoples, some of the production was done by slaves. In these societies, the surplus was larger and was controlled by the rulers, who commanded that it be used to construct monuments and temples (for example, the pyramids). In similar societies where there were significant surpluses and private wealth accumulated, there were methods of redistribution, such as the Jewish custom of "Jubilee,"

1.1 The Sexual Division of Labour among the Pre-European-Contact Cree

In the [Cree] hunting camps a division of labour based on sex was evident. The primary male role was that of hunter and trapper.... They butchered their kills and hauled back meat from the hunt. Men did the heavy work of transporting supplies and setting up camp, and they also manufactured most wooden articles, such as toboggans, sleds and snowshoe frames. Women's tasks were primarily performed in the vicinity of the base camp. They caught fish with set lines and hunted or trapped small game such as hare and ptarmigan.... Women also performed day-to-day tasks in the camp, such as gathering and splitting firewood, replacing conifer bough flooring, cooking meals, and preparing hides and pelts, as well as engaging in constant manufacture and mending of moccasins, mittens and other apparel. Adolescent daughters aided in these tasks and in the care of younger children.

–Alan McMillan, *Native Peoples and Cultures of Canada* (Vancouver: Douglas and McIntyre, 1995), p. 117

---

the redistribution of wealth every fifty years, or the Canadian west coast Aboriginal custom of the "potlatch."

This is not to say there was no trade. Aboriginal peoples in North America traded a number of products, most notably obsidian (a volcanic glass used for making cutting tools), silica stone, copper, shells, and amber. These products were traded for thousands of years and in some cases over many thousands of kilometres, long before the arrival of the Europeans. Trade provided tribes with the opportunity to exchange surplus local production in areas where these resources were plentiful[2] for goods and resources that were not available in that area. Such trade goods may well have also served as a source of food and subsistence goods for nomadic tribes. Trade in perishables also took place between neighbouring tribes. For instance, the Huron Indians traded surplus corn from their cultivated fields for animal products, particularly hides used for making clothing, with their hunting neighbours, the Nippising. However, as the *Historical Atlas of Canada* notes (volume 1, plate 14): "wherever it took place, trade was integrated with local economies that provided for most subsistence needs."

In the feudal societies of the Middle Ages, the responsibility for answering basic economic questions was spread between the family, custom and political (including military) and religious institutions. The market played only a minimal role in determining what was to be produced, who was to produce it and who got the surplus. In large measure, these issues were resolved by the customary obligations that the mass of agricultural workers owed to the hierarchy of upper classes.

The classic example was the European manorial system. The land was technically owned by the king or prince of the region, who parcelled it out to his lords and knights in exchange for tribute and military support. The lords of the manor, in turn, allocated sub-plots to their serfs, agriculturists tied to the land who practised a form of mixed farming. The lord also was required to provide such facilities as a grain mill and a blacksmith's shop, while the serf was obligated to provide the lord with both labour to till the lord's land and a portion of the produce of the serf's land. These obligations—in labour, money or produce—were fixed by custom or, in some cases, by law. The income of the peasant, therefore, was determined by the bounty of nature, the home industry of his family and by the beneficence of his lord.

Again, this does not mean that markets did not exist, particularly for luxury goods not available locally. Rather, it means that the greatest number of people produced for themselves (production for use, not trade), with a portion of what they produced being taxed away to support the political-military superstructure (the ruling classes) and only surplus output entering the marketplace.

State or church regulations usually governed the prices in the markets that this limited surplus was sold in. The doctrine of "just price," laws banning or limiting usury (charging interest on loans) and regulation of wages were all partially successful attempts to regulate markets to achieve societal goals. It was only with the specialization of economic functions, the resulting increase in the complexity of the economy and the rise of capitalism that markets became the dominant institution by which goods and services and incomes were allocated. In the middle of the nine-

> ### 1.2 Potlatch
>
> The potlatch, from the Chinook word *Patshatl*, validated status, rank and established claims to names, powers and privileges. Wealth in the form of utilitarian goods such as blankets, carved cedar boxes, food and fish or canoes, and prestige items such as slaves and coppers were accumulated to be bestowed on others or even destroyed with great ceremony. Potlatches were held to celebrate initiation, to mourn the dead, or to mark the investiture of chiefs in a continuing series of often competitive exchanges between clans, lineages and rival groups. A great potlatch could be many years in the making, might last for several days, and would involve fasting, spirit dances, theatrical demonstrations and distribution of gifts. An intolerant federal government banned the potlatch from 1884 to 1951, ostensibly because of native treatment of property.
>
> –Potlatch, *The Canadian Encyclopedia*, 2nd edition (Edmonton: Hurtig, 1988), vol. 3, p. 1731

teenth century Britain became the first nation to accept self-regulating markets. The results for working people were drastic. Employers were no longer bound by traditional obligations, which often required them to pay their workers enough to survive. Now wages were set in the labour market. Huge cities grew up, and because wages were so low, working people could not afford sanitary housing. The British parliament soon found itself forced to introduce laws to mitigate the anti-social results of unregulated markets. There were limits on the length of the working day and child labour, and regulation of housing. This attempt to undo the negative consequences of unregulated markets was dubbed by Karl Polanyi, a major historian of economic institutions, the "double movement." As the market invaded society and destroyed its social support institutions, new institutions and rules emerged to protect society. He wrote, "for a century the dynamics of modern society was governed by a double movement: the market expanded continuously but this movement was met by a countermovement checking the expansion in deliberate directions." (He was referring particularly to the growth of the union movement and labour legislation controlling wages and working conditions during the second half of the nineteenth century.)[3]

Command Economies

In planned economies with state ownership of the means of production, such as the former Union of Soviet Socialist Republics and its Eastern European allies, China and Vietnam (at least before the widespread introduction of market reforms) and contemporary Cuba, how, what and for whom to produce were political decisions. Because these decisions were communicated to producers as orders, these economies came to be known as command economies. (These societies usually described themselves as socialist societies, because the means of production—capital, natural resources and land—were socially owned, that is owned by the state. They viewed themselves as alternatives to capitalist societies, or societies in which the means of production were owned by individuals known as capitalists.)

In the former Soviet Union the national political body, the Central Committee of the Communist Party and its executive Politburo, would establish goals for the desired output levels of various industrial, agricultural and service sectors. Using these goals, the national economic planning body would establish targets for production of the major sectors of the economy such as steel or wheat. Sectoral and regional planning agencies would then allocate targets and quotas to enterprises, factories and collective farms, usually with some form of incentive for achieving targets or penalties for not meeting them. Government planning bodies also made basic decisions on the proportion of resources (such as coal for the steel industry), raw materials and capital goods (such as tractors for wheat farms) that were to go to different sectors, industries or firms. The prices of these resources were set to represent planning values and not necessarily market values.

The planning proposals were reviewed by local enterprises, which then could suggest revisions that travelled back up the planning chain. After this back-and-forth process a final (usually a five-year) plan was adopted. There were, of course, frequent revisions to the plan, which had to be constantly altered in response to actual performance. Goods and services were distributed through markets and stores but at prices that reflected political and planning priorities with respect to distribution rather than market prices. Thus, for example, bread prices and housing rents were much lower than would prevail in a market economy. The frequent problems of shortages, rationing and lineups for many goods and apartments occurred because people wanted to buy more than the plan called for or that the enterprises could supply at the planned prices.

These economies shared with traditional economies the characteristic that "political" and "distributional" criteria prevailed to a much greater extent in determining what to produce and who would get it than in market economies. In addition, allocation of many goods, such as housing, tended to reflect social or political priorities rather than the ability and willingness to pay that characterizes the market system. In this respect, the Soviet attitude toward housing was similar to Canada's attitude toward health care—both were considered social rights.

This is not to say that markets play no role in real-world command economies. To a greater or lesser extent in the various countries that had, or have, command systems, small firms such as small, private agricultural plots and personal services, and even occasionally larger firms, sold or sell their output in uncontrolled markets. In any case, once the supply of goods and services for consumption is determined, it is usually distributed in large part through consumer markets though, as I have noted, at plan-determined prices.

What happens if the planners err, producing too much of one good and not enough of another? In market economies, prices of goods in short supply would rise and those of surplus products would fall. That is, "rationing" between consumers is accomplished through changes in relative prices. In the command economy, in contrast, planners would attempt to alter the quantities of these goods produced in the following period and resort to rationing or storage in the short run.

Market Socialism

Not all socialist states have relied on political decision-making to determine production, investment and consumption. Market socialist countries, such as the former Yugoslavia, have mixed public ownership of the means of production with markets. As a result, the income that would otherwise accrue to the owners of the means of production (which we usually refer to as *property*) in a capitalist economy belongs to the public. This also affects the motivation of firms: the prime motive for a privately owned firm is to maximize profits; however, a publicly owned firm may best serve its owners' interests by producing higher levels of output at lower prices. This difference in motivation can be seen in public electrical systems and automobile insurance plans in Canada, which aim to deliver electric power or car insurance to provincial consumers at cost-of-production, or close to break-even, prices and not to make profits.

In market socialism, planning takes place primarily to predict what the market *would* accomplish if it were efficient and unrestrained and included *all* of the costs of production and consumption (including such costs as accrue to society at large, like pollution). Planning would also be required to ensure that adequate savings and investments took place and, in the appropriate sectors, to guarantee sustainable rates of income growth and full employment without supply bottlenecks.

There are two main variants of market socialism. The first is similar in many respects to the command system, where planners set "shadow prices" at levels they expect the open market would ideally produce. Consumers and producers would make their decisions on the basis of these prices. If the planners are wrong, the short-run surpluses and shortages would be indicators to alter prices through a series of successive approximations until markets clear—that is, until there are no shortages or surpluses at the planners' prices. The same mechanism would hold for the labour market, allowing free mobility of labour. The elimination of individual non-labour income (interest, profits and rent) would tend to diminish the unequal "voting power" in the market by reducing the spread in incomes. For example, Yugoslavia had the most equal distribution of incomes of any market economy in the 1970s and 1980s.

A second variant of market socialism, involving some form of worker or labour self-management, has become more popular in recent years. Productive capital and resources would be owned either socially (by society), by the workers in each enterprise collectively or by the state, but the management of the individual enterprises would be the responsibility of the workers employed in the firms. Each enterprise would be forced to compete in the marketplace for the consumer's dollar. The primary responsibility of the planners would be to ensure a level of savings and investment that would achieve desired levels of economic growth and employment, and would provide for necessary social and economic infrastructure.

The closest approximation to this form of socialist economy, the former Yugoslavia, used the market to decide what to produce. But how it was produced and the distribution of income was greatly affected by the political institution of social ownership of most productive capacity, its management by the workers and the redistribution of property income under the self-management system.

1.3 The Yugoslav Experience

After the Second World War and the triumph of Marshall Tito's communists over the fascists, Yugoslavia introduced a centrally planned economy on the Soviet model. However, Tito broke with Stalin over economic policy and Yugoslavia was expelled from the Soviet economic block. In any case, the decentralized nature of the Yugoslav economy and the independence of its peasant class made central planning difficult if not impossible and led Yugoslavia into its experiment with worker self-management. State firms were turned into "socially owned" firms and their management turned over to managers appointed by the workers themselves. Workers' councils in the enterprises determined policy including the level and distribution of incomes within the firms and of new capital investment. It is worthy of note that the distribution of income within Yugoslav firms was the most equal of all countries in the world indicating a high preference for equality and sharing among the Yugoslav people. The workers also determined directly and through their delegates to government legislatures how much money was to be put aside from enterprise incomes for schools and hospitals that served the firms.

The initial success of Yugoslav self-management was demonstrated by the country's economic growth rate in the first few decades after the war, among the highest in the world. In the 1980s the system began to falter quite badly, although for reasons not directly related to its self-management market socialist system. Economic difficulties contributed to ethnic rivalries and the eventual breakup of the country. However, it is interesting to note that the most successful republic of the former Yugoslavia, Slovenia, when it abandoned self-managed socialism, adopted a privatization plan that provided for worker buyouts of most socially owned enterprises thus retaining some elements of the former market socialist system.*

* I have written extensively on the economy of Yugoslavia and of Slovenia. For the history of the experiment with self-managed market socialism, see Paul Phillips and Bogomil Ferfila, *The Rise and Fall of the Third Way: Yugoslavia 1945-1991*, (Halifax: Fernwood, 1992). For a description of Slovenia's post-independence economic system, see Paul Phillips and Bogomil Ferfila, "The Legacy of Socialist Self-Management: Worker Ownership and Worker Participation in Management in Slovenia," *Socialist Studies Bulletin*, no. 61 July-September 2000.

Market Capitalism

The defining characteristic of capitalism is, first and foremost, the fact that most of the means of production are privately owned and controlled. That is, individuals known as capitalists own **capital goods**, those goods such as buildings and machinery that are used to make other goods and services. This can be either directly through the personal ownership of a business (a proprietorship or partnership) or through ownership of shares or stock in a corporate form of business; or indirectly through ownership of shares in investment or mutual funds.

But labour, natural resources and money are not commodities produced for the market. For this reason Karl Polanyi called them **fictitious commodities**, factors that are sold on the market as if they were commodities when clearly they are not. Outside of slave systems, children are not "produced" to be sold on the market. Humans do not produce natural resources.

Money is not produced for sale. The markets for these fictitious commodities are often referred to as factor markets, since these are factors of production. Note also that labour earns wages, but rents, interest and profits are paid to the owners of resources and wealth because they own wealth, not because they earn the income. This is significant for two reasons. The first is that the laws of supply and demand do not operate in markets for fictitious commodities; in particular the supply of these products will not go up merely because demand for them increases. The amount of land in the City of Vancouver will not increase merely because the value of land increases, nor will the number of people in Canada decrease if the demand for workers decreases. Second, payment is made to the

1.4 Alternatives to Private Ownership

Private ownership of productive capital can be contrasted to three other forms of ownership—public, cooperative and social. Canadians are familiar with public ownership, primarily in the form of Crown corporations such as the provincial hydro companies, the post office and the Canadian Broadcasting Corporation (CBC). These corporations are owned and directed by government. However, public owner- ship also includes the educational and health authorities that own or run the public schools and hospitals throughout the country.

Most Canadians are also familiar with cooperative enterprises such as the retail consumer co-ops, particularly in western Canada, or the cooperative consumer banks known as credit unions in English Canada and caisse populaire in French speaking parts of the country. In these cases the consumer members collectively own the means of production. The members control the cooperative on a democratic "one member, one vote" basis rather than the private capital system of "one share, one vote." A less well- known form of cooperative is the producer cooperative, where the basic producers or workers, rather than the consumers, are the co-op members. (This is similar to the second type of market socialism model discussed above.)

The most famous such cooperative is Mondragon, in the Basque region of Spain. This huge complex of manufacturing, research and education, sales, agricultural, fishing and financial cooperatives began in 1956, when five young technical school graduates organized by the local Catholic priest, Don Jose Maria Arrizmendiarrieta, took over a local firm making heaters. From these humble beginnings, the cooperative expanded to a huge complex of cooperatives with over 30,000 worker–owners and more than $6 billion in sales. The complex now includes many diverse industrial and service units including schools, a university, technical school and research institution, farm and fishing organizations, manufacturing plants, hotels and retail stores, all centred around a cooperative bank.

Co-op members elect their managers every four years. Wage rates are restricted to prevent the growth of income differentials among workers and between workers and managers. Also, the worker- owners take part in annual meetings and other cooperative councils to determine the priorities and direction of their cooperatives.

A frequent visitor to Mondragon, community development specialist Greg MacLeod, sums up the achievements of the cooperatives:

> Besides being an economic achievement, the Mondragon experiment is a fascinating social experi- ment. The total complex is owned by workers and consumers. Further, an over-riding altruistic sense of community responsibility dominates the total system. In an age of disillusionment with the prevalent social economic systems, the achievements in Mondragon have had a tremendous attraction for reform-minded people in the Western world.
>
> Greg MacLeod, From Mondragon to America (Sydney, NS: University College of Cape Breton, 1997) p. 13.

Social ownership has been defined as "property owned by everybody and by nobody." In theory, the means of production (productive property) are owned by "society," which receives the income from such property either through taxation, a capital charge or collective consumption. Workers have the use of such property, and management may be exercised either by the workers or by the consumers of the goods and services produced, or jointly by both. Society also constrains the workers' or consumers' rights to destroy, sell or remove the property. In Canada, social property has largely been of the "consumer" type in the form of not-for-profit community organizations—cultural, recreational, health and welfare serv- ices—financed, at least in part, by the public purse. They are frequently under the control of self- appointed and self-perpetuating volunteer boards. These **non-government organizations** or NGOs are now sometimes referred to as the third sector of society, or **civil society**, alongside the private and public sectors.

owners of fictitious commodities based on the simple fact that they are said to own the commodity, not because they have in some way earned the income. (The exception to this is the wages that are paid to a worker for putting his or her labour power to work for the employer.)

However, despite the primacy of the **"invisible hand"** of the market in capitalism, a very significant part of production and distribution is determined by political decisions, particularly in countries that may be considered welfare states or social democracies (for example, Sweden, Denmark, Norway, France, Germany and Austria). In most developed Western countries, for instance, the government's participation in the total economy approaches half, in some cases even more than half, of all that is produced. This includes social services, such as health and education, and government transfer payments, such as old age pensions and social assistance.

Finally, where private ownership and markets fail to efficiently deliver politically acceptable levels of production of socially necessary goods and services, the state intervenes to determine, produce or (re)distribute output in order to do so. This is a hugely important function of the state as indicated in part by the large proportion of the GDP produced or redistributed by contemporary governments. As will be detailed later, markets are prone to failure—failure to provide adequate levels of economic and social infrastructure, failure to provide distributions of income that are not socially and economically destructive, and failure to ensure against repetitive breakdowns that call into question the sustainability not only of the capitalist system but of humanity itself.

While private ownership of the means of production[4] is the dominant characteristic of capitalist economies, it is not the only defining feature. Western capitalist economies rely first and foremost on the market to determine what to produce and how to organize production. Adam Smith provided the rationale for this process, arguing that if everyone had the freedom to seek her or his own benefit in the market, the "invisible hand" of competition would maximize output and incomes. Consumers, he argued, would buy goods and services on the basis of their own preferences, constrained by what they are able to pay. Firms would produce based on the demand for their goods and the production costs they face in the marketplace. Smith noted that the distribution of incomes in this system would depend in part on the distribution of ownership of the means of production and of the talents and skills of individuals.

A similar reliance on the market for the distribution of income marks the third defining characteristic of the capitalist system. But for this to happen we must have markets for everything that goes into production. There must be markets for labour, resources, capital goods, *and* the means to purchase capital goods and resources, that is, a market for money. Labour, of course, will earn wages and salaries. Owners of resources will be paid fees known as rents.[5] Owners of capital and monetary wealth will be paid interest, dividends and profits. Thus markets for labour, resources and wealth determine the distribution of income as if these were commodities produced for consumer markets. (In economics, the term commodity is used to describe a good or service that has been produced or provided with the intent of being put up for sale through the market. If you make a sandwich in your kitchen for your lunch, that sandwich is not a commodity. If you make the same sandwich in the kitchen of a fast food restaurant to be sold to customers, it is a commodity. It is the intent behind its creation that makes it a commodity.)

Markets

The central coordinating institution of contemporary capitalist economies is "the market." In fact, of course, there are many markets and they play different roles and have different functions. Markets may be used to distribute surplus production as happens in traditional subsistence economies. Such markets still exist today as can be seen in summertime farmers' markets and roadside stands. Most major markets are not meant for surplus production—they are meant to market specific products. Furthermore, in these markets the organization of production of commodities determines the social relations between workers and capitalists—the employers are the bosses and the workers take their orders from them.

1.6 Government Participation in Selected Capitalist Countries: General Government Total Outlays as Percentage of GDP in 1998 with Projections for 1999 and 2000			
Country	1998	1999*	2000*
Canada	42.1	41.8	41.5
USA	33.6	32.3	32.3
Japan	36.9	39.2	39.8
Australia	32.9	32.6	32.3
Great Britain	40.2	40.8	41.1
Germany	46.9	47.1	46.8
France	54.3	54.1	53.6
Italy	49.1	49.2	48.5
Austria	49.4	49.3	49.0
Denmark	55.1	54.4	53.4
Norway	46.9	47.0	47.0
Sweden	42.2	42.2	41.8
Spain	41.8	41.6	40.5
All OECD	39.4	39.6	39.5
European Union	47.5	47.6	47.2

* Projected

—OECD, Economic Outlook, June 1999

The principal function of goods and services markets is to bring together producers and consumers in a way that determines the prices and quantities of commodities to be produced. The principal function of markets for labour, resources and money is the determination of the distribution of income between workers and the owners of wealth and of resources. Wealth, of course, can be held in more than one way. The wealthy can own factories, buildings, land, equipment and other forms of real capital goods. Alternatively, wealth can be held in the form of money or claims to money such as bonds, mortgages, treasury bills and other forms of paper wealth, which economists refer to as monetary or financial capital.

It is important to distinguish between the functions in commodity markets and in factor markets because markets for goods and services are real; but markets for labour, resources and money, as we have noted, are markets for fictitious commodities and do not behave like ordinary commodity markets.

Adam Smith believed the "invisible hand" of the marketplace would result in the maximum benefit for all. Unfortunately, however, the human and social costs of reliance on self-regulating markets have proved so devastating that govern-

1.7 Farmers are Victims of Market Failure

Modern food production takes place in a chain that includes oil, fertilizer, seed, chemical, and machinery companies on the input side, and grain companies, railways, packers, processors, retailers, and restaurants on the "downstream" side. Almost every link in this chain, nearly every sector, is dominated by between 2 and 10 multi-billion-dollar multinational corporations:

- Three companies retail and distribute the bulk of Canadian gasoline and diesel fuel.
- Three produce most of the nitrogen fertilizer.
- Nine companies make our pesticides.
- Four companies are gaining control of our seed market.
- Three produce most of our major farm machinery.

The situation is the same on the "downstream" side of the food production chain:

- Nine grain companies collect Canadian grain.
- Two railways haul it.
- Two companies dominate the beef packing sector and a few others dominate pork.
- Three large firms manufacture 87% of the pasta in Canada.
- Four corporations mill 80% of Canadian flour.
- Three companies manufacture the bulk of the soft drinks sold.
- Four companies produce most of the [breakfast] cereal.
- Five companies control food retailing in Canada.
- A handful of restaurant chains control a large and increasing portion of the restaurant business.

The single significant exception to this pattern of extreme concentration is the farm link. In Canada, that link is made up of over 270,000 relatively small family farms.

–National Farmers' Union Submission to the Senate Standing Committee on Agriculture and Forestry, The CCPA Monitor, May 2000

ments have been forced by society to limit certain market excesses, to regulate markets or, in some cases, to replace markets altogether. The reason for these human and social costs is that most, if not all, markets are subject to some degree of breakdown—what economists refer to as **market failure**. There are two indications of a market failure. The first is the inability of some markets to function effectively or efficiently without intervention or controls. Second is the tendency for some unregulated markets to produce unacceptable economic and social consequences. In short, the "invisible hand," for some reason or another, does not function in the manner in which Smith envisaged or even if it did, it produces economic results that are simply not socially acceptable.

Further, market failure can be attributed to two major causes, imperfect markets and market breakdown. **Imperfect markets** result from one party in the market having sufficient power to distort the price or income result in a way that it benefits at the expense of the others. The most obvious case is a **monopoly** (one seller) situation. If you, as a consumer, have a problem with the price or service from your local cable provider, you don't have the option of "going to the competition"—there isn't any. The competitive market does not exist. To deal with this situation, most monopolies are either government-owned or have their prices approved by government-appointed regulators.

Pure monopolies such as cable systems are relatively rare, but at the other end of the spectrum, highly competitive markets of the type envisaged by Smith have also largely disappeared. In agriculture, for example, the small independent farmer now faces the monopoly power of a small number of very large agribusiness suppliers and marketing corporations.

What has replaced small competitive businesses as the dominant players in the market place is a small number of very large corporations that tend to control most markets.

Where there are just a few large firms supplying a market, they are know as **oligopolies**. Each of these dominant firms may have market power based on brand names, copyrights, patents, advertising, product differentiation and so on. Alternatively market power can result from control over specific resources. For example, DeBeers has maintained world-wide control of the diamond trade for decades because of its virtual monopoly in the wholesale trade in the precious stones. Or it may be because a company has developed a unique and effective production or marketing technique or practice. The reason the market fails to function as expected is that the few large firms have the power to manipulate their prices and restrict the supply of a product in order to make higher profits at the expense of consumers, suppliers and workers.

Market failure also occurs when the market is unable to allocate the product or the cost of producing the product. There are two major causes of this kind of market failure: public goods and externalities. They are best explained by example.

A **public good** is one that can be supplied to one consumer or to a thousand without significantly affecting the cost. Take fire protection. A fire department can protect one home or a hundred homes with little extra expense. Now assume fire protection is offered by a private, market-oriented firm. If one home owner decides not to "purchase" fire protection, the owner will still get some protection from the fire department since, in order to protect other adjacent insured houses, the fire department must contain and extinguish a fire in the home of the non-purchasing owner. So the creation of a market gives the incentive for homeowners to "freeload"—to accept the protection without paying for it. If enough homeowners do so then there will be no fire service at all, which then becomes a hazard for everyone. For this reason fire departments, police, the justice system, basic scientific research (since knowledge is a public good) and many other public goods are provided by, or financed and administered by, governments.

Perhaps more important (since they threaten the continued existence of humanity itself) are **externalities**—the costs or benefits of production that are not reflected in the market price of a commodity. The most prominent example is pollution. The production of steel to manufacture cars produces greenhouse gasses. The production of cars from that steel produces further greenhouse gasses. The production, transportation and distribution of gasoline for the cars produce more greenhouse gas. The consumption of gasoline to drive the cars produces even more greenhouse gasses. Yet neither the price of steel, nor of cars, nor of gasoline, nor of driving includes the cost to the environment of the production of greenhouse gasses.

Most producers and consumers would howl in protest if they were told to contribute to the cost of reducing the emission of greenhouse gasses or for paying the cost of trying to lessen the effects of the emission. Yet we all pay indirectly in the form of weather disasters, never mind respiratory and other diseases and the taxes to pay for increased costs of healthcare. Because the costs are not included in the price of the product, polluting products are over-produced. Indeed, because of the incentive firms have to avoid paying the

1.8 The Invisible Foot

Herman Daly, former chief environmental economist of the World Bank, coined the term the *invisible foot* as a counter to Adam Smith's *invisible hand* that suggested that without intending to, individual self-interest would lead—through the "invisible hand"—to maximize societ's welfare. Michael Jacobs, a British economist, uses a slightly different body part to describe the the the unintended *negative* effects on society's welfare of individual self-interest (which economists call negative externalities) as the *invisible elbow*. But whatever part of the body trips you up, it is just as painful! As Daly says, "the 'invisible foot' leads private self-interest to kick the common good to pieces."

–See Herman Daly, *Toward a Steady-State Economy* (San Francisco: Freeman, 1973), p. 17; See also Michael Jacobs, *The Green Economy* (Vancouver: UBC Press, 1993), p. 127.

external costs, the market acts not like an "invisible hand" promoting economic welfare but as an "invisible foot" (or "invisible elbow") promoting economic misery.

Not all externalities are negative. A case in point is job training, the cost of which in a fully market-driven society is borne either by the worker or by the employer or by both. However, training benefits not only the individual and the employer but, by increasing the productivity of the worker, reduces the labour cost of products to consumers and, if the worker subsequently moves to another employer, reduces the cost to that employer. But neither the consumer nor the next employer paid for that training. Because these benefits are not rewarded in the market, there is a tendency for worker training to be excessively costly and undersupplied by the market. In both cases, where externalities are either negative or positive, the only solution is government intervention to regulate (e.g., pollution limits), tax (e.g., pollution taxes), subsidize (e.g., training subsidies) or supply (e.g., training programs).

Imperfect markets and market failure are not the only problems with unregulated markets. Markets also fail to achieve acceptable levels of human welfare or to embody human values. Even if the market were to operate effectively in the way suggested by the theoretical models used by most economists, the results would not necessarily be socially or politically acceptable to the majority of us.

There are three major ways in which market outcomes have proven unacceptable to the majority of Canadians. The first is that the market will not, of its own accord, provide a level of social services and social infrastructure—in particular health care and education—that is required for the best welfare of society. The second is that the market produces such an unequal distribution of income that it threatens not only the social cohesion of society but a collapse in the system itself. Third, there is no mechanism in the market system to guarantee full employment and economic growth. Therefore, without continuous and systematic government intervention, the economy is subject to repeated crises (of unemployment, inflation and stagnation).

The market system will not provide for adequate or socially acceptable supplies of education or health services. Low or even moderate income earners do not have the income or access to credit to pay the full cost of education or health insurance or the cost of catastrophic illness or accident. Private insurance is no answer, as has been demonstrated by the experience in the United States, where a third of the population have no, or insufficient, coverage. Even in the United States, the government has realized that it must provide minimal levels of health care for the aged (Medicare) and the low-income earners (Medicaid).

One reason for the failure of the private insurance system is that the poor are more susceptible to illness than the rich. This means that the cost of insurance for the poor is greater than for the affluent. The logic of the market is that insurance companies will only insure the poor at higher premiums than the rich and will not insure for pre-existing health conditions. They may also place limits on the type and amount of treatment the insured receive, creating a two-tier system in which the rich can afford treatments not available to those with basic insurance coverage. The higher cost of premiums means that many low-income people cannot afford insurance and are left uncovered.

The case with education is similar. Without free public education, working-class families would be unable to afford to send their children to school regard-

> ### 1.9 Markets are Fundamentally Amoral
>
> In a market economy, business holds a position of special privilege. It tends to dominate not just the economy, but the prevailing ideology.
>
> The dynamism of business is taken as simple proof of its virtue.... Business embodies freedom. Do whatever the hell you like, as long as the customer buys the product....
>
> But of course this conclusion ignores certain enduring realities about capitalism that have not been repealed by the Information Age.... No matter how hard the enthusiasts of the new corporation try to infer social values from the logic of competition itself, *markets remain fundamentally amoral.* Values need to be found elsewhere—and then imposed on corporations lest they overrun everything we hold dear....
>
> The late Arthur Okun, a fully licensed economist, put it well. "The market deserves a place," he said, "and it deserves to be kept in its place."
>
> –Robert Kuttner, economist and editor of The American Prospect. This excerpt from "Markets are fundamentally amoral," CCPA Monitor, June 1997, was originally published in The American Prospect.

less of the fact that employers *need* educated and trained workers to run their businesses efficiently. Workers know, of course, that if their children get more education they will also earn more when they enter the labour market. But how many such families could afford, or even be able to borrow, the hundreds of thousands of dollars over a period of a minimum of twelve years to provide a private education? The risk is even higher because a student might fail or get sick along the way and never be able to earn the extra income to pay off the debt.

Even though university costs are subsidized by government at approximately eighty percent, the rising student debt loads caused by recent tuition fee hikes have already become a barrier to students attending and completing post-secondary education programs. An inadequately educated labour force not only is a drag on the economy, it also increases inequality in the labour market. According to comparative Canada–U.S. studies, inequalities in wages and salaries between college educated and high school graduates in the U.S. are higher than in Canada, reflecting in part the higher tuition fees in the United States with its heavier reliance on private universities. Thus, in the case of both health and education, the self-regulating market undersupplies the social and economic needs of society.

The market system generally produces wide disparities in income, not just as a result of limiting access to higher education. These disparities are unacceptable not just because they go against the democratic norms of equality, but also because such inequalities contribute to other socially unacceptable consequences. For example, poverty and income inequality contribute to rising crime rates and ill health. As well, wide income inequality risks pushing the economy into recession or depression. Poorly paid workers are unable to purchase many goods and services. This low level of consumption can trigger an economic downturn. Many economists believe that economic inequality was a major contributing factor in causing the depression of the 1930s. In the last two decades, inequality in market incomes in Canada has increased, though nowhere near that in the United States. Furthermore, Canada's tax system and more extensive system of transfer payments has significantly lessened the increase in the income gap. The same has not been true south of the border.

Boom and bust cycles are the third feature of market economies that most people today deem unacceptable. Adam Smith's market system depended on the individual actions of many thousands of independent businesses, workers and consumers. But as the depression of the 1930s demonstrated (and as the great British economist, John Maynard Keynes, proved theoretically), such a system is subject to catastrophic failure when the sum of these individual decisions are not in sync with each other. Since the Second World War, economists and politicians learned how to moderate and control these fluctuations and breakdowns through government economic policies. However, the resurgence of nineteenth-century laissez-faire economics (neoliberalism) and the accompanying growth of right-wing parties and policies have led to a move away from these economic policies. This policy abandonment raises the possibility that the nearly five decades of relatively stable, if not always stellar, economic performance may abruptly come to an end.

What all this suggests is that the wonderful theoretical world of "free-market" economics, what we have called neoliberal thought, is a fragile and unreliable basis for guiding contemporary economy policy. Furthermore, even the ways economists and governments measure how well the economy is performing are terribly flawed.

Measures of Economic Welfare

The standard measure for assessing the performance of the economy is **Gross Domestic Product (GDP)**. It is defined as "the total unduplicated value of goods and services produced in the economic territory of a country or region during a given period. GDP can be measured in three ways: as total incomes earned in current production, as total final sales of current production or as total net values added in current production. It can be valued either at factor cost or at market value."[6]

Devised after the Second World War, this indicator was adopted by the United Nations for international consistency and comparability. It measures the value of all income and expenditure in a country in a given period, usually a year.

The health of the economy is usually gauged by the rate of growth of GDP, while economic welfare is measured by GDP per capita and the growth rate of GDP per capita. International comparisons of economic well-being are usually based on comparisons of per capita GDP as well.

There are many weaknesses with GDP as a measure of welfare. Perhaps the most important is that it either disregards, or counts as positive benefit, not only the "goods" produced in the economy, but also the "bads"—disasters, pollution,

1.10 Gross Domestic Product

Canadian GDP: 2001
(million $s)

	Income		Expenditures
Labour Income	559,102	Personal Consumption	619,860
Profits	129,600	Government	199,683
Interest and Investment Income	53,463	Government Investment	26,423
Net Farm Income	2,963	Business Investment	188,343
Unincorporated Business Income	65,719	Inventory Investment	-6,022
Inventory Valuation Adjustment	-458	Net Exports	55,544
Net Taxes on Factor Payments	56,253	Statistical Discrepancy	567
Net Domestic Income	810,389	Gross Domestic Product	1,084,119
Indirect Taxes minus Subsidies	75,269		
Capital Consumption (Depreciation)	142,498		
Statistical Discrepancy	-290		
Gross Domestic Product	1,084,119		

−Statistics Canada, National Income and Expenditure Accounts (SC 13-001-XPB), 2001

crime, illness, disease and accidents—as long as they have an economic impact.

Also, GDP figures do not include the value of goods produced and work done outside the market, such as housework or volunteer services. This is a serious omission since non-market output in Canada is estimated to be almost half as much as that in the formal market economy.

Other major weaknesses of GDP are more qualitative. GDP per capita gives no indication of the equality of income distribution, of the availability of socially valuable goods and services such as health and education, of the quality and safety of working conditions, of access to and availability of cultural and recreational activities, or of economic security or stability of income. Real standards of welfare should include not just quantitative measures of material income, but also quality of life measures. As the banners of the striking female textile workers in Lawrence, Massachusetts, proclaimed in 1912, "We want Bread—and Roses too."

The GDP only tells us what happens in the market. It does not tell us how well off we really are. This has led to a number of attempts to devise better measures, the best known of which is the United Nations Human Development Index. Since the late 1990s to the

1.11 Natural Disasters, Crime, Illness "Good" for the Economy

When natural disasters are said to be good for the economy, it's time to review what "good" means. Just after Christmas 1999, France was hit by two storms. Winds gusting to 2000 km per hour killed 91 people, cut electricity from over three million people, and snapped off or uprooted 360 million trees. Damage is estimate at $11.8 billion. Insurance will cover around $4.7 billion, the government is contributing $2.5 billion, and the remaining costs will be carried somehow by unfortunate citizens.

The vast amount of materials and labour needed to repair the storm damage will stimulate economic activity. As Denis Kessler, vice-president of France's equivalent to Canada's Business Council on National Issues, has noted: "This disaster will be mostly positive in terms of GDP."

−Mike Nickerson, "Measuring Well-Being in Canada,"
CCPA Monitor, April 2000

1.12 Dung, Kerosene and What Really Counts?

In her critique of the way economists count economic activity and the "real" standard of living, Marilyn Waring has consistently pointed out that "women's work" in and around the home is vital to the real standard of living of society even if their work is never recorded in the national accounts. As a result of the disregard for such work, economists consistently contribute to the undermining of family welfare in developing countries with their market-oriented programs. The following is a particularly telling example.

> Making dung cakes to be used as fuel appears to me to be an entire manufacturing process, with clear inputs and outputs of an economic nature. In mining or gas extraction, for example, paid workers harvest the primary resource. Machines transport it to processing plants. The raw material is refined, the product manufactured. It is sold, then consumed. The traditional economic model is followed: workers process raw materials for the market. This counts. But when dung, the "non-product," is carried as a "service" by "housewives," to sustain land, dwellings and households, then, according to the economic model, nothing happens. There is no economic activity. But dungwork is only women's work, so it is a safe assumption that in the official definitions of productive work it will be invisible.
>
> –Marilyn Waring, *Three Masquerades: Essays on Equality, Work and Hu(man) Rights* (Toronto: University of Toronto Press, 1996), p. 46

present Canada often has ranked as the best country in the world to live in— despite the fact that the country did not even rank in the top ten countries in per capita GDP. The top ranking was due to the fact that the Human Development Index also includes life expectancy, adult literacy and school enrolment as measures of health and education. However, when income distribution is included in the Human Poverty Index, Canada's rank dropped from first to eleventh among the major industrialized countries.

A far more comprehensive attempt to measure welfare is the Genuine Progress Indicator (GPI) project, which has branches in both Canada and the United States. The GPI and GDP measures are compared in Table 1.1. For the United States, GPI figures shows that, despite steady growth in GDP since the Second World War, economic well-being peaked in the 1970s and has declined steadily since.

Dalhousie University's Lars Osberg and Andrew Sharpe, Director of the Ottawa-based Centre for the Study of Living Standards, have developed an Index of Economic Well-being that is a weighted composite of four welfare measures, consumption flows, wealth stocks, inequality and economic security. Measured by this index, economic welfare in Canada peaked in the early seventies, fell sharply after the 1973 oil price increases and subsequent bout of high inflation and low economic growth (stagflation), recovered and peaked again in 1989 before declining steadily through the 1990s.

All of these alternative measures of human welfare, and many others that have not been mentioned, are premised on the belief that GDP is *not* a good measure of well-being. These alternative indexes only indirectly get at the primary cause of income inequality and poor quality of working life: the distribution of *power* in capitalist society. The distribution of power, in turn, is the result of class differences in capitalist societies. Neither class nor power, however, are given much attention by most orthodox economists.

Table 1.1 GPI vs. GDP

Critique of GDP
- GDP ignores the non-market economy.
- GDP takes no account of inequality of income, wealth and spending power.
- GDP treats crime, imprisonment, divorce and other forms of social breakdown as economic gain.
- GDP treats environmental calamity, pollution, war and their cleanup and repair as economic gain.
- GDP does not account for depletion or degradation of natural resources.
- GDP ignores the liabilities of living off foreign assets.

GPI Adjustments
- Adds the value of household and community services.
- Adjusts for the gap between rich and poor.
- Subtracts the cost of crime, auto accidents, commuting, family breakdown and underemployment.
- Subtracts the cost of environmental degradation, pollution and loss of farm- land, forests and wetlands.
- Subtracts the depletion of resources.
- Adjusts for net capital formation and net foreign borrowing.

Source: Mark Anielski, "The Genuine Progress Indicator—A Principled Approach to Eco- nomics," Pembina Institute website <http://www.piad.ab.ca/green/gpi.htm>

Power in Political Economy

With the exception of market power, orthodox economists cannot readily accommodate and quantify power within neoclassical theory. Therefore the analysis of the exercise of economic power in society is left to sociologists, historians and political scientists. This is one of the main reasons that much of the best analysis of contemporary economic issues such as globalization, economic development, labour market segmentation, poverty and gender discrimination comes not from economists but from those trained in other social sciences and even from the humanities.[7]

Classical and contemporary political economists have not suffered from this narrow focus on the market. Adam Smith's 1776 classic, *The Wealth of Nations*, has a great deal to say about power, and the abuse of it, particularly by the business and merchant class. The greatest of the classical economists, Karl Marx, made class power the centrepiece of his analysis. More recently, John Kenneth Galbraith made prominent the concept of "countervailing power" and the power of advertising to create and mould tastes in the 1960s. Harold Innis, the "father" of Canadian political economy, initiated the analysis of the power of information and communications in the 1930s and 1940s. His work has since spawned a whole field of analysis in which Noam Chomsky and the late Marshall McLuhan, a Canadian, are perhaps the best known.

Rather than just listing the various authors and their specific contributions to analysis of the role of power in the economy, we should systematically look at

1.13 U.S. GDP vs. U.S. GPI: 1950–2000

Gross Domestic Product Versus Genuine Progress Indicator

Year	GDP (billions of 1992 US$)	GPI (billions of 1992 US$)	GDP per capita (1992 US$)	GPI per capita (1992 US$)
1950	1,661	810	10,582	5,317
1960	2,263	1,226	12,525	6,783
1970	3,398	1,761	16,569	8,686
1980	4,615	1,982	20,310	8,722
1990	6,136	1,965	24,600	7,879
1998	7,552	1,770	27,939	6,549
2000	8,427	2,451	30,764	8,771

Total Change
1950–2000 +6,766   +1,641   +20,182   +3,454

–Redefining Progress, The Genuine Progress Indicator, 1998 and 2000 updates and author's calculations. Available at www.rprogress/projects/gpi

the sources and instruments of power and how they affect the operations and outcomes of the economy. First we must define what we mean by power in this context. **Power** simply means the ability of an individual or group to affect or control the economic, political and social conditions, decisions, behaviour and values of other individuals or groups. This power can be exercised by one individual or by a group either having the ability to impose rewards or punishments on the other or by influencing the knowledge, values or preferences of other individuals or groups.

There are several sources of power. One source is ideology. Another arises from the division of society along class, gender and race lines. A third source is rooted in those social institutions through which power is exercised—the media, schools, the legal system, property rights, corporations, unions, treaties, religious institutions, indeed the market itself and most importantly, the state.

How is ideology—a comprehensive view of how the world works and should work—transferred into power? The concept of **hegemony**, developed by the Italian social theorist Antonio Gramsci, provides some useful insights. Gramsci was trying to explain how capitalist societies, which he believed did not operate for the benefit of the majority of their citizens, were able to gain the support of most of their citizens. This happens, he said, because the ruling group's ideas about how society should be organized had become accepted as the proper values on which society is to be based. Perhaps no better example is the mantra of Margaret Thatcher, former Prime Minister of Britain. She repeatedly claimed that "there is no alternative" (TINA) to privatization, the replacement of political and social values with market values, market deregulation, contraction of social programs, globalization and a host of other policies harkening back to the economic and social beliefs of the early nineteenth century. It is irrelevant whether or not there are alternatives, as there surely are, as long as the majority can be convinced that there are not.

Neoliberalism has gained economic hegemony over the past three decades.

This ideology reflects the values and interests of the corporate world—owners, major shareholders and senior executives and managers of the big corporations, including the media corporations. A good example of this ideology in action has been the suppression of labour and unions in the last three decades of the twentieth century. The economic woes of the 1970s were blamed on workers and unions who, it was claimed, pushed up labour costs through excessive wage demands, thereby causing price rises and eventually persistently high unemployment. This argument was picked up by many economists who claimed there was a "natural rate of unemployment" and prescribed policies to curb the power of workers and unions. (See chapter 8, box 8.8, Stagflation, Monetarism and the Birth of NAIRU.) In the process, they ignored the other events of the real world— the cartel of oil-producing countries that drove up the price of petroleum by over 300 percent, the inflationary impact of the Vietnam War, and the unilateral abandonment by the United States of the international agreement governing exchange rates, thereby destabilizing international flows of money.[8]

The solution advanced by these economists and the corporate establishment included raising unemployment, lowering wages, dismantling unions and job security programs, restricting the growth of money supply, raising interest rates, and reducing taxes on corporations and those with higher incomes. It was argued that these policies would induce more investment, higher productivity growth and ultimately a resumption of economic and employment growth. Many governments did adopt just this set of policies. However, the ultimate purpose behind these measures was really to transfer income from workers to corporations in order to increase or restore profits.

These policies did work to the extent that unemployment and interest rates rose and unionism and real wages declined or stagnated for two decades. However, productivity did not recover until almost two decades after the medicine was applied. In the meantime, the cuts in taxes to business and the top income groups, combined with higher interest rates, resulted in growing government deficits creating in their minds a "debt and deficit crisis" that could only be countered by massive cuts to social programs. Those cuts took place in the 1980s and, more particularly in Canada, in the 1990s. Cutting social programs meant, of course, cutting the non-market income of the mass of Canadians leading to a further decline in social welfare and real income. This was, in turn, made worse by the introduction of the Goods and Services Tax or GST, a new regressive tax that fell disproportionately on the working class.

This brief exploration of some recent developments in Canadian economic policy is meant to illustrate the effect of the power of a hegemonic ideology. It does not, however, explain how these ideals and values become accepted in the first place or how they are enacted in law, public policies and the market.

Social Division

Individualism is central to the capitalist worldview. In neoclassical economics this preoccupation with the individual is based on the assumption that all individuals have equal, or near equal, access to the levers of economic power.[9] This view was strongly contested by Karl Marx, who put class as the pre-eminent category for economic and social analysis.

The relation between class and power becomes clear when we identify the main classes in a modern capitalist economy. There are those who live off the income earned by their work (the "working class") and those that live off the income that they receive because they own and control large concentrations of the means of production (the "capitalist class"). There are however, other classes. For example, there is the class of "independent commodity producers" such as farmers and self-employed craft workers—carpenters, potters, shoe repairers and hair-stylists—and independent professionals—doctors, architects, lawyers—who not only work at their jobs but who also own and operate their own capital, their farmland, machinery, office equipment or tools. Most of these people don't pack much economic clout but they often identify with the owners of big and powerful corporations, the real capitalist class.

Furthermore, not all members of the big business class operate in the same market sectors of the economy or always have the same economic interests. Owners of capital are divided between those who hold financial capital ("finance capitalists") and those who own and control real capital and resources ("industrial capitalists"). Banks, insurance companies, money market dealers, brokers and the whole financial sector—the people on Wall Street in the United States or Bay Street in Canada—buy and sell money and finance for a profit. This makes them finance capitalists. And they are very powerful politically. But they also can have quite different interests from the big manufacturing, resource, trade and service corporations and the people that control them, the industrial capitalists. Together, however, they comprise the business elite, the capitalist class—and the most powerful group in modern society.

The whole issue of class is also muddled because working-class people today do own some capital, usually in the form of stocks and bonds in pension plans or mutual funds, (though labour's holdings of such capital is minimal and probably declining as pension coverage, and more recently, stock markets shrink). Nevertheless, even though it is a myth, "people's capitalism" (the idea that most people are capitalists because they have small investments in the stock market) has become part of the prevailing ideology.

This myth is also compounded by the notion that business ownership has become separated from the management of business. This is also largely fictitious. Many large firms are run on a day-to-day basis by a corps of professional managers who may or may not own shares in the company. However, they manage these companies *in the interest of the company owners and major shareholders*. Indeed, their pay and bonuses are increasingly paid out in the form of profit sharing or shares and share options, the value of which depend ultimately on the profits of the company.

The power the business elite has is manifest both directly in the market and indirectly through its pervasive influence in perpetuating the ideology of capitalism and through influencing politicians and public opinion. Directly, a relatively small number of capitalists employ the vast proportion of the working class. As Adam Smith attested, there is a large power imbalance between "the masters" and their employees. No one can deny the importance of the power of the employer to deny a worker the right to a job—"the power of the sack!" One potential offset to employer power is unions, although even unionized workers have much less power when unemployment is high or where governments are willing to intervene to limit union power. In any case, less than 20 percent of paid workers in the private sector are currently unionized, meaning that four out of every five private-sector workers do not even have this basic level of protection and power.

Capitalists also have direct economic power in the market. This is exercised through control of patents, trademarks, copyrights, advertising and other means of creating and reinforcing tastes; and by sheer size and financial "deep pockets" that allow large firms to enter and dominate markets and drive out smaller competitors. Further, capitalists have the ability to bring an economy to its knees through a **capital strike.** This takes place when businesses collectively refuse to invest or move their operations to other countries or political jurisdictions in order to protest, block or escape taxation, environmental regulation or any other economic policies they deem will affect corporate profits. These businesses are, in fact, on strike. Alternatively, they can use or threaten to use a capital strike to demand new government policies that will enhance net corporate profits.

> ### 1.14 The Myth of People's Capitalism
>
> A myth has arisen in recent years that we now live in an era of "people's capitalism." The seeming omnipresence of the culture of personal investing—mutual fund scores in the morning paper, stock market tickers flashing on every screen, monotonous market updates interrupting every radio program—has contributed to this myth....
>
> [According to Statistics Canada, the last wealth survey conducted in 1984] painted a surprising picture of a dangerously unbalanced pattern of wealth ownership in Canada.... The richest one-fifth of Canadian households (termed the top "quintile" by the statisticians) owned over two-thirds of all household wealth. Excluding the value of residences, land and other real assets, the top quintile's share of *financial* wealth was even larger: the top fifth of households owned an incredible three-quarters of all net financial wealth. The bottom 60% of households, on the other hand, together accounted for just 6% of net financial wealth—one-tenth of its share of the population. Not surprisingly, the poorest segments of society actually reported *negative* net financial wealth.
>
> —Jim Stanford, *Paper Boom* (Toronto: Lorimer and Canadian Centre for Policy Alternatives, 1999), pp. 257, 259

Institutional Power

Capital also has great power through its indirect control of values, information, tastes and opinions. The most obvious case is the control of most of the media—radio, television, newspapers and even, increasingly, the Internet—by corporate conglomerates. In Canada, there is the possible exception of the publicly owned Canadian Broadcasting Corporation (CBC) though even the CBC displays the values and perceptions of capital through its TV advertising. Even "non-commercial" CBC radio regularly reports on the Toronto Stock Exchange, the Dow Jones and NASDAQ stock market indexes, despite the fact that very few of its listeners hold any stocks. At the same time both the private media and the CBC seldom report on the state and health of the unions or labour generally, except to give largely negative coverage of strikes, demands for increases in minimum wages or for restitution of unemployment insurance benefits. Indeed, the media as a whole has consistently supported the political and economic agenda of corporate Canada.

Through donations to pro-business political parties and the funding of a host of opinion-influencing special interest groups and think tanks with a neoliberal, right-wing bias, capitalists also influence the policies of government to the benefit of business. The most well-known of these right-wing institutes and organizations include the Fraser Institute and the C.D. Howe Institute and advocacy bodies such as the Business Council on National Issues, the Canadian Federation of Independent Business, the Canadian Taxpayers Federation and the National Citizens Coalition. While none of these organizations represent the mass of Canadian workers or citizens, they do appear to have the sympathetic ear of government and the media.

The Canadian author Murray Dobbin has documented the influence of the business class and its agencies in the dismantling of much of Canada's social network and the promoting of privatization, deregulation, income tax reductions, "free trade" and globalization, and in his book, *The Myth of the Good Corporate Citizen*, Dobbin writes:

> For almost twenty years the most important policy directions taken by Western governments have been discussed, refined, and agreed upon not in the established democratic forums but in closed, exclusive clubs established for this purpose. Such consensus-building organizations and forums as the Trilateral Commission, the World Economic Forum, and the Bilderberg forum have not been established by or even acknowledged by governments. Yet they, and their nationally based counterparts like the [Canadian] Business Council on National Issues [BCNI], are among the most important policy forums in the world. Officially recognized or not, they have an enormous influence on the lives of ordinary citizens in every country, in every village, in the world.[10]

The BCNI established its own virtual shadow cabinet with supporting task forces on "taxation, international economy and trade, social policy and regional development, labour relations and manpower, government organization and regulation, foreign policy and defence, competition policy, education, and corporate governance."[11] The Business Council went as far as presenting the Mulroney and Chrétien governments with draft legislation and pressuring them to adopt it, which, by and large, both the Conservative and Liberal governments did.[12] Nor has Dobbin been the only social critic to chronicle the rise to power of the modern corporation in Canada.[13]

This pervasive business influence has not been restricted to government and public policy. Commercial interests have been partially successful in entering school classrooms with advertising tied to news and information programming in exchange for "free" computers. School boards have, in numerous cases, been willing to enter into such agreements because they lacked alternative sources of funds to buy such equipment. This was, in turn, a result of cuts in provincial funding to education.

Corporate influence in the education system extends to exclusive concession contracts in public schools, giving brand or corporate names to university departments chairs, programs and buildings, providing tied research grants, even providing corporate-friendly textbooks for use in the schools.

A similar example could be described of the attempts to introduce two-tiered, for-profit medicine into the health care system in Alberta. The excuse was the failure of the public sector to deliver the required funding to provide an adequate level of medical care. Deliberately obscured was the fact that the funding failure was the result of neoliberal governments being unwilling to allocate sufficient money to public services in order that these governments could channel more income to the private and corporate sectors. It is a case of what economist John Kenneth Galbraith identified as "public squalor and private opulence," a direct consequence of the imbalance of power between classes and of the creation of institutions that translate that imbalance into a misdistribution of the output of the economy.

The point is that the power wielded by the capitalist class is not only direct in its dealings with its workers or its consumers, but also indirect through its influence in conditioning information, decision-making, behaviour and values in society. These values are conveyed through institutions that control society such as the state, including its laws, legal system and distribution and extent of property rights; the media, advertising and promotion agencies; schools and education institutions; and opinion-making organizations.

> ### 1.15 Silent Coup: The Corporate Takeover of Canada
>
> Our political leaders are engaged in nothing less than the systematic dismantling and restructuring of the socioeconomic system that was built up in Canada over the past 60 years. Corporate Canada has all but succeeded in its mission to eradicate the Keynesian social welfare state in this country.... In the final analysis, we are now living under a system of corporate rule that is dealing death blows to democracy in this country. What the Trilateral Commission targetted as "excess democracy" 20 years ago has all but been wiped out. Not only have citizens' rights been subverted in favour of investors' rights, but our society is rapidly moving in the direction where virtually only corporations can be said to have full citizenship status....
>
> –Tony Clarke, "Silent Coup: Confronting the big business takeover of Canada," CCPA Monitor, vol. 4, no. 3, July/August 1997

Property Rights and Power

One of the most important legal aspects of capitalism is the concept of property rights. Private property rights are at the centre of self-regulating market logic and of corporate power. Adam Smith over two centuries ago put his finger on the relationship between the state and property when he wrote: "Civil government, insofar as it is instituted for the security of property, is in reality instituted for the defence of the rich against the poor, and for the defence of those who have property against those who have none." But there is no natural system of property rights. As a senior judge of the American courts has written: "Property is never for long anything more or, really, anything different from what some politically appointed court says it is."[14]

The fact is, property rights are not just a single right of ownership. Rather they are a "bundle of rights" that include the right to own, sell or destroy property, to control the income generated by property, to utilize and manage property and to prevent others from access to the use or enjoyment of property. These are the property rights that allow corporations to shut down factories, expropriate jobs and transfer them to a low-wage country. These are the property rights that allow businesses to buy up resource areas and deny people the right to enjoy the lakes and wilderness of those areas. These are the property rights that

1.16 Adam Smith on the State and Wealth

Till there be property there can be no government, the very end of which is to secure wealth, and to defend the rich from the poor.

—*Adam Smith*

allow firms to dictate working conditions and wages of employees and to deny the workers jobs if they won't agree to those wages and conditions. These are the property rights that are the *source* of corporate power.

The degree and nature of the restrictions placed upon an "owner's" use and enjoyment of property has varied through time as our legal system has developed and changed. Restrictions on the unfettered property rights of capital in the postwar period can be seen as a mirror of societal values, the desire of society, through its legal system, to promote public interest, safety and values of security and equality. These are the restrictions on private property rights that have been stripped away in the neoliberal counter-revolution of the last two decades.

This is exceedingly important at the present time. Business and governments, led by the U.S.A. and the European Union, with the support of Canada, are expanding the property rights of corporate capitalists beyond the boundaries of their nation states through international treaties such as the North American Free Trade Agreement (NAFTA), the World Trade Organization (WTO), the Multilateral Agreement on Investment (MAI), the General Agreements on Trade in Services (GATS) and Trade Related Intellectual Property Rights (TRIPS). (See chapter 10.)

Fortunately, opposition from labour, environmental and social action groups, and non-governmental organizations was sufficiently strong to derail, at least temporarily, a couple of the most offensive extensions of corporate power, the MAI and expansion of the agricultural and intellectual property rights provisions of the WTO. However, business is using its political, media and economic power to continue the process of expanding its global property rights at the expense of the social and political values of the majority of society.

Power and Political Economy

Considerable attention has been paid to the issue of power in the determining of what is to be produced, how it is to be produced, and in particular for whom it is to be produced. This is necessary because orthodox economists have largely ignored the subject. Power does not fit into their conception of "efficient markets," in part because it explains a great deal more about how the real economy operates than the competitive market theories of which most economists are so enamoured. It is impossible to adequately understand how markets work, how tastes, prices and costs are determined, and how income is finally distributed without an equivalent understanding of how power originates and is exercised in the economy. The place to start our investigation is in the institutions of production and exchange.

Notes

1. Anthropologists often use the term "primitive" to describe the early non-market societies that did not have an established state or governmental structure.
2. Economists call this practice of trading goods surplus to local needs as "a vent for surplus."

3. Karl Polanyi, *The Great Transformation* (Boston: The Beacon Press, 1944), pp. 133-134.
4. We use the terms "means of production," "(productive) property" and "(real) capital" more or less interchangeably in this book. We do have to distinguish, however, between *real* capital and *financial* capital. Real capital refers to the plant, buildings, machinery, equipment, land and resources used to produce output. Financial capital refers only to the paper that represents monetary claims on the accumulated wealth of an economy—bonds, bills, debentures, stocks, shares, mortgages, money—any form of "IOU" that a person holds. Ownership of these IOUs gives their owners a paper claim to real capital. Thus we often refer to ownership of real capital as *real wealth*, ownership of paper claims to capital as *paper wealth*. Other writers refer to the financial and related sectors as the "paper economy" as opposed to the rest of the goods and services industries that compose the "real economy."
5. During the period when the classical economists were writing, the prime economic resource was agricultural land for which tenant farmers paid rent. Therefore, the three factors of production were deemed to be labour, *land* and capital, while land was paid *rent*. This terminology has tended to be maintained among economists. However, land should be seen in the broader context of natural resources and rent as the income accruing to owners of the "bounties of nature."
6. *Statistics Canada*, National Income and Expenditure Accounts *(SC 13-001-XPB)*. Gross Domestic Product (GDP) differs from Gross National Produce (GNP), the measure that used to be used in Canada to estimate economic output, in that GDP measures output produced within the country whereas GNP measures income received by people in Canada. Thus, GNP is equal to GDP plus investment income received from non-residents, less investment income paid to non-residents. Because of the high degree of foreign ownership in Canada, GDP is significantly lower than GNP because of the net outflow of interest, profits and dividends.
7. Doug Henwood, for instance, author of the insightful book on the operations of American financial markets, *Wall Street*, and author and editor of the economic newsletter, *Left Business Observer*, has a Ph.D. in English literature.
8. "In July 1944, in Bretton Woods, New Hampshire, representatives of forty-four nations met to establish the standards by which international trade and finance would be conducted once the Second World War had ended. This included not only specification of the exchange and payments system that would prevail, but also of provisions for helping 'Third World' nations develop in the post-colonial world." [John Harvey, "Bretton Woods System," *Encyclopedia of Political Economy*, Philip O'Hara, ed. (London: Routledge, 1999), p. 44.]

    The bodies established as a result of the Bretton Woods Agreement were the International Monetary Fund (IMF), the World Bank (WB) and the General Agreement on Tariffs and Trade (GATT), now the WTO. However, the original Bretton Woods system fell apart in the early 1970s when the United States abandoned its fixed exchange rate tied to gold.
9. The assumption is formally known in economics as "methodological individualism."
10. Murray Dobbin, *The Myth of the Good Corporate Citizen* (Toronto: Stoddard, 1998), p. 153.
11. Dobbin, p. 167.
12. Dobbin, pp. 170ff.
13. For a year-by-year chronology of the legislation of the neoliberal program see "How the corporate agenda was legislated by Liberal and Tory governments, 1980-1997," *CCPA Monitor*, vol. 4, no. 6, November 1997, pp. 14–15.
14. David Bazelon, "What is Property?" in David Mermelstein, ed., *Economics: Mainstream Readings and Radical Critiques* (New York: Random House, 1970), p. 59. This article is well worth reading because he traces how contemporary property rights were established through the political and legal process.

Chapter 2

Institutions of Production and Exchange

Organization of Production and Exchange

It is common to focus on the market as the central political–economic institution in contemporary capitalist economies. In all the discussion of the transformation of the economy of the former Soviet Union, for instance, the emphasis was on two processes: the transition to a market from a planned economy and the privatization of state-owned enterprises. The emphasis on the market, however, puts the cart before the horse. We can get a better understanding of how capitalism works, not by looking at the end result, the market for goods and services, but rather by focusing on the major decision-making unit: the business enterprise.

Business enterprises can take many shapes and sizes and can operate in different kinds of markets. They can be large, multinational corporations like IBM, or they can be small, unincorporated family businesses. They can be involved in relatively competitive markets, as is the case with most family farms; or they can exist in highly monopolized markets such as the newspaper business or natural gas distribution. They can produce for consumer markets; or they can produce for other businesses or for government. They can be owned privately by a few individuals or by a family; they can be widely owned by many shareholders; or they can be owned by the state, by the community or, as in the case of cooperatives, by the workers or by consumers. Furthermore, they can be profit-seeking businesses; or they can be "not-for-profits," such as non-governmental agencies providing health, cultural, recreational and other community services. Also, they can be involved in production activities, for example, the manufacture of brake shoes; or they can operate in exchange activities, such as retailing car parts.[1]

The two most common ways to classify firms are by the sphere of the economy in which they are engaged and the structure of the market within which they operate. The term **sphere** refers to whether the firm is primarily engaged in the production of goods or services, or in the exchange of goods or services. The example above distinguishes between a manufacturer of brake shoes and a retailer of car parts. The manufacturer of brake shoes is engaged in the production of a product, brake shoes. Those shoes are then sold wholesale to a retailer of car parts. The retailer sells the shoes to the final customer. Rather than producing the shoes, the retailer sells them, or exchanges them for the customer's money. Many firms, of course, do both but we classify them by their primary function, either production or exchange.

The term **market structure** refers to the degree of power that firms enjoy in any particular market. At one extreme, where there are many small firms producing or distributing relatively similar goods or services, a **competitive** market structure

2.1 Profits or Surplus?

In Marxist political economy, the concept of surplus is used rather than profits. **Surplus** is a similar though slightly broader concept: it measures the amount that owners receive after subtracting explicit costs only. Profits and surplus accrue to the owners by virtue of their ownership and/or control of the means of production and distribution (that is capital and resources, or **property**.) Owners of capital and resources receive the surplus (including profits) simply because they own or control property, not for any contribution to producing the surplus. Perhaps this can be made clearer by the following schematic, which sets out how surplus is generated and distributed in the two spheres and by the two market structures.

Generation and Distribution of Surplus by Sphere and Market Structure

By Sphere
Production: Surplus = (Net Output Price - Labour Cost) x Output
Surplus in production is generated by the difference between the selling price (minus the cost of materials and energy used in the production process and depreciation of capital equipment) minus the labour cost.

Exchange: Surplus = (Net Final Price - Purchase Price) x Units Sold
Surplus in exchange (commercial surplus) is generated by the difference between the value of final sales (minus the cost of labour to conduct these sales) minus the cost of purchasing the goods resold.

By Structure
Competition: Surplus is the value of the owner's labour (the "wage" he or she would earn working for someone else) plus the "normal" return to the owners' investment (the interest he or she would have earned by investing the money in a bond or other safe monetary investment.)

Monopoly: Surplus is the "wage" value of the owner's labour and the interest-equivalent return on owned investment as in competition *plus* a return to market power in the form of a selling-price premium due to restriction of output reflecting the exercise of market power.

is said to exist. At the other extreme, where there is but one firm producing or distributing a product or service with no close substitutes, the market is **monopolistic**. In fact, the major share of our contemporary economy is controlled by a small number of very large firms. Because of their limited number and the fact that they have differentiated products (similar but sufficiently different to convey market power— for example, Pepsi and Coke), privileged access to raw materials or monopoly control over a production technology, these firms have a degree of monopoly power in a given market. In orthodox economics textbooks, these firms are called **oligopolies**—meaning "a few sellers"—rather than monopolies, though all oligopolies have some degree of monopoly power that allows them to generate greater surpluses than would be possible in more competitive markets. They can generate higher profits by reducing the output they put on the market allowing them to raise prices to the consumer. (If a competitive firm tried to reduce its output and raise its prices, its competitors would just replace its former output at the old prices.)

As much as business leaders, politicians and academics may talk about the virtues of competition, capitalists do not like competition. Competition reduces their ability to generate profits. This is why companies make every effort to differentiate their products through advertising and promotions or to patent and copyright their products and production processes—anything to make their markets less competitive. Indeed, the "flight from competition" by business came very early in the history of capitalism. Late in the nineteenth century businesses began forming combines, trusts, holding companies and mergers with the goal of reducing the number of competing firms. The First World War provided the economic conditions for the consolidation of "big business" and marked the transition from an era called competitive capitalism to that of **monopoly capitalism**.

Even in orthodox neoclassical economics, *there are no profits in competition*, at least in the long run when new or existing firms have the opportunity to set up or expand to take advantage of temporary profit opportunities. If a firm wants to realize a surplus above its costs in the long run it must maintain a monopoly position and exploit the market power created by that monopoly position. It should be clear that firms are in business to make profits, not to generate competition that reduces profits.

Profits, as conventionally defined by economists, are the amount of money left over after the firm pays not only the explicit costs of materials, energy, machinery and buildings and labour; but also the implicit costs of the labour of the owners and a return to their investment.

Take a simple example of a hairdressing salon. The owner pays the employees, the rent, heat and electricity, and the suppliers, a figure that might come to $4,000 per month or $48,000 a year. But she also invested $50,000 in equipment. If she had bought Canada Savings Bonds with that $50,0000 instead, she would receive interest of approximately $3,500 (at an interest rate of 7 percent). In other words, her capital investment is costing her $3,500 a year. Also, if she didn't run the salon she could work for another salon and make a salary of $15,000 per year. Thus, running her own shop is also costing her $15,000 in lost salary. Her total cost, therefore, is her explicit cost of $48,000 a year plus her implicit costs of running her own business of $18,500. To break even, she must take in $66,500 a year. If she takes in less, she makes a loss and will likely end up going out of business. If she takes in more than $66,500, she will make a profit. That is what is meant when we say that profit is what is left over after *all* costs—including the (interest) return on one's investment—are paid. And this is why there are no profits in competition, because if our salon owner is making profits, some other hairdresser (perhaps even one of her own employees) is likely to set up a shop expecting also to make a profit. But as more and more hairdressing shops are set up and try to attract business by lowering prices, the revenues of all salons fall until there are no profits left.

The large corporation is the dominant economic institution in our contemporary capitalist economy. That is, the predominant structure is monopoly in terms of the total value of production and sales and, hence, the designation in political economy of the current economy as monopoly capitalism. However, these large firms often engage in both production and exchange. For example, Safeway produces its own milk products under the brand name Lucerne and sells them through its own supermarkets. These large monopoly corporations are supplemented by thousands of small, competitive firms.[2] In the mid 1970s, (the last year that comprehensive statistics have been published) the top 200 non-financial firms (i.e., 0.01 percent of all firms) owned approximately half of the total productive assets in Canada and accounted for close to a third of total sales. The

2.2 Top 100 World Economies (1999)

(Corporations in italic)

Country/Corporation	GDP/sales ($mil)			
1	United States	8,708,870.0	51 Colombia	88,596.0
2	Japan	4,395,083.0	52 AXA	87,645.7
3	Germany	2,081,202.0	53 IBM	87,548.0
4	France	1,410,262.0	54 Singapore	84,945.0
5	United Kingdom	1,373,612.0	55 Ireland	84,861.0
6	Italy	1,149,958.0	56 BP Amoco	83,556.0
7	China	1,149,814.0	57 Citigroup	82,005.0
8	Brazil	760,345.0	58 Volkswagen	80,072.7
9	Canada	612,049.0	59 Nippon Life Insurance	78,515.1
10	Spain	562,245.0	60 Philippines	75,350.0
11	Mexico	474,951.0	61 Siemens	75,337.0
12	India	459,765.0	62 Malaysia	74,634.0
13	Korea, Republic	406,940.0	63 Allianz	74,178.2
14	Australia	389,691.0	64 Hitachi	71,858.5
15	Netherlands	384,765.0	65 Chile	71,092.0
16	Russian Federation	375,345.0	66 Matsushita Electric Ind.	65,555.6
17	Argentina	281,942.0	67 Nissho Iwal	65,393.2
18	Switzerland	260,299.0	68 ING Group	62,492.4
19	Belgium	245,706.0	69 AT&T	62,391.0
20	Sweden	226,388.0	70 Philip Morris	61,751.0
21	Austria	208,949.0	71 Sony	60,052.7
22	Turkey	188,374.0	72 Pakistan	59,880.0
23	General Motors	176,558.0	73 Deutsche Bank	58,585.1
24	Denmark	174,363.0	74 Boeing	57,993.0
25	Wal-Mart	166,809.0	75 Peru	57,318.0
26	Exxon Mobil	163,881.0	76 Czech Republic	56,379.0
27	Ford Motor	162,558.0	77 Dai-Ichi Mutual Life Ins.	55,104.7
28	Daimler-Chrysler	159,985.7	78 Honda Motor	54,773.5
29	Poland	154,146.0	79 Assicurazioni Generali	53,723.2
30	Norway	145,449.0	80 Nissan Motor	53,679.9
31	Indonesia	140,964.0	81 New Zealand	53,622.0
32	South Africa	131,127.0	82 E.On	52,227.7
33	Saudi Arabia	128,892.0	83 Toshiba	51,634.9
34	Finland	126,130.0	84 Bank of America	51,392.0
35	Greece	123,934.0	85 Fiat	51,331.7
36	Thailand	123,887.0	86 Nestle	49,694.1
37	Mitsui	118,555.2	87 SCB Communications	49,489.0
38	Mitsubishi	117,765.6	88 Credit Suisse	49,362.0
39	Toyota Motor	115,670.9	89 Hungary	48,355.0
40	General Electric	111,630.0	90 Hewlett-Packard	48,253.0
41	Itochu	109,068.9	91 Fujitsu	47,195.9
42	Portugal	107,716.0	92 Algeria	47,015.0
43	Royal Dutch/Shell	105,366.0	93 Metro	46,663.6
44	Venezuela	103,918.0	94 Sumitomo Life Insur.	46,445.1
45	Iran, Islamic Republic	101,073.0	95 Bangladesh	45,779.0
46	Israel	99,068.0	96 Tokyo Electric Power	45,727.7
47	Sumitomo	95,701.6	97 Kroger	45,351.6
48	Nippon Tel & Tel	93,591.7	98 Total Fina Elf	44,990.3
49	Egypt, Arab Republic	92,413.0	99 NEC	44,828.0
50	Marubeni	91,807.4	100 State Farm Insurance	44,637.2

–Sales: Fortune, July 31, 2000. GDP: "World Bank, World Development Report 1000," CCPA Monitor, vol. 7, no. 9, March 2001

other half of the country's productive assets were distributed among approximately 200,000 firms.

In manufacturing in the mid-seventies, the largest 100 firms controlled 60 percent of total sales in Canada. In both manufacturing and utilities, the top 20 companies controlled half of total sales. It has even been estimated that eight families control one-half of the companies whose stock is traded on the Toronto Stock Exchange.

That concentration of economic power, of course, was before the recent waves of corporate takeovers and mergers. Comparable information on market control has not been published in the last couple of decades and the situation has become complicated somewhat by the spread of "free-trade" agreements and the accompanying "globalization" of capitalism that has occurred, particularly in the 1990s.

Capitalist globalization has increased competition between multinational firms, a competition that some have credited with preventing the re-emergence of inflation as unemployment fell during the second half of the 1990s, particularly in the United States. To maintain or increase profits these same companies cheapened their labour costs by using their economic power in labour markets—downsizing, contracting out, de-unionizing, cutting wages and benefits, moving to low wage regions in Third World countries or the low wage states of the southern United States. At the international level these competing multinationals have begun to merge to restrict competition and create global monopoly power, with automobile manufacturing leading the way. Typical was Germany's Daimler–Benz takeover of U.S.-based Chrysler Corporation. The other major car companies have also taken over or made alliances with Japanese, European and Korean companies, placing the three (formerly) U.S. auto giants in the top 28 economies in the world. In short, market power exercised in national markets by monopoly corporations is being extended to deregulated global markets with global corporations now exceeding in size and economic power most countries in the world.

The Production Decision: The "Black Box" of Production Economics

The centrality of the business firm is illustrated in Figure 2.1. (This is simplified to exclude the international sector, government and the financial sector. These will be given later.) The production decision is the place to begin understanding the behaviour of firms. Deciding to produce is simultaneously a decision to hire labour and make an investment in real capital. How much, and at what price, is determined by the power relations not only in the **factor markets**—the markets for resources ("land"), labour and capital; but also in the **product markets**—the markets for goods and services. These power relations depend on a number of factors.

The first is the degree of competition between buyer and seller, between buyers, and between sellers. A huge firm like Wal-Mart faces limited competition in the retail discount department store market in Canada. It utilizes extensive advertising, "big box" marketing and favourable locations to augment its market power. Perhaps the only close rival to Wal-Mart nationally would be Zellers. On the other side of the market, however, it buys from thousands of closely

Figure 2.1: The Aggregate Flow of Income

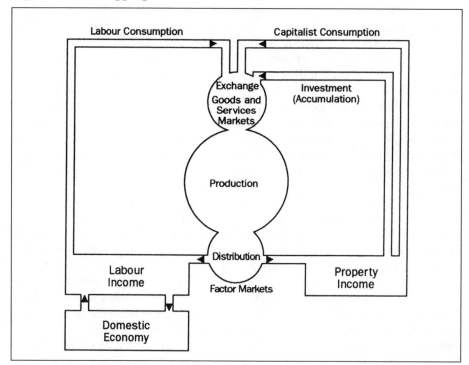

competitive clothing, toy, small appliance and similar manufacturers, a number of them "sweat shop" operations in Third World countries. Because these suppliers compete among themselves to turn out products to Wal-Mart's brand specifications they possess little or no economic power. This power imbalance means that the small producers create part, if not all, of Wal-Mart's surplus. Because it is so big Wal-Mart can demand lower prices and bigger wholesale discounts. Companies that refuse to meet these demands lose out to their competitors who do.

Wal-Mart exercises similar power in the labour market. The company can choose sales and other employees from a large supply of non-unionized workers, predominately women. With over a million unemployed Canadians competing for jobs, Wal-Mart can find the people it needs and at the same time keep its wages low.

Corporate power is not unlimited. In the labour market, for example, there are a number of institutions that restrain employer power, the most important being unions. Unions, in the words of the economist John Kenneth Galbraith, act as a "countervailing power" to employers. The stronger and better organized the labour unions are, the greater the limitations on corporate labour market power. Adam Smith recognized that employers enjoyed more bargaining power than workers because of their wealth and the laws which at that time outlawed labour combinations (unions). One would never know this from listening to those neoliberals who *selectively* extol Smith's insights today. Unions are not the only constraint on employer power. Governments provide minimal standards for wages and working conditions by law—minimum wages, maximum hours, holidays and vacations, health and safety and similar labour standards legislation. However, such standards, never very high, have fallen over the last three decades, reflecting the political power of business.

Traditionally, the balance of power between labour and corporations has depended on the state of the labour market—that is, to the level of unemployment. Whenever unemployment falls to low levels, a somewhat rare event in capitalist economies over the last two centuries, labour's bargaining power has increased, since employers are forced to begin to compete for qualified workers by bidding up wages, and improving benefits and working conditions. Though unionized workers are better able to take advantage of this improved market power, the unorganized also find their bargaining position improved. More frequently, however, workers face high levels of competition for jobs. Marx called these people the "reserve army of unemployed," an army that swells as the economy slows down and/or goes into recession or depression and erodes labour's bargaining power. Under these conditions unorganized workers and those without specialized skills experience the greatest loss in bargaining power.

The move to free trade and unregulated capital mobility in the last couple of decades has significantly shifted the balance of power away from labour, whether unionized or not, and toward capital. All the low-wage labour of the Third World and—since the collapse of the Soviet system—also that of Eastern Europe, have effectively become part of the "reserve army" competing for jobs with workers in the industrial capitalist countries. This global labour market has undermined the ability of unions to exert countervailing power against the international corporations.

2.3 The Capital Market

The term **capital market** is confusing even to economists. This is partly because we use the word capital to mean different things. Capital refers to **capital goods**, those goods such as buildings and machinery that are used to make other goods and services. Our stock of capital goods is measured by the **value** of accumulated capital goods. The problem is, trying to figure out the value of accumulated capital led to one of the greatest and most protracted controversies in all economics, which neoclassical economists have still not resolved.

But we also use capital to refer to **finance capital**, the money that is used to finance the purchase of capital goods. Finally, the term capital is used by political economists to refer to an **employment relationship** in the sense that capital employs labour.

When we use the term capital market, economists are usually referring to the market for finance capital, loans of money to purchase capital goods. The price of purchasing the use of money to finance investment in capital goods is the interest rate. The total cost of capital, therefore, will depend both on the interest rate and the prices of capital goods, which will vary from capital good to capital good and so on.

2.4 The Rise of Corporate Political Power

Much of the increased power of corporations in Canada has developed with the advent of the Free Trade Agreement and NAFTA ... corporate bills of rights. The deals give rights to corporate "citizens," rights to profit from investment with ever decreasing obligations to employees, community, environment, and consumers. The deals give corporations political rights by making it possible for them to stop governments from acting in ways that might affect their profits or growth. In vast areas of public policy, conflict between the interests of citizens and corporations is decided in favour of corporations by laws that are unchangeable by Parliament, unchallengeable in court.

—Murray Dobbin, The Myth of the Good Corporate Citizen, p. 2–3

2.5 The Cost of Job Displacement to Workers

The evidence is that workers displaced by techno-logical change, corporate downsizing and restruc-turing do pay a price. Recent U.S. experience, for instance, shows that not only do displaced workers face considerable periods of unemployment, many who do find new jobs end up in "nonstandard em-ployment arrangements—temporary work, perform-ing work they used to do on a contract basis, starting a consulting business selling their services, or working part-time involuntary—outcomes gener-ally associated with lower pay.... Workers who find new jobs frequently receive lower wages than in their prior positions. It has been estimated that five or more years after displacement, displaced workers earn 10 to 18 percent below what their counter-parts who were not displaced earned."

–Francine Blau, Marianne Ferber and Anne Winkler, The Economics of Women, Men, and Work (Upper Saddle River, NJ: Prentice-Hall, 2002), pp. 280

Women are affected worse than are men. Not only are displaced women more likely to drop out of the labour force (become "discouraged workers") and be forced into nonstandard employment arrange-ments, they also suffer a larger drop in income on average than do men. An Ontario Labour Ministry study reported in 1993 that, when displaced, "women take an average $2,283 greater pay cut than do men. This confirms an earlier 1980–82 Ontario study that reported that women took a 42 percent cut in pay after displacement compared with only 25 percent of men."

[Paul Phillips and Erin Phillips, Women and Work (Toronto: Lorimer, 2000) p. 126]

Technology also affects the distri-bution of power in the labour market. This has been evident from the early years of the British industrial revolution when British hand weavers destroyed the new mechanical weaving machines that their employers had brought in to eliminate their jobs. These machine breakers, who were known as Luddites because they often claimed to be work-ing under the direction of the fictitious general Ned Ludd, were not mindless opponents of technology. Instead, as the British historian Eric Hobsbawm points out, they were engaged in a primitive form of collective bargaining to save their jobs. Technological change has almost always had the effect of destroying jobs, whether it be by ma-chines replacing skilled workers, robots replacing production line employees, or computers and electronic devices re-placing clerical, sales or technical work-ers. It is possible, as the technological optimists argue, that over time the economy may create as many or more new jobs as technological change de-stroyed. But in the short run, temporary unemployment, the threat of job loss and the insecurity of workers faced with finding a comparable job are real and undermine the bargaining power of un-ions. The bulk of the evidence is that the majority of workers displaced by technological change suffer a reduction in pay when they do find new jobs. This is particularly true in recent years, where workers displaced from the manufacturing sector are finding work only in the low-wage service sector.

As so eloquently noted by Adam Smith, the distribution of income and wealth also tips the balance of power in the labour market toward capital. With little wealth to fall back on, workers are dependent on their wages for day-to-day subsistence. As a result they have scant bargaining power in any protracted dispute with employers. Low-income workers in particular simply cannot hold out for long enough to put enough economic pressure on employers for decent wages. This holds whether labour is unorganized, as was required by law in Smith's day, or whether it is unionized as is permitted, if not encouraged, in our era.

Even today over two-thirds of workers in Canada are not organized in unions. In the United States, the situation is even worse with over four-fifths of the work force unrepresented by unions. All that unorganized workers can do is go, cap-in-hand, and beg for improvements in wages and working conditions. Only workers possessing specific skills or knowledge that employers require to operate and who are scarce in number relative to the employers' needs have any individual countervailing power to that conveyed to employers by their control of jobs, income and wealth.

So far, we have talked mainly about market and bargaining power in production decisions and factor markets. A similar analysis could focus on the interaction between the production decision and consumer markets where large corporations have market power because of advertising and promotion, patents and copyrights, control of production technology, costs of entry and access to capital. We will return to this later in the book.

Some production sectors are not included in Figure 2.1. One is the household, or domestic, sector, which does not normally produce a flow of money. Despite this, the sector is nevertheless important for raising and maintaining the labour force.[3] The informal economy, that legal and illegal productive activity that is either not represented or is under-represented in any official picture of the economy, is also not represented in Figure 2.1.

The Domestic and Informal Economies

The **informal economy** is economic activity that produces goods and services (or real income) but which is rarely, or only partly, included in official measures of economic output or income such as GDP. It is excluded primarily because the goods and services in the informal economy are not produced for, or distributed by, a market (or at least by a visible market) and, therefore, there is no record or measure of this activity. The activities of volunteers, such as referees and coaches for community hockey leagues or candystripers in Canadian hospitals, constitute a good example of unrecorded work. Some argue that domestic work has been excluded from official measures of economic output because it has traditionally

Figure 2.2: The Domestic Economy

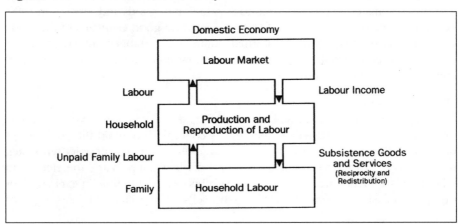

been "women's work," and in our patriarchal society women's work has not counted. The informal economy has also been excluded because many of its transactions are illegal or quasi-legal, and/or are concealed to avoid paying taxes. The subsectors of the informal economy can be seen as made up of the **domestic and volunteer** economy, the **grey** economy and the **illegal** (or underground) economy, indicating a declining ranking in legal and social acceptability.[4]

The Domestic and Volunteer Economy

The most important part of the informal economy is the domestic, or household sector (Figure 2.2), which involves food preparation, child care and nurturing, clothing provision and maintenance, household services, repairs and maintenance. It is in households that much work and productive activity goes on, goods and services produced and consumed. A study by Statistics Canada published in 1994 concluded that this household activity contributed an equivalent of between 32 and 54 percent of GDP in 1992.[5] This was down moderately from earlier decades as unpaid housework is being replaced by marketed goods and services, with more and more women, particularly married women, having entered the labour market. One prime example is the growth of prepared and take-out foods replacing home-cooked meals. Another is the replacement of home-laundered cloth diapers with disposable diapers. This is the reverse of the trend that Keynes noted when he said that one way to *reduce* the GNP is for a gentleman to marry his housekeeper. (The work that the employed housekeeper did showed up in the GNP, but once she became a wife she would continue to do the same work but it would no longer count as part of the GNP.)

Alongside the household are the efforts of the community, voluntary, mutual and cooperative aid organizations. In the early days of settlement, barn- and house-raising "bees" and similar cooperative/mutual aid activities were a regular feature of many communities in rural and northern Canada. With urbanization, these activities have declined in importance. They remain significant in the North where food, clothing and bedding production obtained by hunting, fishing and trapping, and wood fuel and lumber production are estimated by Ross and Usher to provide 10 to 30 percent of the income of families.[6] Volunteer and charitable organizations such as churches, Meals on Wheels, food banks and candystripers were also estimated to produce around $4.5 billion of goods and services in 1980, equivalent to around 2 percent of GNP. We have no good estimates of the value of youth babysitting services, informal community arrangements such as car pools or barter and skill exchanges, nor of how much amateur recreation and cultural organizations contribute.

The Grey Economy

The grey economy is market type activity that is not reported to government. It is usually conducted by barter or cash and is concealed to avoid the payment of taxes and licences, because the work is often done by people who lack qualifications, or to avoid regulations or standards. Examples are: the electrician who installs a kitchen range for a relative on his or her own time in exchange for unreported cash payment; the farmer who sells uninspected chickens, eggs or raw milk to neighbours at a farm gate stand. It includes the individuals who make their living with garage sales but who do not purchase a peddler's licence.

How significant is the grey economy? Some years ago, the Italian GNP was re-estimated upward by 15 percent to account for this informal economic activity. In Hungary in the latter days of the communist regime it was estimated that fully two-thirds of the population participated in the grey economy. In some Eastern European economies in those days, it was proposed to encourage the grey economy by legalization in order to increase the rate of economic growth and to reduce shortages in consumer services.

The introduction of the Goods and Services Tax (GST) in 1991 prompted numerous claims that the underground economy in Canada was exploding in size as consumers and business alike attempted to avoid paying the new tax. The Canadian Federation of Independent Business had even charged that the underground economy had reached a level of 15 percent of GDP.[7] To assess these claims, Statistics Canada conducted a second study in 1994, a companion to their study of the value of household work. They divided the underground economy into four categories: legal activity both market and non-market, and illegal activity both market and non-market. Some of the underground economy was already measured in GDP. Unreported income, for instance, may be included in some of the expenditure measures they use. Statistics Canada estimated that the *unmeasured* legal component reached a maximum of only 2.7 percent of GDP, the *measured* legal component 1.5 percent for a total grey economy of just 4.2 percent of GDP in 1993.[8] This was approximately 1 percent more than the maximum estimate a decade earlier, not the explosion that special interest business groups, anti-taxers and right-wing think-tanks had been claiming.

The Illegal, Underground Economy

The underground economy is criminal. Perhaps the most important components are tax evasion, organized crime (in particular the drug trade), prostitution, smuggling and illegal gambling. The underground economy does produce goods and services, however undesirable, which are not measured in GNP. Some estimates are as high as 10 to 15 percent of GNP in Canada, supporting some 150,000 jobs.[9] However, the Statistics Canada study put the estimate of illegal activity at only 1 percent of GDP. This figure appears to be rather low if media accounts of the extent of illegal drug operations in Canada, including the widespread cultivation of marijuana, are true. As well, crime, in effect, double-counts the contribution of the underground economy to GDP. Because comparable amounts of goods and services are spent in suppressing underground activity (police, courts, penal system) and in repairing the damages inflicted by this activity (insurance, hospital, medical and social facilities), it gets counted twice.

Taken together, the unmeasured informal economy, in both its positive and negative forms, makes an important contribution to real economic activity, though primarily in the form of household and volunteer work. In Canada it may be perhaps 40 to 60 percent of GDP. The tendency of orthodox economists to ignore the informal economy is, therefore, a major weakness in much contemporary economic analysis, and serves in particular to degrade the value and importance of "women's work."

2.6 The Flight From Competition

"Men go into business to earn a living. There are often circumstances which seriously interfere with their ability to do so. The greatest of these is competition."

–Canadian Grocer, 1981

The Dominion Wholesale Grocers' Guild was one of the most visible and persistent business organizations in the forefront of a massive flight from domestic competition in the 1880s and 1890s, hard on the heels of the barriers to foreign competition erected by the National Policy tariff. Businessmen formed guilds, associations, pools, trusts, and mergers with the aim of restricting the free market in every form of enterprise—transportation, manufacturing, finance, and distribution.... Other businessmen had turned to organic mergers rather than loosely knit trade associations as a way of ending open competition. Although the classic merger movement of 1909–1912, in which some 275 individual firms were reduced to 58, was largely defended in terms of the desirability of achieving economies of scale in production and distribution, the need to eliminate "wasteful" competition was obviously a factor in some of the outstanding mergers.

–Michael Bliss, A Living Profit (Toronto: McClelland and Stewart, 1974) pp.33–34, 39–40.

The Monopoly Sector

The monopoly sector is known by different names—"the planning sector," "monopoly capitalism," "corporate capitalism," "big business," "core, or centre, firms." Firms in this sector are (1) big (frequently multiproduct, multiregional, multinational); (2) bureaucratic; and (3) in possession of market power.

The first real "big businesses" were the railways. The tremendous cost of building railways made price competition ruinous. As other industries became more capital intensive and technologically sophisticated, business sought ways to limit competition. The most effective was for smaller companies to merge, creating large companies known as combines or trusts. There was a wave of these consolidations in the U.S. in the 1890s. In Canada the first merger movement peaked a little later—approximately 1907–1912. Only in some industries was this effective in restricting competition. Hence, in the second half of the 1920s there was a second wave of corporate mergers. This has been followed by peaks in the late 1950s, the 1960s and then the 1980s and 1990s. In the late 1980s more money was spent on takeovers and consolidations than was spent on new investment. Since then, the pace of mergers and takeovers has actually accelerated in response to the increase in global competition. The result is more and more mergers among existing multinational corporations, such as the merger of the giant German car manufacturer, Daimler–Benz, with Chrysler, the third largest U.S. auto firm. The resulting German–American consolidation DaimlerChrysler (including Mercedes–Benz) also has ownership shares in Mitsubishi of Japan and Hyundai of South Korea. The goal of these consolidations is to augment market power by reducing effective competition on a global basis.

Market power means that each firm has a significant influence on the prices it charges. They do not necessarily accept a given market price but try to select market prices that will maximize their profits over the long term. Firms in this sector are "price searchers," not "price takers." It is this longer-term profit horizon that is conveyed in designating this sector, the planning sector. Their size and control of assets allows these companies to look beyond the immediate period even if it means taking short-term losses. Small firms with limited resources do not have the same capacity. It is ironic to see staunch apologists for contemporary capitalism attack the idea of Soviet style central planning since there is no better example of central planning than the modern global corporation.

What is the source of this market power? In general the competition these firms face is limited because they have a degree of monopoly power. This monopoly power allows the company to restrict supply and thereby raise prices, though not without limit, to the level that maximizes its long-term profits. What are these factors that confer this power?

The most obvious is the case of a **natural monopoly**— that is, where it is cheaper (in economic language, "more efficient") for a single company to provide a good or service than for two or more firms. This is the case for firms such as the traditional (wire) telephone companies or electrical distribution companies, since only one set of telephone or hydro poles is required to deliver the service or the power to the consumer. If there were two firms, the cost of providing two sets of poles and wires would effectively double the cost of providing the same level of service. Most utilities such as natural gas distribution, water and sewage provision, cable television and internet services, and fire protection services fall into this category. It is also the reason why the prices charged for these utilities are usually controlled either by public utility boards or by public ownership and by regulation of these companies or services.

2.7 The Efficiency of Private versus Public Utilities

Part of the neoliberal agenda of the 1980s and 1990s was privatization and deregulation of utilities on the grounds that public ownership and regulation was inefficient relative to private, unregulated utilities. However, the empirical evidence has been that there is no support for the supposed superior efficiency and performance of private utilities. Indeed, if anything, the evidence points to exactly the opposite conclusion—that public utilities produce cheaper electricity than private utilities.

Economist George Chuchman in a paper that summarizes six detailed studies of American electrical utilities, writes:

> [T]he most surprising aspect overall has been the lack of any consistent evidence in these studies that public owned electric utilities are inefficient in the operations or that the inefficiencies of regulation of monopolies are of major significance....
>
> It appears that the study with the strongest conclusions, that public sector electric utilities set lower prices than private utilities, is the very recent study by [John] Kwoka. ["Pricing in the Electric Power Industry: The Influence of Ownership, Competition, and Integration," American Economic Association Meetings, Boston, 1993.]

–George Chuchman, "Regulation, Competition and Privatization in the Electric Utility Industries," Department of Economics, University of Manitoba, 1995, pp. 13,17

The claim that public power is cheaper is supported by evidence comparing the monthly cost of electricity by publicly owned Canadian utilities compared with privately owned U.S. utilities. The basis of comparison is the monthly cost of 1,000 kilowatt hours. (Data supplied by Hydro-Quebec)

New York	$ 191.08	Halifax	$ 94.00
San Francisco	$ 169.75	Toronto	$ 92.30
Boston	$ 165.74	Ottawa	$ 73.55
Miami	$103.31	Vancouver	$ 61.16
Montreal	$ 60.33	Winnipeg	$ 58.94

The cost of deregulation was also illustrated by the electricity crisis in 2000 in California and Alberta that followed deregulation of their power systems. The California debacle contributed to the bankruptcy of one of the world's largest energy supply companies in 2001.

The majority of cases of monopoly or near monopoly are not, however, "natural." Some are deliberately created by law, some by the dictates of economics and technology, some by the purposeful creation of market advantage or

2.8 Pharmaceuticals, "Free Trade," and the Rising Cost of Medicare

In 1980, drugs accounted for only 8.9% of the overall costs of Medicare. By 1992 that figure had risen to 14%, or $9.2 billion, and is still climbing.

The escalating cost of prescription drugs can be traced to the enactment of two bills passed by the former Tory government, Bill C-22 in 1987, and Bill C-91 in 1991. These bills extended the period of patent protection for brand-name pharmaceuticals to 20 years. During that period, generic drug manufactures are not allowed to manufacture and sell cheaper versions of the brand-name drugs. The makers of these drugs have been granted a 20-year monopoly on their use....

Previously, generic drug makers were licensed to make and sell cheaper "no-name" versions of most drugs, thus lowering our drug costs by nearly $500 million a year. The Canadian-owned generic firms also employed over 2,200 people.

–CCPA Monitor, May 1995

By the end of the decade of the 1990s, drug costs exceeded the cost of physicians' services under Medicare and remained the fastest growing segment of Canada's health insurance system.

control over knowledge and technology.

Knowledge is naturally a public good—that is, once knowledge is created it costs nothing to share it with everybody. But if it was shared with everybody, it wouldn't be scarce and therefore would not bring anybody profits. The only way knowledge can be used to bring profits to corporations is to privatize it. This is the whole purpose of patent and copyright laws. They create private property rights in knowledge and information such that the owner can gain monopoly control over it. The private owners can then limit the supply of products made with that knowledge, driving up the price and creating monopoly profits.

Perhaps the best examples of this are the pharmaceutical companies and, more recently, the computer software industry. Under present Canadian legislation drug patents are valid for a period of twenty years. This means that a new or redesigned drug created by a single pharmaceutical manufacturer cannot be copied or made by any other company for twenty years unless it purchases that right from the original developer of the drug. This allows the original developer to raise the price of the drug over the cost of production either by limiting how much it will manufacture or by licensing the right to manufacture to other firms for high fees. Pharmaceutical companies argue that this right, and the resulting profits, are necessary to cover the cost of research and development. The level of profits generated by the major pharmaceutical companies, however, would suggest that this protection right is excessive.

The software industry is similar in that individual programs and products are copyrighted. This allowed Microsoft to first protect its Windows operating system from competition. Then it used this monopoly power to promote its other applications, in particular its Internet platform Internet Explorer, at the expense of other platforms, in particular Netscape. It was this use of Microsoft's monopoly control of the Windows platform that led the U.S. Department of Justice to bring charges of abuse of a monopoly position under American anti-trust law. The resulting conviction and order to break up Microsoft are still being contested before the U.S. Courts by some states, though the federal government has accepted a compromise agreement with Microsoft that imposes a much lesser standard of competitive behaviour.

The prevalence of legal monopoly through patent and copyright is increasing, particularly with the spread of information and bio-technology and the development of "new" products such as genetically altered seeds. However, it is probably the **high cost of entry** into an industry that is the most potent source of market power for large corporations. What are these cost barriers to the entry of new competitors in an industry? One is the amount of investment, particularly for industries that are capital intensive. Take for example a pulp and paper mill. Building such plants costs about a quarter of a million dollars per worker. For an oil refinery initial investment can be a million dollars or more per worker. That means a refinery that employed only 50 employees would have a start-up cost of $50 million or more.

But the high entry barrier is not just in the initial cost. Many mass produced products require the establishment of sales organizations and dealer systems. An automobile company, for instance, requires a dealer and service system and a supporting parts distribution system. But even that investment isn't the end of it. For automobiles, where each individual company faces competition from the other car companies, market power can only be maintained by convincing consumers that each car is actually different (even though most manufacturers make near-identical models for each market niche). The cost of large-scale advertising campaigns is huge and since success is not guaranteed a risk cost must be factored in. Furthermore, developing a complex product itself may be a very long and expensive project. The longer and more costly the process, the greater the risk that the product may not find a market when it finally becomes available. Over a decade ago, the cost of bringing a new car onto the market was estimated to be $6 billion. In all, therefore, these costs are out of reach for all but a few large companies.

With new firms blocked by the high cost of entry, the existing large firms in established industries compete for market share, not normally through price, but through advertising, promotion and technological and stylistic innovation. Firms in these industries retain sufficient market power to make profits well above those earned by competitive firms.

Firms can develop monopoly power also through process innovation. Henry Ford's adoption of the production line allowed him to lower the price of his standard Model-Ts to a level that captured the majority of middle and lower income market. By the time other firms had converted to production line organization and technology Ford dominated the market. In Canada, Timothy Eaton entered the catalogue and mail-order retail market early in the last century, allowing Eaton's to become the first retail department store to capture a nation-wide market. Others copied it but only after Eaton's had become a household name across the country. Coca Cola developed a secret formula that remains both a trade secret (i.e., a monopoly) and the secret of its success in holding on to a major share of the soft drink market. McDonald's developed a distinctive marketing strategy that catered to children that few other fast food chains have been able to duplicate.

Many other examples could be given, but the basic point remains: innovation can give a firm a degree of monopoly power in a market. Small competitive firms usually cannot compete in these markets because they either do not have the institutional capacity for research, product development, marketing or promo-

2.9 Mergers and Takeovers: Boon to Investors, but Not to Consumers

Hardly a day passes without an item in the business pages announcing yet another merger or takeover. The tone of coverage is typically upbeat: bigger is better, we are told, and the winners will be consumers...(1999) was a record year for global mergers and acquisitions (M&As).... global M&As were valued at US$608 billion during the first nine months of 1999 alone. And this on the heels of 1998's record merger boom valued at US$544 billion, itself a jump of 60% from 1997....

Increasing market dominance by global oligopolies and monopolies is bad news for consumers, as any first-year economics student can tell you. The praise of economists for competition, in theory, is for a variety where there are many producers and consumers, none of which on its own can influence the market price. In practice, competition may exist to some degree in the biggest, most profitable markets. But those on the periphery could be at the whim of monopoly power, with consequent high prices and poor customer service—or worse, be left without service at all.

–Marc Lee, "Business takeovers boon to investors, but not consumers," *CCPA Monitor*, February 2000

tion, or do not have the access to the necessary capital. Software companies are to some extent an exception. However, for the most part, once their product becomes accepted or begins to carve out a niche in the market, they sell out to larger firms in order to further develop the product and expand the market. They do this because the small firm simply doesn't have access to the resources to build the mass sales market. As a result of these barriers, there are a small number of large firms in many product markets (oligopolies, rather than monopolies). It is, however, possible to have one dominant firm and a number of smaller firms hiding under its protective price umbrella.

Many monopoly firms have relationships (sometimes referred to as interlocks) with other dominant firms. Some may be directly related, as with subsidiaries. Safeway's subsidiaries, for instance, include MacDonald's Consolidated in wholesaling and Lucerne Dairies and Empress Foods in the food processing industry. Alternatively, firms may have interlocking directorships. This is the case where company directors sit on the boards of two or more otherwise unrelated firms. This is very common with production firms and major financial corporations—banks and trust companies. Bank and trust company directors, for instance, may sit on the boards of manufacturing companies and vice versa. These interlocks increase the power of these large firms because it gives the manufacturing firms not only a source of information on what is going on in the economy, but also gives them easier access to loan markets to finance investments.

The motor of the capitalist system is the search for profits.[10] This search can be broken down into two types of competitive activity which, using military terminology, one can call tactical and strategic. **Tactical activity** is usually short-run, devised to take advantage of or respond to a particular situation in the market. This takes the form of an advertising campaign or promotion, a product modification, a price change or rebate, a "sale," "loss-leaders," reduced finance charges, etc. In this tactical form of rivalry, price competition (the sustained cutting of prices to minimum levels compatible with the continued existence of the firm) plays a minor, even insignificant role. Price cutting is, however, used as a tactical weapon to gain more market control through a larger market share, or by driving smaller competitors out of business. Large corporate chain stores, for instance, may initiate a price war when they enter new markets in order to "buy" sufficient market share to be cost competitive.

Strategic activity is designed to secure greater control of a market on a much longer time horizon. This usually takes the form of a significant investment aimed at obtaining a major cost advantage or a strategic position in a specific market. For instance, a national grocery chain will invest in a supermarket in a new urban development long before there are enough people living in that area to make the store profitable. Once established, however, the store will have a local monopoly that will generate profits as soon as the population of the development increases. Its existence, at the same time, acts as a barrier to any competitor considering building in that region.

There are many other investment strategies that firms can use to increase their market control. One is to invest in a new market, such as Eastern Europe or China, or in the development of new technology. The automobile manufacturers, for instance, are investing in new "hybrid" (gas and electric) car technology, all hoping to be first with an economically viable model. At the same time, they are moving production of some models and components to low-wage countries in the Third World in an attempt to get a cost advantage over their rivals. There are still other long-term investment strategies, such as developing a new product mix; diversification to reduce risk; integrating ownership with suppliers or buyers (called vertical integration) or with rivals (called horizontal integration) as the automobile companies are doing; all strategies designed to increase their control of their markets.

Although price is sometimes used as a tactical weapon, what we call competition in the monopoly sector tends not to be price competition but rivalry to increase market control and profitability and to achieve cost reductions, all through tactical and strategic activity. Strategic rivalry in this sector takes place through investment designed to lower cost, raise productivity or introduce new products in order to control markets and undercut rivals. If this means that smaller, less advanced firms are driven from the market, this is good, according to business and orthodox economists. Because this process lent the monopoly sector and capitalism their dynamism, Austro-American economist, Joseph Schumpeter called it **creative destruction**. But it also gives the capitalist system its roller-coaster tendency marked by periodic overinvestment and the resulting crises that we call recessions and depressions.

The Competitive Sector

The vast majority of Canadian firms are small, employing less than 100 employees, particularly if we include farmers as businesses. Even the larger small businesses (50–100 employees) usually have very little market power and tend to be price takers rather than price searchers. Many will be in industries where there are no dominant firms, particularly in agriculture, and other "easy entry" sectors such as light manufacturing (eg., clothing or furniture), retail sales and service (eg., clothing stores and quick-print centres) and personal services (such as hairdressing salons, photography studios or family-type restaurants). Others, however, are small firms in industries dominated by a few large firms. In these cases the small firms enter the "nooks and crannies" of the market where the large firms do not find it profitable. These nooks and crannies are what the business pages refer to as "niche marketing."

An example is the mom-and-pop corner store that fills the demand for convenience (of location, hours, credit, delivery, etc.) that the dominant super-markets do not meet. Prices may be somewhat higher to reflect the cost of convenience and low level of sales. But the small retailer has very limited discretion in pricing in order to compete with the major stores and, since entry costs are low, with other convenience stores. Other competitive markets are those restricted to a local area for a variety of social reasons, such as a kosher butcher shop near a Jewish residential area, flower shops near a hospital or candle shops near a Catholic church.

The essence of the competitive sector is the relative ease of entry. It is this ease of entry that quickly eliminates any market power that a small firm might have. There are no great barriers of technology, investment, patents, access to raw materials, brand control of markets or differentiation of product that prevent the entry of a new firm. Consider, for example, a qualified hairdresser who wants to set up shop. What are the costs? Outside of a business licencse, a sign and some supplies, the salon itself can be rented and, normally, the equipment required can be leased or purchased over time. That means the start-up or initial investment costs are very limited and there are few, if any, other barriers to getting into business. There is no exclusive technology, no dominant firm in the market and no significant economies of scale that would give a big firm a cost advantage. This means that if profits are being made in this sector, there will be an incentive for our hairdresser to set up shop. The increased competition of such new firms, however, will quickly erode any excess profits and drive prices down to minimum levels. It is in this sector that the "law" of supply and demand that economists so often speak of can be observed in action. Firms operating in the monopoly sector need pay little attention to this law.

Some small businesses can achieve monopoly profits that are not necessarily competed away. Classic examples might be firms of architects, artists, graphic designers, rock bands, doctors, dentists and lawyers. In these cases the market power results from a naturally given—and scarce—talent, by an institutional limitation of supply such as enrollment limits in professional faculties in universi-ties, or by the regulation of minimum prices such as those established in the egg, chicken and milk markets.[11]

Profit in the competitive and in the monopoly sectors are subtly but importantly different. A small business usually invests to provide an income for the owner(s) comprised of the wage equivalent of their labour plus an income on their investment, the equivalent at least to what can be obtained from reasonably safe financial investments (bank deposits, bonds, term deposits, Canada Savings Bonds, guaranteed investment certificates, money market mutual funds, etc.). Income above this is "excess" profit. If other people get wind of such excess profits they will be inclined to enter into or expand their operations in the industry, thus driving out these excess profits. In this sense, *there are no long-term profits in competition*.

Expansion of small, competitive businesses is usually financed by borrowing from the owner's savings or using such savings as collateral for a loan, perhaps by mortgaging a home. In other words, investment is financed from the savings of the owners from their previous labour and investment income.[12] Investment may take place in the expectation of extra profits, but without past savings either in the form of financial assets or in debt-free collateral assets, small firms will be unable to get the financing to expand or enter an industry.

The heyday of competitive capitalism was in the first three-quarters of the nineteenth century, before the combination and merger movements produced big business. This does not mean that the role of small firms in the economy is necessarily declining, even today. Indeed, in terms of employment growth in the last couple of decades in particular, smaller firms have been especially important as the large corporations adopted a new generation of labour-saving production technology and consumers shifted their demand towards services, resulting in a major expansion in retail sales firms.

It must be noted that the lack of market power tends to make small firms very unstable. Less than one-half of new small firms last five years. Some small firms do not grow to be middle or large firms, though this is most frequently the result of achieving monopoly market power through control of technological innovation (a classic example being Microsoft that patented the DOS operating system and then built the proprietary Windows platform on it). For the majority of small businesses, however, access to a fortune is achieved most readily by growing just large enough to attract the attention of, and being bought out by, a larger firm attempting to limit competition to itself.

The Competitive and Monopoly Sectors: Some Final Observations

Little time has been spent discussing competitive markets and the competitive firm in this outline of the major business institutions in our market economy. The reason is not that small competitive firms are few in number (there are hundreds of thousands of them) or that they employ few workers—small firms with under 100 workers employed 44.4 percent of all workers in Canada in 1992 and have been creating jobs faster than large firms over the last couple of decades according to the most recent Statistics Canada study. The reason is that small competitive firms are laggards, not leaders. Their contribution to the economic out-

> ### 2.10 Small Firm Instability
>
> The generally positive job-creation record of small firms hides a lot of churning and turmoil under the surface of the aggregate employment statistics. In addition to being the largest creators of jobs in the modern labour market, small businesses are also the largest *destroyers* of jobs. Rapid job turnover, the frequent bankruptcy of small firms, and other sources of instability mean that employment with small firms is generally quite insecure.
>
> –Jim Stanford, *Paper Boom* (Ottawa and Toronto: CCPA/Lorimer, 1999), p. 129

> ### 2.11 Galbraith on Economists and Modern Economics
>
> The problem of economics here, once again, is not one of original error but of obsolescence. The notion of the consumer so distributing his income as to maximize satisfactions that originate with himself and his environment was not inappropriate to an earlier stage of economic development. When goods were less abundant, when they served urgent physical need and their acquisition received close thought and attention, purchases were much less subject to management. And on the other side, producers in that simpler and less technical world were not under compulsion to plan. Accordingly they did not need to persuade—to manage demand. The model of consumer behavior, devised for these conditions, was not wrong. The error was in taking it over without change into the age of the industrial system. There, not surprisingly, it did not fit.
>
> –John Kenneth Galbraith, *The New Industrial State* (New York: Signet, 1967), p.225

put of the nation is far less than either their numbers or their employment would suggest. Their productivity, investment and wages are low and they are dependent upon the large monopoly sector and government for their growth. As Jim Stanford suggests in his book *Paper Boom*:

> Most small businesses in Canada are destined to play an inherently secondary or subsidiary role in the economic progress of the nation as a whole, by virtue of the fundamental nature of the goods and services which they produce. Most smaller firms depend on sales to one or two markets: either the consumer purchases of individuals who already have jobs with other companies, or else purchases by those other companies of supplies and services used in their own operations....
>
> Most small businesses need some *other* employer to do something *first*, therefore, before they can sell their own product and create their own jobs. In this sense, most small businesses cannot "lead" the development of the broader economy. They can only follow it....
>
> Even if small business continues to account for a disproportionate share of new jobs created, the job-creation is itself dependent on prior expansion in the base industries whose performance ultimately determines the rise and fall of the economy as a whole. In the vast majority of cases, those base industries are dominated by large companies and public agencies.[13]

If we wish to understand the political economy of Canada today, we must begin with the institution that leads, drives and shapes the economy, the large corporation which, collectively, is called the monopoly sector. It is interesting and revealing that most neoclassical and neoliberal economists are preoccupied almost exclusively with competitive firms and competitive markets, and that any attention they pay to monopoly power is to treat it as a market distortion or market failure. Their tail wags their dog.

Notes

1. For the classic, and still relevant, analytic descriptions of American firm structure see Robert Averitt, *The Dual Economy* (New York: Norton, 1968) and John Kenneth Galbraith, *The New Industrial State* (Boston: Houghton Mifflin, 1967). Canada's corporate structure is discussed in Eric Kierans and Walter Stewart, *Wrong End of the Rainbow* (Don Mills: Collins, 1988).

2. "Competition," as used here, is not just "perfect competition" as defined in neoclassical economics. Economists define perfect competition as markets composed of many small firms producing identical products. An example might be wheat farming or lobster fishing. The competitive sector, however, also includes what economists refer to as "monopolistic competition," markets where many small firms compete with slightly different products or different locations. Examples might be ethnic restaurants, "mom and pop" corner stores, women's clothing boutiques and barbershops.

3. See S. Clark & M. Stephenson, "Housework as Real Work," in K. Lundy & B. Warme, eds., *Work in the Canadian Context* (Toronto: Butterworths, 1981).

4. These three subsectors of the informal economy have also been referred to as the "White," "Grey" and "Black" economies, from traditional use of the term black to refer

to illegal transactions as, for instance, in the expression "black market" or "buying on the black." Similarly, "grey" has traditionally been used to refer to transactions that are partly legal and partly illegal. The term "underground economy" is frequently used to refer to both the grey and the illegal economies. Here, however, we will use it exclusively to refer to the illegal economy.

5. Statistics Canada, "Households' Unpaid Work: Measurement and Valuation," (13-603-E, no. 3), 1994, p. 7. This publication includes an extensive discussion of how the various estimates were obtained. For one earlier, detailed discussion of the informal economy in Canada, see David Ross and Peter Usher, *From the Roots Up* (Toronto: Lorimer, 1987), ch. 5. Their estimate of the value of housework was between 35 and 44 percent of GNP.

6. Ross and Usher, *From the Roots Up,* p. 81.

7. Statistics Canada, "The Size of the Underground Economy in Canada" (13-603-E, no. 2), 1994.

8. Statistics Canada, "The Size of the Underground Economy In Canada," 1994, p. 50.

9. Ross and Usher, *From the Roots Up,* p. 97.

10. In conventional economic theory, the term profits is used somewhat ambiguously to refer to several different income flows to capitalists. "Normal" profits refers to the minimum return to capitalist to induce them to remain in a business. "Excess" profits exist in competitive industries only until new firms enter, driving down prices and profits to "normal" levels. In the long run "excess" profits can only exist in monopolized industries where firms possess market power and are therefore sometimes called monopoly profits.

    In Marxian theory a similar, though different, concept is used, that of *surplus* or *surplus value*. Surplus value, the source of capitalist profits, is the difference between the amount of money the capitalist pays for the means of production and for labour power to produce commodities and what she or he sells these commodities for. (The analogous concept to the rate of profit is the rate of surplus value, which is equal to the surplus value divided by the payment for labour power, sometimes referred to as the rate of exploitation.)

11. In the case of agricultural marketing boards, minimum prices were set, not to create monopoly profits for farmers, but rather to prevent their incomes from falling to the point were they would be forced out of business. However, what it does mean is that some of the more efficient farmers in these sectors consistently do make "above normal" returns to their labour and investment though few become rich in the process.

12. Symbolically this is: $\Delta K = I = f(S)$ where S = savings of the small business owners out of labour and investment income.

13. Jim Stanford, *Paper Boom* (Toronto: Canadian Centre for Policy Alternatives and Lorimer, 1999), pp. 136–141.

Chapter 3

Production Theory

Why Firms Behave As They Do

As demonstrated in the last chapter, the behaviour and performance of firms vary between price takers (competition) and price searchers (monopoly). The term price searchers doesn't really describe what such firms actually do in their pursuit of market power. Therefore, the explanation of why firms behave as they do must also distinguish between competition and monopoly. Though the latter dominates the contemporary economy, it is competition that is usually dealt with first in standard economics texts and is used to justify the "efficiency" of the unregulated market economy, though it is not efficient, either in theory or in the real world. Nevertheless, we will follow convention and deal with competition first.

The Competitive Sector

The competitive firm is forced by its relative insignificance in the marketplace to accept the prices prevailing both in the markets it sells to and also in the markets in which it hires its labour and buys its equipment and supplies. This applies to any small or medium size business—a family farm, independent retail store, restaurant or hair salon, small manufacturer or welding shop. These enterprises buy materials, hire labour and produce and sell products or services that are all pretty much the same, or at least consumers perceive them to be much the same, as those of all the other firms in these markets. Consumers will certainly have a preference for Pepsi or Coke, but not for AAA Shoe Repairs or CityWide Shoe Renu. How many people care whether the milk they drink comes from farmer Jones or farmer Goertzen?

> ### 3.1 The Myth that Deregulation is Good for You
>
> California's deregulated power industry, in which producers can sell electricity for whatever the traffic will bear, was supposed to deliver cheaper, cleaner power. But instead the state faces an electricity shortage so severe that the governor has turned off the lights on the official Christmas tree—a shortage that has proved highly profitable to power companies, and raised suspicions of market manipulation....
>
> How might market manipulation work? Suppose that it's a hot July, with air-conditioners across the state running full blast and the power industry near the limits of its capacity. If some of that capacity suddenly went off-line for whatever reason, the resulting shortage would send wholesale electricity prices sky high. So a large producer could actually increase its profits by inventing technical problems that shut down some of its generators, thereby driving up the price it gets on its remaining output.
>
> –Paul Krugman, "California screaming," *New York Times*, December 10, 2000

Given that the firm must accept these competitive prices, it will try to produce as much as it can, at least up to the point that the price it can charge no longer exceeds the costs it takes to produce more output. Economists have long argued that costs to produce a commodity rise as a firm approaches its maximum capacity.

Figure 3.1

Price

Supply

Quantity of Output Supplied by
Competitive Firms

This is known as the **law of diminishing marginal productivity**.[1] If the price in the market were to rise, the firm could afford to hire additional labour and produce more. If the price fell, it could not afford to produce as much and would reduce its output and employment. This argument is the basis of the **"law" of supply**, which simply states that the higher the price, the more the quantity of goods and services a competitive firm will be willing to supply (and vice versa). This does not seem to be an unreasonable assumption.

Since all competitive firms are similarly affected, the supply of a good or a service to the market can be illustrated as a curve, as in Figure 3.1. What does it say? Merely that if the price prevailing in the market rises (measured on the vertical axis), the amount of goods or services provided by competitive firms to the market (measured on the horizontal axis) will also rise. Again, we have no reason to question this assumption.

3.2 The "Laws" of Supply and Demand

The story is told that during an election in the 1950s in Saskatchewan the Minister of Agriculture in the Cooperative Commonwealth Federation government was addressing a large election rally in a rural constituency. He was in full flight, criticizing the federal Liberal government for the low price of grain and falling farm income, when he was interrupted by a red-faced farmer at the back of the hall who shouted, "Hey, Toby, what about the law of supply and demand?"

Toby Nollett, the agriculture minister, hardly missed a beat, glared at his heckler and responded, "And who do you think passed those laws anyway?"

Of course, the laws of supply and demand are not laws and they may not even be true all the time. They are what economists consider usual or normal behaviour in markets: consumers want to purchase less when the price goes up and firms want to supply more when the price goes up. This means that if the price is high suppliers will usually want to supply more to the market than consumers want to buy. As a result a surplus will appear and, *if there is competition among producers*, prices will be bid down until the demand and supply are equal and the surplus disappears. If the price begins too low, the opposite normally happens, providing consumers are able to compete among themselves and bid up the price.

To figure out how the price is determined, we need know what consumers are willing and able to pay for the good or service. Normal, rational, human behaviour suggests that consumers will buy more as price declines. There are two reasons to support this assumption. One is that if the prices of tomatoes fall and those of avocados don't, some consumers will be willing to substitute tomatoes for avocados in their dinner salads. The second reason is that if the price falls, consumers can buy more for the same amount of money. If a can of pork and beans is priced at one dollar a tin you can buy two tins for a "Toony." But if the price is lowered to 66 cents, the same consumer can by three tins for the same two dollars.

This is the **"law" of demand**. It says that the higher the price, the less the quantity of a good or service a consumer will want to buy or demand (and vice versa). Taking all consumers together, the demand (curve) can be

Figure 3.2

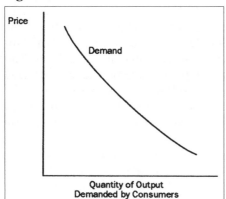

Figure 3.3

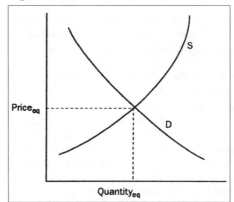

illustrated as in Figure 3.2. Again, it merely indicates that as price falls, the quantity of the good or service demanded will increase. We still, of course, don't know what the price will be and, therefore, what quantity of our commodity will be purchased. In order to determine that we must include both demand and supply. This is done by putting supply and demand together (Figure 3.3). Now

we can determine what the price and the quantity of goods and services will be in the market. No other price could exist in the market except the one where the supply offered by firms is equal to the quantity demanded by consumers. This price is called the **equilibrium price** (P_{eq}). If the price is higher than the equilibrium price (P_{eq}), then supply would be greater than demand and firms with unsold production would reduce prices. If the price is lower than P_{eq} then demand would be greater than supply and consumers would want to buy more than was available, inducing firms to raise prices. This mechanism of price setting is most obvious at an auction, such as the flower market in Holland, where the auctioneer keeps lowering the price of the flowers made available by growers until all are sold to buyers purchasing the flowers for the export market. Auctions where the auctioneer keeps increasing the price until the supply is sold to the highest buyer occur daily in North American livestock markets.

3.3 Value Theory: A Tale of Scissors

In the nineteenth century, economists debated what appeared to be a paradox. Why were diamonds, which were otherwise of little practical use except as ornaments, very expensive to buy, while water, the most essential of all products for human life, was virtually free?

The classical economists, in particular Adam Smith, David Ricardo and Karl Marx developed one answer based on the labour theory of value. However, it was Alfred Marshall, a British economist, who is credited with the theory that has become the mainstay of modern orthodox economic theory. Marshall argued that you need two blades of the scissors in order to cut paper. One is not good enough.

What he meant was that it was not enough to know that water was more in demand than diamonds. You also had to know that diamonds were rare and expensive to supply while water was readily available and cheap to supply. It is the interaction of the two blades of the scissors that cut the paper. It is the interaction of supply *and* demand that determines market value. And diamonds are not always valued more than water.

Just ask a person lost in the middle of a hot desert. "What would you pay more for, a flask of water or the world's biggest diamond?"

3.4 Stanford on Small Business

The unprecedented growth of low-wage, low-productivity small business employment in Canada, especially prominent during the 1990s, in many ways represents a shift toward a third-world pattern of economic development. The number of well-paying, productive jobs available in the "core" of the economy (larger firms and public agencies) has stagnated, thanks in large part to the slowdown in real capital accumulation by those same employers. Through economic necessity more than choice, many Canadians have responded to the dearth of "good" jobs by trying to make their own jobs. Government has promoted this trend with tax breaks and outright subsidies, as a relatively cheap way of dealing with the overall unemployment crisis.

–Jim Stanford, *Paper Boom*, p. 142

What would happen if the equilibrium price meant that firms were making losses? In the long run, some firms would go out of business. This happens all the time in agriculture. The world prices for grain and oilseeds have been so low in recent years that many farmers' incomes have plummeted to levels below what they could earn by leaving the farm and working in a "city job." As a result, more and more farmers "give up the ghost" and leave agriculture. This should reduce the supply on the market (Figure 3.4), raising the price from P_{eq} to P'_{eq} until losses cease. Unfortunately for Canadian farmers, however, there are so many farmers worldwide and the governments of some countries have been subsidizing their farmers so that they don't leave farming, that the effect on total world supply, and thus on grain prices, has been minimal.

What would happen if P_{eq} meant that firms were making (excess) profits? In the long run, other firms would enter the business to attempt to cash in on the profits. The increase in supply should soon eliminate the profits as prices fall from P_{eq} to P''_{eq} (Figure 3.5). Thus, it is easy entrance and exit in small competitive business that adjusts prices and demand and tends to limit all but temporary profits and losses. In this sense, competitive business is controlled by the market rather than controlling the market.

One result of this is that when there is a downturn in the economy or when certain costs (for example, indirect taxes, workers' compensation assessments, interest rates) rise, competitive firms cannot adjust as easily as monopoly firms. If they start to lose money, the only way out is to reduce costs, and the largest cost they can control is usually their labour cost. This tends to make small business

Figure 3.4

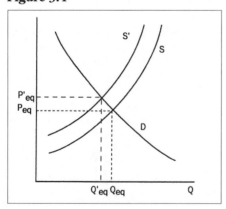

Figure 3.5

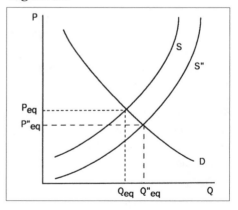

particularly hostile to unionism, minimum wages, unemployment insurance and welfare (all measures that tend to, or perhaps more importantly are believed to, hold up wages). On the other hand, small business is frequently more favourable to the regulation of competition, minimum prices and labour subsidies than is big business.

While Canadian farmers do not employ many workers, they have used their political power to exempt farm labour from minimum wage laws and workers' compensation coverage throughout Canadian history. Farmers are also more likely to blame workers rather than the monopoly companies they buy from for the cost of their inputs. Given their limited use of wage labour, therefore, farmers have in the past tended to try to control or reduce costs through cooperative buying and marketing or through regulating supply or markets. The two best examples of supply control and regulated markets are the marketing boards in the dairy and "feather" (eggs, chicken and turkey) industries and the Canadian Wheat Board, which is the monopoly marketer of wheat and barley produced by Prairie farmers.

However, the growth of global agribusiness and the attack on market regulation under the North American Free Trade Agreement and the World Trade Organization have severely undermined both the cooperative and regulatory systems that were put in place to try to protect farmers. It is probably only a matter of time before the average farmer becomes essentially a "waged worker," working for the international agri-corporations that will contract out all their agricultural input needs. This is already the case for many specialty crops and is widespread in the hog industry.

3.5 Marketing Boards

There are three types of marketing boards in Canada. The first is that represented by the milk and feathered industries boards. They are what are known as **supply management** boards in that they have the power to restrict supply through the allocation of quotas to farmers to ensure that the Canadian supply of these commodities equals Canadian demand at a price that provides farmers with a stable income at a reasonable standard of living. That is, they attempt to replicate a competitive market outcome in a market where there is monopoly power by processors and wholesalers that would otherwise be able to exploit the independent farmers. These kinds of marketing boards have been remarkably successful in stabilizing farmers' incomes while at the same time promoting productivity growth and restraining consumer prices.

The second type of marketing board is exemplified by the Canadian Wheat Board (CWB). It has a monopoly on the sale of all wheat and barley from the Prairie region. It does not, and cannot, control supply, although it may limit deliveries through individual quotas in years where there is more grain produced than can be sold on the international market or stored in the grain system in that year. The CWB is a **"single-desk seller."** This allows it to act like huge multinational grain companies and exert its monopoly selling power offsetting the power of the multinationals—only in this case in the interest of the farmer, not the multinational corporations. Studies have shown that single-desk selling has returned to the farmers many millions of dollars each year over what they would have received without the Wheat Board. It is this effective defence of the farmer that has made the CWB the target of the multinational grain corporations who have been attempting to use U.S. trade law, NAFTA and the WTO to have it abolished.

The third type of marketing board are the **voluntary boards**, such as the Manitoba Pork Marketing Board. These behave very much like any other private or multinational marketing corporation and are usually in competition with them. The only advantage to the farmer is that they are farmer owned or controlled and are non-profit such that the farmer gets the full return from all market sales.

The Monopoly Sector

Monopoly sector firms[2] have more options both in the short and long run. These large firms have a controlling interest in the sectors they serve—heavy manufacturing, corporate retail chains, resource industries, the media and so on. Because the firm has a degree of monopoly in its markets, consumers have less opportunity to bid off one producer against another. This means that if the firm raises its price, the loss in the quantity demanded will be much less than for a firm in a more competitive market. This is illustrated by the demand curve in Figure 3.6.

Second, the firm can advertise its distinctive characteristic—its unique or monopoly characteristic, be it real or imaginary—to shift the demand curve (Figure 3.7). This gives it the option of raising the price (to P_2) for the same quantity (Q_1), to sell more (Q_2) at the same price (P_1), or to arrange some combination of increased price and quantity that will optimize its profits. (This is why such firms are called price searchers.)

Third, the company can use its market power to attempt to lower costs for raw materials, supplies, transportation and especially labour. In the longer run, it can get more out of its workers by introducing speedups, downsizing (described by one major Canadian capitalist as "drowning the kittens"), contracting work out to non-union suppliers, union breaking, increased mechanization and so on.

Fourth, it can use the political power that flows from its economic power. Big companies lobby for tax concessions, subsidies, wage controls, reduced pollution controls, safety and health standards, reduced unemployment benefits or to shift costs from the firm to the public treasury (e.g., costs of transportation routes, utilities, pollution control, training, research and development, etc.). Perhaps the most visible example of this recently has been employer pressure on the government to increase immigration or to create a new category of "guest workers" to fill job openings. Governments give in to these demands rather than force these employers to pay competitive wages, improve working conditions or absorb the cost of training unemployed Canadian workers to fill the jobs.

A business's total revenue equals the quantity of output it produces and sells times the price for that output. A business's total costs equals what it pays for raw materials and energy, for labour (wages and salaries), for interest on money borrowed to purchase equipment and to provide working capital, for deprecia-

Figure 3.6

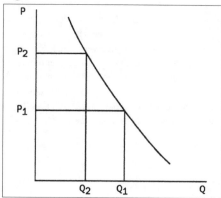

Figure 3.7

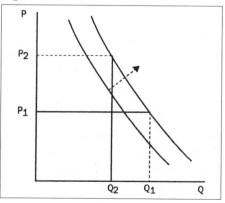

tion and for indirect taxes. Income taxes on business profits are not a cost of production since they are only paid on any profits *after* the output is produced and sold.[3] While this is also true of the competitive sector, it does not have the same economic or political muscle to lobby governments for special treatment on taxes, subsidies, or exemptions from environmental, health and safety, and other regulations.

How does the monopoly sector determine its prices and level of output? It is important to remember that because these firms are so big it is not easy for them to enter and exit the marketplace. As a result, there is no equivalent to supply and demand pricing as in the competitive sector. Monopoly firms use what economists call **markup pricing** or what noted economist John Kenneth Galbraith called "the Revised Sequence" of price determination.

Oligopoly firms begin by setting a target rate of profit, usually approximately 20 percent return on capital invested, after income taxes. Firms then estimate (on the basis of engineering data and expected prices) their costs of raw materials, labour, interest on borrowed money, depreciation and taxes

---

3.6 The "Revised Sequence" and the Myth of Consumer Sovereignty

In virtually all economic analysis and instruction, the initiative is assumed to lie with the consumer. In response to wants that originate within himself, or which are given to him by his environment, he buys goods and services in the market. The opportunities that ... are the message of the market to producing firms. The flow of instruction is in one direction—from the individual to the market to the producer. This is called consumer sovereignty ... (and) may be denoted the Accepted Sequence.

The mature corporation has readily at hand the means for controlling the prices at it sells as well as those at which it buys. Similarly, it has means for managing what the consumer buys at the prices which it controls. This control and management is required by its planning. The planning proceeds from use of technology and capital, the commitment of time that these require and the diminished effectiveness of the market for specialized technical products and skills....

It follows that the accepted sequence is no longer a description of the reality and is becoming ever less so. Instead the producing firm reaches forward to control its markets and on beyond to manage the market behavior and shape the social attitudes of those, ostensibly, that it serves. For this we also need a name and it may appropriately be called "The Revised Sequence."

–J. K. Galbraith, *The New Industrial State* (New York: New American Library, 1967), pp. 221–2

---

at varying levels of output. As a general rule the cost per unit of output declines as the scale of production increases. This allows firms to estimate the price required to produce their target rate of profit. Market prices are then set at the estimated cost of production plus the target rate of profit.

If costs decrease as output increases, the market price the firm will charge will also decrease as output increases. Firms must, therefore, estimate not only costs at various levels of output but, in addition, the expected demand at the varying prices. Given these expected costs and demands, the price and quantity is determined where the cost plus the target rate of profits intersects with the demand. When building, expanding or downsizing its operations, the firm usually designs its plant to be operated at around 80 percent of capacity.

Why would a business deliberately plan to have 20 percent extra capacity over what it requires to meet its expected market sales? The answer lies in the fact that no firm can be totally sure of the accuracy of its anticipated sales figures. What happens if demand actually exceeds what was expected? What happens if demand fluctuates both up and down around the expected level? If there is no

Figure 3.8

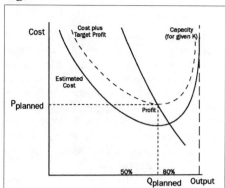

Figure 3.9

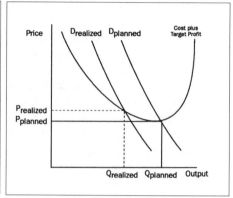

excess capacity, the firm cannot respond in the short run and will lose market share to rival firms producing a similar product. On the other hand, particularly if cost per unit of output continues to decline until production approaches full capacity, firms can expand output to meet the demand and, without raising prices, realize extra or super profits over their target levels. This process is illustrated in Figure 3.8.

What happens if either demand or costs are not what are expected? For example, what happens if the expected demand does not materialize? Firms have several options: they can increase advertising to increase demand, but this will also increase costs and hence reduce profits. Alternatively they can increase advertising and prices to attempt to recover the increased costs or, third, they can maintain prices and accept temporarily less-than-target returns. Finally, they have the option of laying off workers, reducing output and increasing prices. This option is illustrated by the price Pr in Figure 3.9.

So, for the monopoly sector, the normal result of a decline in expected demand is either reduced profits or increased prices or a combination of both. A reduced demand producing an increase in prices is a perverse market result—yet it happens all the time. That is, when demand for a product declines or is less than expected, prices frequently rise to compensate. This tendency is called **perverse pricing**.

What if demand is insufficient to allow higher prices to be passed on? What happens, for instance, when government and Bank of Canada policy causes overall demand within the economy to drop resulting in a recession or a weak economy? In this case, initially profits will fall, creating what is known as a **realization crisis** (so called because businesses cannot realize expected levels of profit). When profits fall or fail to meet expectations, investment tends to decrease or even cease. Large firms then turn their attention to cutting costs or gaining control of more market. North American industries have been experiencing a realization crisis since the mid-1990s.

To cut costs, companies have a number of options, most of which involve reducing labour costs. This can take the form of attempting to reduce wages and salaries, though this can prove difficult, though certainly not impossible, when the workers are unionized. Maple Leaf Foods in Manitoba recently used the threat of plant closure to force its workers and their union to agree to contract cuts. Maple Leaf is hardly unique in this tactic. Employers have conducted a concerted campaign to break unions and to prevent unions from representing workers in the first place, even to the extent of closing businesses, as McDonald's Restaurants have done in two recent cases, rather than accept negotiating with a union. In this they have been aided by conservative provincial governments, particularly in Alberta and Ontario, which have catered to employers by passing restrictive labour legislation and reversing many of the legislative gains labour had made in the post-Second World War period.[4]

Despite union opposition, many employers introduced two-tier wage systems in the 1980s and 1990s. In these systems current employees stay at their wage rates, but there is a reduced starting rate for new employees. Even more common was the practice of contracting out to lower wage or non-union subcontractors. Factories, for instance, would contract out cleaning services to low-wage cleaning companies and lay off their unionized cleaners who were making wages comparable to the plants' production workers. This was a particularly prevalent practice with all levels of government, including hospital and school boards.

Wages and salaries may also be reduced by moving production to low-

3.7 Perverse Pricing: Rising Prices as Demand Drops

In the economic downturns at the beginning of the 'seventies and 'eighties, there were numerous examples of firms such as tire manufacturing companies and Japanese car makers announcing price increases because of excessive "competition" which, when you read the explanation, translated into reduced sales. To maintain revenue, the firms claimed, they had to increase prices.

Examples of corporations raising prices to maintain target profits when demand drops or fails to meet expectations have been rare in recent years for two reasons. One has been the growth in the economy in the last half of the 1990s so that there have not been many cases of major corporations facing falling demand. Second, global competition has temporarily reduced the market power of large corporations and thus their ability to raise prices. However, the response to the Asian crisis and the decade-long recession in Japan has been intense merger and acquisition activity integrating competing multinational companies. This has been led by the automotive industry and has resulted in growing international market power by the merged companies.

Since the economic downturn in 2001, moreover, examples of perverse pricing are again beginning to be seen. For instance, the *Globe and Mail* (September 5, 2001) reported: "As the recent economic slump puts new pressure on corporate budgets, Microsoft is doing everything it can—*including raising its prices on some software licences*—to ensure its sales don't fall flat." [emphasis added]

More recently, Microsoft has announced that its profits have risen, in part as a result of these price increases. Rebecca Buckman wrote in the *Wall Street Journal*: "Microsoft has recently gotten a revenue kick from a controversial new software pricing program that has raised prices for many customers" [reprinted in the *Globe and Mail* (July 26, 2002)].

wage areas such as the "sunbelt" states in the U.S. or to Mexico, moves made more feasible by the adoption of NAFTA. With the spread of such free trade agreements and the growing strength and coverage of the WTO, corporations can also move their operations or their subcontracts to other Third World countries, particularly those that repress labour to hold down wages, such as Korea, China or Guatemala. Merely the threat of such a move has proved a major tool of North American employers in lowering wages and busting union s.[5]

A further alternative has been to replace regular, full-time workers with a

3.8 Restrictive Labour Legislation in Alberta

Virtually every area covered, from certification to internal affairs, to the right to strike, saw coercive restrictions on labour. Changes to the Code included provisions forcing unions to hold votes on an employer's "final" offer and/or the recommendations of a mediator, and harsh sanctions for union non-compliance with mediation. Even when workers might choose to strike under these onerous conditions, they had now to provide seventy-two hours notice to the time and location of such action and restrict picketing to members of the union concerned. In the case of construction workers, the restrictions on the right to strike, providing for concurrent votes by large majorities across a number of unions, were especially onerous. Picketing was subjected to tight controls at the discretion of the Labour Board. Of particular importance was a new provision requiring a certification vote even where all the employees in the unit signed membership cards. In addition, the provision allowing the Board to certify a union when management interfered in an organizing drive was now eliminated from the *Labour Code* [passed in June 1988]. All this obviously reflected the Bill's pre-eminent focus: the enhancement of capital's flexibility to respond to "the competitive world-wide market economy," dutifully acknowledged in the preamble.

–Leo Panitch and Donald Swartz, *The Assault on Trade Union Freedoms*, (Toronto: Garamond Press, 1993) pp. 106–107.

"contingent" labour force, sometimes referred to as "just-in-time" labour, which command wages well below the traditional—male—labour force. These contingent workers—part-time, temporary, contract, casual labour—tend to be disproportionately women, youth, immigrants and visible minorities, and Aboriginal people.

Another option has been government legislated wage controls or ceilings. Corporate support for direct controls has never been strong because it would involve government intervention in the affairs of business. In inflationary periods, such as the second half of the 1970s, Canadian governments tried to hold money wage increases at or below the rate of inflation. The difficulty in implementing such direct controls and opposition from the corporate sector have led governments in Canada to impose indirect controls by freezing public sector salaries or imposing wage settlements on their unionized employees below the rate of inflation. This and the recession of the early 1980s gave private employers the market power to impose similar settlements in the private sector.

Increasing the intensity of work or lengthening working hours can also lower wage costs. Many employers find it profitable to lay off regular workers, requiring the remaining employees to work paid or unpaid overtime. In 2000, the Ontario Conservative government of Mike Harris took the extraordinary action of introducing legislation to lengthen the standard work week (before overtime rates apply) to 50 hours from 45 to accommodate employers in intensifying the exploitation of their workers. Paying overtime rates is usually cheaper than employing more workers because employers are not required to pay for benefits, pensions or payroll taxes on the overtime wages, nor do they have hiring and training costs for additional employees.

One of the most prevalent forms of work intensification over the last two decades has been what is popularly known as "Japanese management," "total quality management (TQM)" or "team work." The basic principle of TQM is to organize the workers into teams. These teams are expected to find ways for the work to be done more efficiently and with less labour and to motivate the workers to work "harder and smarter" by delegating supervision to a team leader. This eliminates the jobs of some middle layer supervisors and managers. Workers are enticed to accept teamwork by the promise that they will be able to make their own decisions and improve the quality of their jobs. Once workers came to realize that TQM speeded up work and reduced the number of jobs, resistance to TQM built up. As a result, management has moved on to new flavour-of-the-month labour management techniques. (A fuller examination of management techniques is included in the next chapter.)

The intensification of labour can also occur through automation and computerization. Once purchased, programmable robots do not have to be paid wages, can work around the clock, are not charged payroll taxes and never go on strike for higher wages. Another organizational innovation is just-in-time production (JIT). With JIT, manufacturers, assemblers and service providers receive their required components just in time for manufacture, assembly or sale. This eliminates the cost of holding inventory, including the wage costs of warehouse employees, who lose their jobs.

Finally, employers can attempt to reduce their costs or increase their net profits by demanding cuts in taxes, both in the indirect (payroll and capital) taxes and the direct (corporate income and capital gains) taxes on profits. Many such tax cuts have already taken place or have been promised. This was clearly the top item on the corporate political agenda as shown in the elections in both Canada and the United States in 2000, where the leading corporate parties all campaigned on the promise of a reduction in taxes, mainly directed at corporations and the wealthy.

The monopoly sector markup model implies that cost increases can be passed on, in whole or in part, to the consumer even in the event of a decline in demand. Competitive markets imply, on the other hand, that cost increases cannot be passed on except in a market characterized by increased demand. What this means is that under monopoly capitalism, it is quite possible to have both a rising average price level and rising unemployment, something that is not considered possible within the capitalism envisioned by conventional economic analysis.

> ### 3.9 Class Analysis: Ford vs. Reuther
>
> Henry Ford II and Walter Reuther, the head of the United Auto Workers at the time, were touring a brand-new engine plant that they were scheduled to officially open. As they walked along the catwalk overlooking the production floor where large automated machines were churning out the blocks with only a few men looking on and monitoring the process, Ford turned to Reuther and said jokingly: "Well, Walter, you aren't going to get many union dues out of the men at this plant."
>
> Reuther was quick to respond. "No, Henry, but you aren't going to sell them many cars either."

> ### 3.10 Most Business Firms Pay Low Tax—or No Tax
>
> Almost two-thirds of all business firms in Canada with annual revenues of less than $15 million—as many as 716,000 of them—paid not a dime of federal income tax between 1995 and 1998. Neither did as many as 41 giant corporations with annual revenues of more than $250 million.
>
> Among the big corporations' subsidiary companies, 40% of them—about 2,664 in all—were also completely tax-free.
>
> That information was derived from two internal Revenue Canada reports recently obtained by Canadian Press under the Access to Information Act.
>
> One of the studies looked at federal taxes paid by Canada's banks and other financial institutions between 1996 and 1998. It found that in 1998 the total amount they paid in taxes to Ottawa dropped by an "astounding" $1.6 billion—a decline of 44%.
>
> –CCPA Monitor, July/August 2001

Notes

1. Technically, the law of diminishing marginal productivity (often mistakenly called the law of diminishing returns) states that in the short run, when at least one factor (usually land or capital) is fixed, the hiring of additional units of a variable factor (labour) will sooner or later result in a fall in the amount of extra output that additional labour will produce. (Obviously, if additional labour is producing less and less additional output, the cost of producing that additional output will rise.)

2. The rise and exercise of monopoly power in the United States and Canada is developed in Samuel Bowles and Richard Edwards, *Understanding Capitalism* (New York: Harper and Row, 1985), chs. 6–7; Alfred Chandler, *The Visible Hand: The Managerial Revolution in American Business* (Cambridge, Mass.: Harvard University Press, 1977); Wallace Clement, *The Canadian Corporate Elite*, Carleton Library No. 89 (Toronto: McClelland and Stewart, 1975); and Jorge Niosi, *Canadian Capitalism: A Study of Power in the Canadian Business Establishment* (Toronto: Lorimer, 1981).

3. Firm revenues and costs can be summed up with the following equations:
   Firm revenue = Price x Quantity = PxQ
   Firm costs = cost of raw materials and energy + wages and salaries + interest + depreciation + indirect taxes = rm + (w + i + dep + Ti)
   The difference between revenue and costs is gross profit (p). Therefore: p = P x Q - rm - (w + i + dep + Ti).

4. For a detailed discussion of the progressive curtailment of labour rights in Canada up to the early 1990s see Leo Panitch and Donald Swartz, *The Assault on Trade Union Freedoms* (Toronto: Garamond, 1993).

5. In a study for the Labor Secretariat of the North American Commission for Labor Cooperation (part of the labour sub-agreement to NAFTA), "The Effects of Plant Closing or Threat of Plant Closing on the Right of Workers to Organize," Kate Brofenbrenner of Cornell University documented the use of threats by employers to "run away to Mexico" to defeat organizational drives by unions and strikes in the United States. A summary of the full report is provided in chapter 10, box 10.15.

Chapter 4

The Labour Process

Most orthodox economists do not really consider the way employers organize, motivate and discipline their workers. This is left to "human resource management" and "industrial relations" specialists. It is, in Marx's descriptive language, a "hidden abode." Indeed conventional economics has a great deal of difficulty in dealing with the organization of work. Economist and Nobel laureate, Ronald Coase, in the late 1930s set out what has become the dominant position of mainstream economics. He argued that the complexity of coordinating and integrating labour in a cooperative (or interdependent) production process meant that using markets to organize and reward labour within a firm was not only unfeasible but also inefficient. Since markets for labour could not be used to organize work, it had to be done by an autocratic planning system controlled by management. The right to dictate the organization and speed of work was one of the rights of business ownership.[1] The problem is, orthodox economics does not, and cannot, deal with the distinction between labour power and realized labour, two of the key concepts discussed in this chapter.

Human resource management and industrial relations experts assume that the interests of workers and employers are the same. Their job is to improve the coordination of labour and management to achieve the goals of the corporation. Consider the following quotes from a human resource management text:

> [Business] organizations are the most inventive social arrangements of our age and our civilization. It is a marvel to know that tens of thousands of people with highly individualized backgrounds, skills, and interest are coordinated in various enterprises to *pursue common institutionalized goals...*[2]

> People and organizations depend upon each other. Individual employees rely on organizations for jobs, and increasing resource constraints coupled with rising societal expectations mean that they have to use the available resources more effectively.[3]

Note that it is assumed that workers are dependent on business for their livelihood, that the goals of the corporation are the same as those of the workers and that, given increasing constraints and rising expectations, labour must be used "more effectively" by the corporations. But are these assumptions necessarily valid? The goal of the corporation is to make maximum profits even if that means downsizing, laying off workers, lowering pay, contracting out and a host of other

4.1 Participation and Productivity

Many studies have shown that involving workers in making management decisions not only improves their motivation but also increases output and the rate of technological improvement at the workplace. The reason is really very simple. Any worker who is doing much the same job from day to day very quickly recognizes all sorts of ways the job can be made easier or faster, or the product or service made better or cheaper. These include everything from altering or adding a machine or tool or changing the order in which different tasks are done to modifying the size or shape of an envelope or order form to make them easier to process. If the employee can have some say in these kind of matters, such produc-tivity-increasing changes can be quickly and easily introduced into the workplace. The most interesting question is why more businesses do not involve their workers more in decision-making. The answer ap-pears to be that employers would lose much of their power over workers. Furthermore, there is consider-able fear among managers that workers would come to the realization that they don't need bosses but could do the job themselves. [See chapter 8, box 8.4, Participation, Productivity and Power]

management practices which conflict with workers' interests. Using labour "more effectively" can also mean part-time employment, speedups, shift work, excessive mandatory overtime, and so on. Human resource management has come to mean attempting to improve relations between employer and worker or to devise management systems that are more acceptable to workers so as to reduce turnover and absenteeism, in-crease worker motivation and morale, and facilitate on-the-job training. This is the current end-product of the evolu-tion of modern management, the prime task of which has been to extract the maximum amount of work from em-ployees.

However, the conflict between workers and employers is endemic. The workplace in the normal capitalist firm has two characteristics: (1) the relation-ship between employer and employee is authoritarian and (2) the employer and employee constantly struggle for control of the job—the employer to maximize output, the employee to maximize job satisfaction.

Labour Potential—Labour Power

Employers try to reduce labour costs by increasing labour productivity, the output of each hour a worker toils, or increasing the rate of exploitation of labour, the difference between the output workers' produce and the wages they receive. Unit labour costs can be reduced in two ways. Employers can structure the labour market in order to increase their economic power over labour (see the next chapter). They can also structure the work process to increase the amount of work done by workers. That is, employers can try to control the amount of work done by structuring how work is organized, mobilized, motivated and controlled.

When an employer purchases labour on the labour market, the employer only purchases a certain number of hours of the workers' time. The employer does not hire a specified quantity of work but of time in which to work. That is, the employer purchases a potential capacity for work, **labour power**, not any fixed quantity of actual labour. What do "bosses" do? Their problem is to convert as much potential work as possible into **realized labour**. In other words, their problem is to maximize the actual amount of work done during the hours the workers are being paid.

Thus, though we treat labour as a commodity to be bought and sold (like sacks of potatoes or computers), labour is in fact a fictitious commodity. It is fictitious because a commodity is defined as a good or service produced for the market. Labour, on the other hand, is a human capacity and humans (outside of slave-breeding farms) are not bred and reared for sale on the market. Also, what the employer purchases is not a unit of labour but a potential. The question for the employer is how to maximize or optimize **work effort**. Employers want workers to work as hard as they, the employers, think is "fair."

In economic terms, the employer's goal is the minimization of unit labour cost (ULC or the cost of labour per unit of production). ULC depends on the wage rate, the **efficiency** with which labour is utilized and the **intensity** with which it is employed.[4] Efficiency, in this context means how well the employer organizes the work of his employees. For instance, it may be a physical matter such as the placement of work stations so as to minimize the amount of walking workers must do. Or it could be an organizational matter, such as assigning routine data entry to low-paid clerks rather than to higher-paid bookkeepers or accountants. Intensity is simply how hard or fast the employees work.

4.2 Speenhamland and the New Poor Law

In the late eighteenth century, as industrial capitalism was taking control of the British economy, destitution and poverty was the fate of masses of the agricultural classes as rural overpopulation and the excess of agricultural labour drove down wages and raised unemployment. In 1795, the Berkshire magistrates met in Speenhamland in emergency session to seek some way to alleviate the suffering and distress.

[They] decided that subsidies in aid of wages should be granted in accordance with a scale dependent upon the price of bread, so that a minimum income should be assured to the poor *irrespective of their earnings*. The figures varied somewhat in various counties, but in most cases [across the country] the Speenhamland *scale* was adopted.... [until it was abolished in 1834 by the adoption of the New Poor Law.] Two years earlier, in 1832, the middle class had forced its way to power, partly in order to remove this obstacle to the new capitalistic economy. Indeed, nothing could be more obvious than that the wage system imperatively demanded the withdrawal of the "right to live" as proclaimed in Speenhamland—under the new regime of the economic man, nobody would work for a wage if he could make a living by doing nothing.

–Karl Polanyi, *The Great Transformation* (Boston: Beacon, 1944), p. 78

Carrots and Sticks

People working for themselves (for example, farmers, independent contractors, truck drivers, craftworkers and artisans) make their own decisions about how hard, how long and how they will work depending on their priorities between material income, leisure and job satisfaction. This is what people mean when they say they prefer "being their own boss." Indeed, almost universally people prefer being their own bosses. Historically, physical force or the threat of starvation was usually necessary to induce people to move from self-employment to employee status, even when they might be paid more for waged work.

How then do bosses convert labour power into real labour, to maximize efficiency (at least from the employers' perspective) and the efforts of the workers? In general, there are two strategies for any given technique of production: **carrots** (incentives to hard and efficient work) and **sticks** (disincentives to slack or inefficient work).

4.3 Disciplining Labour: Corporal Punishment and Black Holes in Industrializing Canada

The early factories in Canada were disproportionately staffed with women and children, in part because they could be paid lower wages, in part because they could be subjected to industrial discipline that many adult men would not. Here is evidence before the Royal Commission on the Relations of Labour and Capital 1889 of a 14 year old journeyman cigar-maker from Montreal. Questions are by commissioner Helbronner.

Q) How old are you? A) I was 14 on the 10th January last.

Q) When you call yourself a cigar-maker, you mean that you have served your apprenticeship, do you not? A) Yes, sir.

Q) How long? A) Three years.

Q) You began working at 11 years? A) Yes, sir.

Q) What wages do you get now? Are you paid by the piece? A) Yes, sir.

Q) You receive the same wages as the workingmen? A) Yes.

Q) What wages did you get during your apprenticeship? A) One dollar a week for the first year, $1.50 for the second year, and $2 for the third year. When I worked extra I got more.

Q) When you worked extra you got more? A) Yes.

Q) What do you mean by working extra? What was the amount that you were expected to do? A) We got 10 cents by 100 cigars, and when we made a certain quantity above that we were paid 10 cents a hundred.

Q) Did you have any fines to pay during your apprenticeship? A) Yes, sir.

Q) Many? A) A good number.

Q) Do you remember how many? A) No.

Q) Do you remember the most you paid in one week? A) Twenty-five cents.

Q) This is the highest you paid? A) Yes, sir.

Q) How many hours did you work a day? A) Sometimes ten hours, other times eight hours. It was just as they wanted it.

Q) Do you remember why you paid these fines? A) Sometimes for talking too much; mostly for that.

Q) You were never licked? A) Yes; not licked so as any harm was done me, but sometimes they would come along, and if we happened to be cutting our leaf wrong, they would give us a crack across the head with the fist.

Q) Was it usual to beat children like that? A) Often.

Q) Were you beaten during the first year of your apprenticeship? A) Yes, sir.

Q) That is, you were beaten at eleven years? A) Yes, sir.

Q) You were never sent before the Recorder? A) No, sir.

Q) Have you seen other children beaten? A) Yes, sir.

Q) Did you see them beaten worse than yourself? A) No, sir.

Q) Do you know of a factory where there is a blackhole? A) Yes, sir.

Q) Have you seen children put in that blackhole? A) Yes, sir.

Q) How old were these children? A) I could not tell the age.

Q) Younger than yourself? A) No, sir.

Q) Why were they put into the blackhole? A) Because they lost time.

Q) Who put them into the blackhole? A) The man who kept the press.

Q) Do you know whether this man wears a constable's medal? A) Yes, sir.

Q) Do the children cry out? A) No, sir.

Q) Were they taken to the blackhole brutally? A) No, sir.

Q) How long did they stop in the hole, as a general thing? A) Some of them stopped there till seven o'clock.

Q) When were they put in? A) In the afternoon.

Q) Was it seven o'clock in the evening or seven hours of time? A) Seven o'clock in the evening. They put them in during the afternoon until seven in the evening.

Q) At what time do the men leave the factory? A) Generally five o'clock and sometimes at six.

Q) Do you mean to say that those children were kept in the blackhole after the men had left the factory?

A) Yes, sir.
Q) Who let them out? The same that put them in? A) Yes, sir. I think so, but I never saw him.
Q) Was this blackhole heated? A) I don't know, sir.
Q) In what floor of the factory is this blackhole? A) In the cellar.
Q) Is there a furnace in the cellar? A) Yes, sir.
Q) Is the blackhole near the furnace? A) No, sir.
Q) Is there a window therein? A) No.
Q) When children were shut in there, you never heard them cry to get some one to let them out? A) No, sir.

–Royal Commission on the Relations of Labor and Capital, Reports, "Quebec Evidence" (Ottawa: Queen's Printer, 1889)

Sticks

In earlier times sticks were more common than they are today. Employers in Canada have used whipping, corporal punishment, beatings, "black holes" (holes dug out under the factory floor to confine child labourers who broke company work rules by talking or playing instead of working), fines and imprisonment. Today the big stick (called by labour arbitrators the "capital punishment" of employers) is unemployment or dismissal. There are also lesser punishments, such as suspensions, loss of seniority, demotion, docking from pay, reduced hours and other reductions in pay or benefits.

The use of sticks has become less prevalent due to factors such as the evolution of human rights laws, the growth of unions and collective bargaining, public opinion, the complexity of technology and capital intensity of production, the growth of welfare provisions, fuller employment, and perhaps the realization that negative sanctions are not very effective. However, the threat of unemployment remains the most effective weapon in the hands of employers today in controlling work effort.

Carrots

As the use of sticks declined, the use of carrots, or incentives, has increased. Carrots can be divided into **material** and **psychic** (or **prestige**) incentives. Material incentives are the most important in modern capitalist societies. Probably the most common of material incentives is "payment by results" such as piece work, bonuses tied to individual or group productivity, commissions, merit pay or rewards for particular effort or contributions (such as suggestion boxes rewards) and prizes for highest sales or production levels. A second common incentive is a job ladder where loyalty and hard work are rewarded by promotion to a better and higher paying job. There are many other "perks" or incentives that can be handed out by management. Hard work may be rewarded by better working conditions, larger offices, longer holidays or perhaps just a higher ranking in the choice of when to take holidays, travel opportunities, choice of shift and even the proverbial "key to the executive washroom."

Not all rewards are material, however. There are also psychic or prestige incentives. Remember your grade school teacher who put a gold star on your essay to reward you for your brilliant prose? These vanity awards have been widely utilized by employers to recognize and encourage exemplary work. Robert Owen, the brilliant and humane capitalist and textile manufacturer in nineteenth-century Britain (who has also been proclaimed the "father of British socialism"), put coloured cards above each worker's machine. High producers would get a red card, good producers a yellow card, and mediocre producers some other colour. In the Soviet system, exceptional workers would be named "Hero of the Soviet Union." In the Canadian civil service, "rug ranking"—the size and depth of carpet in the civil servant's office—is an indicator of an employee's power and rank. "Good" workers are also more likely to be rewarded by more autonomy in their work and less direct supervision.

But perhaps the most important psychic benefit derived from hard work is the satisfaction the individual gets from doing the job well. The German sociologist, Max Weber, called the will to work hard and well the "protestant ethic"; while the great American dissident economist, Thorstein Veblen, called it the "instinct of workmanship." The protestant ethic teaches us that it is godly to work hard and produce much, and that sloth is a sin. Veblen argues that people have an inherent instinct to be productive and to produce as much as they can and that this causes a conflict with business owners who wish to restrict output to raise prices and profits. Thus employers want to maximize the output of individual workers but restrict total production. But we will leave this larger aspect of political economy to a later chapter.

Managing the Labour Process: Approaches

It is not sufficient to think merely of carrots and sticks as the means of managing work. Workers are very ingenious at evading management work rules and finding ways to extract a "fair day's pay for a fair day's work." For instance, when wages are low, some workers have frequently resorted to pilfering to supplement income and obtain a "just" or living wage. Also, whatever the penalties or incentives, workers have their own ideas of what is an acceptable work effort beyond which, collectively, they will not work. How does the employer police the production process?[5]

There are several managerial strategies for controlling the workplace: direct control, technical control, bureaucratic control and autonomous control. Depending on the type of work or worker an employer may use more than one type of control.

Direct control is probably the one that most people think of when they picture the traditional workplace. In this case, the supervisor, the foreperson, or in small firms probably the owner, watches over "her" or "his" workers and drives them to intensify their work with threats or promises. Talking among workers is discouraged, even penalized, and the relationship between supervisor and worker can often be abusive. Railway gangs, garment and boot and shoe factories in both developed and Third World countries, much furniture and labour intensive manufacturing, agricultural labour and most unskilled service work is organized in this way. In recent years computers have even increased the scope for direct control by reducing the cost and difficulty of monitoring work intensity. For instance, among checkout clerks, data and word input clerks, and telephone and call centre operators, computers can maintain a constant record of the speed and quality of the employee's work. Supervisors are then able to set minimum standards for speed and quality and to easily monitor the workers to ensure these standards are maintained.

Direct control was widely practised in the early stages of competitive capitalism. However, the "second industrial revolution," the phase of monopoly capitalism, introduced machine-driven production lines. As a result, direct control gave way to a large extent to **technical control**, particularly in manufacturing. In this case, the pace, organization and productivity of work is determined and monitored by the machine rather than by direct personal supervision. This does not mean that there is no longer any need for supervisors. They still monitor quality, try to maximize the speed of the production line, and deal with any technical or breakdown problems. The auto assembly plant is a good example of machine, or technical, control. Workers are given specific tasks at a station on the production line, for example, installing seats. When the car arrives at the worker's station, the worker has so many minutes to install the seats before the car moves on to the next station. The worker is instructed on how exactly to install the seats, what order to insert the fastenings while the power tool that tightens the bolts is set to apply the correct tension. As a result, the speed, content and intensity of work is completely controlled by the speed and design of the production line.

There are many jobs, however, where direct supervision is either not feasible or too costly but where there is also no production line or machinery to control the quality and intensity of work.

4.4 Bureaucratic Management and Work Rules

The use of bureaucratic management in modern corporations involves the establishment of an elaborate web of rules and norms to control the effort and performance of workers. Richard Edwards describes such a system of rules at Polaroid Corporation in the 1970s.

Defining Work Tasks and Directing Workers

Each job within the Polaroid plants has been analyzed and summarized in an "approved description."...Such descriptions, in addition to stating pay, location, and entry requirements for each job, set forth in considerable detail the tasks that the worker must perform.

The approved description for a machine operator who assembles SX-70 film provides a useful example. All the regular duties of such operatives are set forth in considerable detail, including the operation of the automatic assembly machine and responsibility for clearing jams and making adjustments, monitoring the machine's output, and maintaining the machine. For example, duty number seven (out of eighteen) states that the operator must make adjustments for web tracking (using automatic Servo control units for adjustment to tapered mask), and component feed failures. Check for proper operation of missing components detectors. In addition, precise directions are given for responsibilities in the event of the crew chief's absence (the operative is responsible). Finally, even the irregular duties are spelled out: training new operators, conducting special tests for management to improve productivity or quality, and so on.

–Richard Edwards, *Contested Terrain* (New York Basic Books, 1979), pp. 136–137

Take, for example, office workers who are involved in typing (or inputting in the case of computers), photocopying, mailing, filing and perhaps answering the telephone. Individual supervision may even be counterproductive, since most workers would react negatively to having someone constantly "looking over their shoulders." In these cases, most employers, particularly the larger ones, use **bureaucratic control**. Bureaucratic control simply means that the employer, either unilaterally or through negotiations with a union, establishes a set of institutional rules and duties governing employees' work. As long as the individual worker abides by the rules and performs the duties satisfactorily he or she will be rewarded. The office worker who arrives regularly at work on time, does all the duties assigned, takes just the specified ten-minute coffee breaks and half-hour lunch break, observes the dress and courtesy code, and doesn't make any horrific mistakes will normally be secure in his or her average paying job. Among larger employers and in many public sector jobs such as teachers, civil servants and nurses, it is company policy as much as supervisors that control work. However, the recent spate of downsizing, contracting out, creation of part-time and temporary jobs, and cuts to public services have considerably reduced the job security of even those who satisfactorily work by the rules.

Finally, there are also numerous jobs where none of these control systems are appropriate or effective. Take for example a research scientist, a university professor, a software writer or many other professionals and highly-skilled, technical workers. While they are all to some degree subject to bureaucratic control and some loose direct control, for the most part they are allowed to design and control their own work. The average university professor, for example, is required to teach around six or nine hours per week during the university term, which covers about eight months of the year. Although the course names and their general content are determined by the individual university departments, the organization, specific content, and method of evaluation are, within some broad regulations, at the discretion of the individual professor. In addition the professor has considerable control over how much time over and above the required classroom hours are spent in teaching activities. There is a general understanding that the average professor will spend about forty percent of working time on teaching, forty percent on self-directed research and twenty percent on administrative duties, but there is wide latitude for individuals to concentrate on one or other of these general areas. The contract between the professors and the university specifies the amount of holidays a teacher is entitled to, but when, if, and where they are taken is left to the individual, subject only to the requirement that scheduled classes be taught. There is little or no direct monitoring of teaching, research or administrative work. Professors are required to file an annual activities report including a list of publications, which is used as the measure of research productivity and the various committees sat upon as a measure of administrative work. Teaching is only very partially monitored by annual student evaluations.

Autonomous control is the name given to such situations where the organization and pace of work is controlled by the individual worker whose rewards are tied to recognition of accomplishments over a much longer time period of time. In fact, we can say that autonomous workers largely *self-manage* their work and usually are evaluated only by annual performance reviews or are required to file regular reports on their activities.

Scientific Management and Other Systems

Such methods of controlling individual workers, however, are just part of larger management systems. It is necessary for the capitalist not only to control and supervise workers on the shop floor, but also to establish a **system of management** within which control is exercised. A particular company will use different forms of workplace control for its various workers. A manufacturing firm may produce its product under technical control, have its shipping employees under direct control, its office employees under bureaucratic control and its sales force and engineers under autonomous control. Management systems, therefore, are ways of managing, motivating and controlling workers, within the context of the whole firm.

Prior to the late nineteenth century, a common form of management was internal subcontracting, a system prevalent in mining and metal works. In the textile mills, direct control through a traditional foreperson system prevailed. External subcontracting, on the other hand, was widely practised in railway and canal construction.

Internal subcontracting was the system by which employers would hire skilled workers on a piece rate basis, paying them so many dollars per unit of output. For example, the factory owner would pay skilled moulders five dollars for every stove they produced. The moulders would hire their own assistants and unskilled labour, paying them out of the five dollars received for each stove. The moulder were more or less independent, self-employed workers, while the unskilled workers and assistants were under their direct control. The factory owner merely provided the building and raw materials and marketed the manufactured stoves. The technology and knowledge embodied in making the moulds and casting the iron and in planning and supervising the process rested in the hands and mind of the skilled workers. This created a problem for the factory owner since the skilled workers controlled not only the technology but also the intensity and speed of the work, not only for themselves, but for everyone involved in making stoves. In internal subcontracting, the employer could only use the price paid to the master worker to try to change the number of stoves produced.

Direct entrepreneurial or hierarchical control was dominated by a single employer, by forepersons or by a hierarchy of supervisors and managers acting on behalf of the employer. In this system the internal subcontractor was replaced by the employer or foreperson who personally supervised and disciplined the workers on a day-to-day basis. Machine technology also determined the pace and intensity of work. Most textile workers in Quebec in the nineteenth century worked in the direct entrepreneurial system. In both systems, most firms were still fairly small by today's standards, though the rise of the industrial factory marked the beginning of the end of competitive capitalism and the transition to monopoly capitalism.

External subcontracting was the practice of contracting jobs to subcontractors, who normally hired and supervised their own labour, though not infrequently would further subcontract parts to smaller sub-subcontractors. This was the dominant system, for instance, in the building of the railways across Canada beginning in the 1850s and extending to the First World War. Subcontractors were responsible for hiring and supervising their own "navvies," as the unskilled railway construction labourers were known. The navvies, many of whom were immigrants, lived a precarious existence, vulnerable to threats of deportation, of fines or imprisonment, or unemployment and as a result, of starvation. Little technology was required on the job, while planning was in the

4.5 Work and Wages in a Quebec Textile Mill in the 1880s

Testimony of a Machinist at the Hochelaga Cotton Factory before the Royal Commission on the Relations of Labour and Capital, 1889.

Questions by commissioner Helbronner:

Q) Do you know how many hands are engaged in that mill? A) There are about eleven hundred hands.

Q) To the best of your knowledge how many men are there? A) About 400 or 500.

Q) How many women are there? A. 500 or 600, I should say.

Q) Do you know how many women and girls above fifteen years age are at work in that factory? A) There are about 500.

Q) How many children are there? A) There are a couple of hundred of children.

Q) So far as you know, how old is the youngest of these children? A) There are children of ten years old working there; perhaps some even younger; but I know of several ten years old.

Q) Of those whom you know to be ten years old, have they worked a long time in the factory? A) They have been working a couple of years.

Q) What are the average wages of these children? A) Twenty-five, thirty cents a day.

Q) What are the average wages of the girls? A) The girls can earn about 75 cents to 80 cents a day.

Q) Do they work by the piece? A) There are some who work by the day, but the majority do piece work. In my department, which is the department of weaving, women there all work by the piece.

Q) What are the average wages of the men? A) From eighty cents to one dollar a day. There are several who make much less and there are men having families who earn sixty cents a day.

Q) Are there times when you work longer than others? A) Yes; often we are pressed with work and we are obliged to work extra.

Q) What are the working hours? A) For a couple of months work we have been working ten hours a day— sixty hours a week.

Q) Which is the longest day of work that you have had? A) Thirteen hours.

Q) Do the children work as long as the men stay in the factory? A) The same thing. When some work all work. If any one dares not want to work, the next morning he is fined.

Questions by commissioner Kerwin:

Q) Is it true that the children work in the factory barefoot? A) Yes; several do.

Q) At the present time? A) Yes, sir.

Q) Is it true that the agent of this factory goes into the Saguenay district and brings back whole families to work in that factory? A) Yes; I know that they go down to the Saguenay to engage hands.

Q) Are there many of these people brought from down there? A) Yes; the great part of the employees of the factory down below are people brought from the Saguenay.

Q) Are you aware whether it is true or not that the majority of these Saguenay people do not know what a bank note is of the denomination of one dollar, and that they do not know the difference between the notes of the several banks? A) I know that there are some of that sort, but I could not give the names of the parties.

Q) Do you know whether the pledges given these people have always been redeemed? A) They have not been redeemed.

Q) Those people who came from the Saguenay on the strength of the promises made them, when they learnt from the other employees that they did not receive the amount of wages pledged to them, did they demand an increase? A) Yes; they demanded it.

–Royal Commission on the Relations of Labor and Capital, Reports, "Quebec Evidence" (Ottawa: Queen's Printer, 1889)

hands of engineers, and direct supervision and discipline was meted out by the forepersons employed by the contractors.

With the emergence of large, monopoly firms employing thousands of people it was no longer possible for the owner or even the forepersons to personally supervise each worker. New forms of management arose when the old subcontracting and entrepreneurial control methods began to break down. Perhaps the most famous of these new systems was scientific management, the system designed by Frederick Winslow Taylor around the turn of the twentieth century. Taylor was the leader of a whole movement of engineers, management consultants and efficiency experts that transformed the work process at the time of the rise of monopoly capitalism late in the nineteenth and early in the twentieth centuries.

Scientific management is now a generic term referring to the rationalization of work, designed to take control of production out of the hands and minds of skilled workers, particularly the skilled internal subcontractor. Taylor saw that the knowledge and know-how of the first industrial revolution was in the minds and skills of the craftspersons. To gain control of work, the employer had to appropriate the knowledge and skills of the craftspersons

---

4.6 Contracting on the National Transcontinental

The letting of a railway contract for the building of several hundred miles of grade on a new transcontinental is a matter of some import. In the case of the National Transcontinental Railway such matters were handled from Ottawa, the several contracts being let by the National Transcontinental Commission, representing the Dominion Government. As each section of the new road was ready for a start on construction, a call for tenders was published broadcast throughout the country, and the contract, ostensibly, was let in open competition. That, however, may often be a mere formality. It is obvious that only certain firms will engage in railway construction and the competition lies wholly within well-known groups. Between the dates of calling for tenders and the final letting of the work there is much struggle and stress, or plain wire-pulling, on the part of the men contending for the contract....

The relation existing between the head-contractor and the sub-contractor, however, seems but to whet the appetite for more sub-letting. At any rate the sub-contractors invariably proceed where possible to sub-let in another form, which final form is in fact the most acute. From the experience gained in his relations with the head-contractor he hastens to let out his work again to small work-groups in "stations" of one hundred feet each. Some groups will take five, eight, or eleven stations, and they in turn undertake to build their portion of the road up to grade level. In the system of sub-letting, station-work is about the fourth circle out from the head-contractor.

The agreement which the station-men enter into is a replica in substance of that which the sub-contractor has already signed with the head-contractor, with the exception of the rates paid for yardage and the prices charged for goods. The sub-contractor sees to it that his margin on both is sufficient to help defray his debt at the headquarters camp and to insure a safe return on the work he has already undertaken.

The peak of the contract system in railway building was reached on Canada's last transcontinental. There, too, was its weakness most in evidence: sub-letting became an art. Men and officials in the possession of large contracts traded on their holdings, and intermediaries sought profits from transferring their various interests. How did such relations affect wages?

—Edmund Bradwin, The Bunkhouse Man (Toronto: University of Toronto Press, 1972), pp. 44–52

Needless to say, Bradwin's evidence is that subcontracting had disastrous effects on the wages and living conditions of the navvies who were disproportionately new immigrants.

---

and subject them to the control and discipline of the managers. To do this, Taylor developed his three basic principles of scientific management: separating planning from doing; centralizing knowledge, conception and planning in management; and breaking down jobs into their simplest parts that can be done by the least skilled worker.

Scientific management so alienated workers they could not be counted on to remain loyal to the employer or to do consistent or quality work. Such discontent could also lead the workers to join unions. In an effort to keep unions out, some employers improved living and working conditions and introduced pensions and other welfare programs for their members. This strategy, often referred to as corporate welfarism or paternalism, was intended to cause workers to identify with the company, thereby reducing turnover, increasing productivity and forestalling unionism. It reached its peak in North American in the 1930s though paternalism is still a major management system in contemporary Japan.[6]

4.7 Taylor on "Scientific" Management

This is a famous application of the principles of "scientific" management as recounted by Taylor himself:

The task before us, then, narrowed itself down to getting Schmidt to handle 47 tons of pig iron per day and making him glad to do it. This was done as follows. Schmidt was called out from among the gang of pig-iron handlers and talked to somewhat in this way:

"Schmidt, are you a high-priced man?" ... "Well, if you are a high-priced man, you will load that pig iron on that car to-morrow for $1.85." ...

"Vell did I got $1.85 for loading dot pig iron on dot car to-morrow?"

"Yes, of course you do, and you get $1.85 for loading a pile like that every day right through the year. That is what a high-priced man does, and you know it just as well as I do."

"Vell, dot's all right. I could load dot pig iron on the car to-morrow for $1.85, and I get it every day, don't I?"

"Certainly you do – certainly you do." ...

"Well, if you are a high-priced man, you will do exactly as this man tells you to-morrow, from morning till night. When he tells you to pick up a pig and walk, you pick it up and you walk, and when he tells you to sit down and rest, you sit down. You do that right straight through the day. And what's more, no back talk. Now a high-priced man does just what he's told to do, and no back talk. Do you understand that? ... Now you come on to work here to-morrow morning and I'll know before night whether you are really a high-priced man or not."

This seems to be rather rough talk. And indeed it would be if applied to an educated mechanic, or even an intelligent laborer. With a man of the mentally sluggish type of Schmidt it is appropriate and not unkind, since it is effective in fixing his attention on the high wages which he wants and away from what, if it were called to his attention, he probably would consider impossibly hard work.

Schmidt started to work, and all day long, and at regular intervals, was told by the man who stood over him with a watch, "Now pick up a pig and walk. Now sit down and rest. Now walk-now rest," etc. He worked when he was told to work, and rested when he was told to rest, and at half-past five in the afternoon had his 47 tons loaded on the car. And he practically never failed to work at this pace and do the task that was set him during the three years that the writer was at Bethlehem. And throughout this time he averaged a little more than $1.85 per day, whereas before he had never received over $1.15 per day, which was the ruling rate of wages at that time in Bethlehem. That is, he received 60 per cent higher wages than were paid to other men who were not working on task work. One man after another was picked out and trained to handle pig iron at the rate of 47 tons per day until all of the pig iron was handled at this rate, and the men were receiving 60 percent more wages than other workmen around them.

–Frederick W. Taylor, *The Principles of Scientific Management*, quoted in Harry Braverman, *Labor and Monopoly Capitalism* (New York: Monthly Review, 1974), pp. 104–105

Fordism, as the dominant management system has been called, emerged out of the Second World War. It was the successor to direct control and incorporated much of the organization of scientific management. Like welfarism it was meant to reduce the labour turnover that resulted from scientific management. But it was also a response to the rise of the militant industrial unionism associated with the Congress of Industrial Organizations (CIO) in the United States and its Canadian counterpart, the Canadian Congress of Labour (CCL). While it often fought these unions, it also sought to tame them and incorporate them into the production process. The system began, as the name suggests, with Henry Ford, who introduced the production (or flow) line with its method of machine control. Ford combined this organization of work with a combination of higher wages, *after* a demonstrated period of employment stability; and with a paternalistic concern with some aspects of the non-working life of the employee. His workers had to demonstrate acceptable personal habits, such as cleanliness, prudence, and abstinence from tobacco and alcohol.

At the broader economic level Fordism meant **mass production for mass consumption.** At the shop floor, mass production involved complex, specialized production equipment tended or operated by semi-skilled (or, more correctly, work-skilled) operatives. Mass consumption was made possible by union-negotiated wages that guaranteed labour its share of rising productivity resulting from technological change. Not all workers benefited. Jobs that didn't require specific training or work-learned skills were relegated to what we now term the "secondary labour market," where wages and working conditions were much inferior. [See chapter 5 on segmented labour markets.] Fordism, combined with these job and wage distinctions, is still perhaps the most common management system today, at least in heavy manufacturing. Globalism, the decline of the manufacturing sector and the rise of the service and new technology industries, however, have severely undermined the predominance of Fordism. Different systems of management emerged in the different sectors of the labour market, in new industries such as information technology, and in different production processes. Firms that had previously operated more than one control system in different parts of its operations, now increasingly sub-contract those departments of the firm that do not fit the Fordist pattern, such as janitorial, cafeteria and security services, out to separate firms. As a result, many political economists simply call the present management system (or systems) **post-Fordist**.

Most orthodox economists and neoliberals generally ignore the whole subject of systems of control. Technology and work organization are seen as givens and are not considered part of the purview of economics. The division of the labour market into non-competing groups is explained by treating labour that has "invested" in education and training as capital goods. Indeed, this is openly recognized. Wage differentials and job segmentation are "explained" by **human capital** market theory. That is, workers are paid wage premiums and assigned to different labour markets on the basis of their investment in education or training in job skills. Investment in education and training is treated the same as if it were investment in new plant or machinery. For most economists, the process of converting labour power into real labour is just as much a "hidden abode" as it was in Marx's time.

4.8 Volvo Kalmar

The Swedish car making firm Volvo was one of the first major world manufacturers to respond to the labour problems associated with "Fordist" moving production line organization. In 1974 it opened its Kalmar plant, making it, as Christian Berggren notes, "the world's first auto assembly plant without mechanically driven assembly lines." He describes the genesis and organization of the plant in his book *Alternatives to Lean Production.*

> Volvo at Kalmar was conceived as the answer to the severe personnel problem plaguing the auto industry at the start of the 1970s, when turnover rates of 100 percent and higher were not uncommon....
>
> One of the central ideas was that the building's construction should facilitate working in teams....
>
> A precondition for such a construction ... was a transport system that was more flexible than a mechanical conveyor belt. Here—in the battery-powered, automatically guided vehicles (AGVs or "carriers") ...—lay Kalmar's greatest technical innovation....
>
> The novelties in the design of the building and in the production flow became the basis for a series of other features of the plant: the team culture, extensive prospects for job rotation, and the functional assembly.... Together, these features expressed the core idea of the project: efficient production by motivated, capable co-workers....
>
> —Christian Berggren, *Alternatives to Lean Production* (Ithica, N.Y.: Cornell University Press, 1993), pp. 120–121, 236

As a postscript to this story—after Volvo was sold to a major European carmaker, the Volvo plants reverted to traditional assembly line production.

The Question of Technology

Many people, including most economists, consider technology and technological change as something that comes from outside the economy. When a new technology emerges from the realm of science or from an inventor, businesses adopt and develop the new technology to increase not only their own productivity but also the productivity of their workers. Thus, technological change is considered to benefit both workers and business.

But is that necessarily so? The employer who introduces a new machine that replaces thirty workers and throws them into unemployment doesn't say "the Devil made me do it" but rather "new technology made me do it." There is, though, a different interpretation— that businesses select from available technology, or develop alternative technology, to maintain or increase control over workers and production. This means that, at least in part, technological change is determined by conflicts between employers and their workers. Technology plays a large role in the intensity and productivity of work. Once a particular production technology is adopted it determines how work is organized and what skills are necessary. Thus the choice of technology, something employers decide by themselves, is one that will give them the most control over the rate of work, how much is produced in a day and ultimately the most profit. While the continued existence of the company is important to workers—their jobs depend on it—they also have an interest in the safest, easiest and most satisfying technology. Workers' interests normally will receive little or no consideration in that choice.

The way work is organized—the labour process—and the choice of technology, of course, are not independent of the labour market. The availability and wages of workers—the labour market—is an important factor determining what technology is adopted and how work is organized. This does not detract from the central problem of management, that of extracting the most work and effort from the labour it hires; or of converting labour power (or potential labour) into the most realized labour possible. This is the very definition of management efficiency. It does not, however, include consideration of the workers' welfare except when improving wages and working conditions contributes to increasing a business's productivity.

Notes

1. This, of course, makes nonsense of the assumption in most economics texts, including that of fellow Nobel Prize winner Paul Samuelson, that it doesn't make any economic difference to the behaviour of the firm whether capital owns the firm and hires labour, or the workers own the firm and hire capital.It should also be noted that the prize in economics is not a "Nobel Prize" but rather a "prize in honour of Alfred Nobel" and was introduced, not by Nobel as was the case with the other Nobel Prizes, but rather by the Swedish central bank. The committee that awards the prize is selected by the bank and, critics have argued, represents a very narrow conception and evaluation of contributions to economics. In any case, even neoclassical economists have recognized that it does make a difference whether capital hires labour or labour hires capital. See, for instance, Jaroslav Vanek, *The Participatory Economy* (Ithaca: Cornell University Press, 1971).

2. Robert Granford Wright, quoted in William Werther, Keith Davis, Hermann Schwind and Hari Das, *Canadian Human Resource Management,* 3rd edition (Toronto: McGraw-Hill Ryerson, 1990), p. 5. [Emphasis added.]

3. William Werther, et al., *Canadian Human Resource Management*, p. 6.

4. Symbolically, ULC = function of $(w/d+e)$ where w = wage rate; e, the efficiency with which work is done; and d, the work effort or work done per hour.

5. For a systematic treatment of the historical development of the various types and systems of control, see: Harry Braverman, *Labor and Monopoly Capital* (New York: Monthly Review Press, 1974); Samuel Bowles and Richard Edwards, *Understanding Capitalism* (New York: Harper and Row, 1985), chs. 8–9; Richard Edwards, *Contested Terrain* (New York: Basic Books, 1979), chs. 1–8; David Gordon, Richard Edwards and Michael Reich, *Segmented Work, Divided Workers*, (Cambridge: Cambridge University Press, 1982); and Craig Littler, *The Development of the Labour Process in Capitalist Societies* (London: Heinemann, 1982).

    Canadian material can be found in: Craig Heron and Robert Storey, eds., *On the Job* (Montreal: McGill-Queen's University Press, 1985); Gregory Kealey, ed., *Canada Investigates Industrialism: The Royal Commission on the Relations of Labour and Capital 1889* (Toronto: University of Toronto Press, 1973); Harvey Krahn and Graham Lowe, *Work, Industry and Canadian Society,* 3rd ed. (Toronto: Nelson, 1996); Graham Lowe and Harvey Krahn, eds., *Working Canadians* (Toronto: Methuen, 1984); Graham Lowe and Harvey Krahn, eds., *Work in Canada* (Scarborough: Nelson, 1993); and James Rinehart, *The Tyranny of Work,* 3rd ed. (Toronto: Harcourt Brace, 1996).

6. Paternalism was not common in Western businesses except among smaller and religiously-oriented employers, many of them Quakers. Welfarism was in part an expression of a real, paternal concern for "their" workers, not just a method of motivating and controlling them. However, at least until the decade-long economic slump that beset the Japanese economy in the 1990s, paternalism found its dominant expression in the large firm sector of the Japanese economy where the total economic and social welfare of the male worker was almost completely dependent on lifelong dedicated service to a single employer. Lifetime employment and the paternal benefits associated with it, however, began rapidly eroding in the face of the deteriorating economic situation of Japan, particularly after the Asian financial crisis of 1997.

Chapter 5

The Labour Market
Part One

Characteristics of the Labour Market

One of the very odd assumptions made by most orthodox economists is that the labour market can be treated as if it were just any other commodity market like the market for potatoes, copper or natural gas. The labour market is fundamentally different from any other market, differing from commodity markets in two ways, both of which have already been touched upon.

First, labour is a fictitious commodity. A real commodity is good or service produced by human activity to be sold on the market. As noted in chapter 1, labour, like money capital and natural resources, is not created to be sold on the market. For this reason it does not respond to the laws of supply and demand. No matter how great the demand for computer programmers may become, women will never start giving birth to fully grown computer programmers.

Second, each unit of labour has a unique and individual will; that is, **human agency**. In this way, labour differs not only from factor commodities such as goods and services, but from land and money capital, the other fictitious commodities.[1] Because labour has a human agency, it may act, individually or collectively, for a positive end, such as forming unions and demanding better working conditions. Machines, piles of copper billets or stacks of money obviously can't act in similar or meaningful fashion. Even the most advanced computer or robot can only do what some human programmed it to do. It has no will of its own. Hal, the nasty computer of the movie *2001*, remains a figment of a science fiction writer's fertile mind.

Third, labour is heterogeneous. That means no two workers are identical. They have different personalities, different attitudes and aspirations, different physical and mental attributes and capabilities, different skills and education, and different families. They are of different sexes, come from different ethnic and racial backgrounds, and are of different ages. Once again, this does not hold true for most other commodities on the market, though obviously resources in their natural state can vary considerably in quality. Services can also vary considerably in quality but this is mainly because they are provided by different workers.

An important dimension of heterogeneity of individual workers is the differences in their education, training and work experience. Economists call this investment in the skills and knowledge of workers **human capital.** It is considered analogous to employers' investment in machinery and capital equipment, which is referred to as physical capital or capital goods; and, as some would argue, is equally subject to obsolescence and depreciation. Investment in human capital, as with

5.1 A Whimsical View of Human Capital Theory

A man with a degenerative brain disease that was considered terminal went to the organ transplant bank to purchase a replacement for his decaying mind. After a series of tests to gauge compatibility and suitability of a donor brain, the organ bank technician informed him there were only two possible brains available, both from middle-aged donors. One was from a school teacher and one from a bank economist, both of whom had been killed in automobile accidents.

"How much would they cost?" he asked.

"The teacher's brain is $5,000," the technician replied. "The economist's brain is $20,000."

"Why is the economist's brain worth four times that of the teacher's?" the man asked.

"Oh, that's simple," the technician replied, "It has never been used."

investment in physical capital, is thought to raise the productivity of labour. There is, however, a major difference. Human capital belongs to the worker and is inseparable from that individual. Not so with capital goods, which can be transferred from worker to worker or employer to employer. There can be no second-hand market for used human capital.

Fifth, labour power is non-storable. If a worker becomes unemployed, neither she nor her employer can store up her potential work in a vault for use at some later date. Like Darling Clementine, "she is lost and gone forever, dreadful sorry…" poor unemployed. Not so for unused machines, billets of copper or tonnes of wheat.

Finally, the assumption that the supply and demand of a commodity will tend to adjust in response to market pressures so that there are no persistent shortages or surpluses only occasionally applies to labour markets. The fact is, over the last two or more centuries, the labour market has rarely achieved full employment—in economics terminology, the labour market has seldom "cleared." The supply of workers has almost always been greater than the demand, resulting in unemployment. Unemployment and/or underemployment has been, and remains, a chronic problem in all capitalist market economies, not least of all, in Canada.

In all these characteristics labour is different from all other commodities or factors of production, and labour markets are different from all other markets. In contrast much orthodox economic theory treats labour markets as if all labour is the same, there is no unemployment, and wages always adjust to reduce labour shortages or surpluses. The neoclassical labour market treats labour as if it were a commodity subject to the laws of supply and demand. This means that as wages rise, workers will be willing to supply more labour. Further, it is assumed that labour markets are stable and that the market will always tend to produce full employment. Also, labour is considered to be homogeneous (all workers are the same). Differentials in worker productivity and wages, therefore, are the result of investments in human capital (education and training). Consequently, workers that receive low wages do so because they failed to invest in education and training in their formative years.

The demand for labour by each firm is determined in the orthodox labour-market model by the extra net income the firm receives when it hires one additional unit of labour. A business will only want to hire an additional worker if that worker brings to the firm at least enough new income to pay the worker's wages and to cover additional material and capital costs. Total demand for labour is the sum of the demands of all firms in the market. Employers will hire more

5.2 Unemployment in the Twentieth Century

Canada did not begin to measure unemployment on a systematic and statistical basis until well into the twentieth century. Official Statistics Canada estimates have been calculated for the years since 1926 and other studies have estimated and produced statistics for earlier years. We know, for instance, that there were periods of depression and high unemployment in the 1870s, '80s and '90s, though we have no reliable figures. We also know there was an unemployment crisis just before the First World War.

Detailed estimates of unemployment after the First World War are graphed in chapter 8, box 8.9. However, a rough description of twentieth-century unemployment would be that after the First World War, a sharp depression raised unemployment to around 6 percent. This is not high by today's standards but given that most families had only one income earner and close to half the population was rural, this meant that a significant proportion of urban families had no income at all. Unemployment rose to around 20 percent in 1932–33, in the winter months to as much as 25 percent. Among young single men, the rate probably approached 50 percent or more. The results were devastating and prompted the introduction of unemployment insurance on a reluctant federal (Liberal) government in 1940.

The Second World War brought full employment and much more government involvement in economic management policies to regulate and manage the economy. These policies were based on the ideas of the English economist, John Maynard Keynes. The average rate of unemployment in the war period was around 2–3 percent and, at one point, fell to less than half of 1 percent. In the postwar boom—"the golden age of capitalism"—the rate varied between 3 and 5 percent. The exception to this was the "Diefenbaker recession" between 1957 and 1961 when the (tight-money) policies of Bank of Canada Governor, James Coyne, raised the rate to 6–7 percent. At the time the Economic Council of Canada, a relatively non-partisan government advisory agency, estimated full employment in Canada at between 3 and 4 percent.

However, unemployment began to rise steadily after the Bank of Canada adopted a high interest rate policy (known as monetarism) and repeated Coyne's mistaken policies after the mid-1970s. Unemployment rose from 7–8 percent in the late seventies to over 12 percent in the recession of the early eighties. There was some recovery in the second half of the decade, but unemployment never fell below an average rate of 7.5 percent by the end of the decade. At that point monetary policy (high interest rates), tax, and trade agreements drove the Canadian economy back into recession and unemployment again skyrocketed to double-digit levels. Unemployment did fall in the second half of the decade, but the experience of unemployment was made far more onerous. This was because Liberal governments had gutted the unemployment insurance system in 1993/94 and 1996/97 to the particular disadvantage of women workers. How much unemployment will be caused by the recession beginning in 2001 and how long it will persist remains to be seen and will depend on whether the United States slips back into a "double-dip" recession as some economists fear.

---

workers, therefore, as wages fall, since employers can hire more labour even if the productivity of the new workers hired is falling, as long as wages are also falling. This is simply because as productivity falls, the wage will also be lower.

Wages and employment levels are determined by the classical supply and demand mechanism. Where supply and demand cross, wages are equal to the value of what the last worker hired is able to produce. This wage is known as the marginal product of the last hired worker. It also assumes that all workers who wish to work at that wage can find employment. This means that once the market stabilizes, there is no *involuntary* unemployment. Everybody who wants to work at the market rate can find employment. This is known as the **marginal productivity theory of wages and employment**.

It is, however, a very different understanding of how the labour market works from that which the general public perceives and that which political economists generally favour. In fact, I consider the normal labour market to be quite different than this idealized view. Workers are not the same (that is, they are heterogeneous) and they are segmented into different isolated markets. Furthermore, usually there is unemployment, which means that the labour market is in disequilibrium, resulting in frequent and persistent surpluses and shortages of specific types of worker. Wages and working conditions are not determined automatically and smoothly in the market but are responsive to class conflict and the wage demands of unions. Finally, most labour markets are very poorly defined in that workers are constantly moving into, out of and between different labour markets. Labour markets are a bit like airports. Some people are entering from the local community; others embarking from arriving aircraft; some people are leaving for other airports or heading for home or a hotel; some are just sitting and waiting—waiting to leave or waiting for someone to arrive. The main difference is that not many travellers or those waiting to greet them remain sitting in the airport for a very long time, while most workers remain in their jobs for months, years, or even a lifetime. Nevertheless, the picture we must have of the Canadian labour market is like that of a network of airports, each with its own characteristic travellers, size and dynamics. This should all become clear as we look at the segmented labour market model.

Labour Market Segmentation

After the Second World War, a number of labour economists who had cut their intellectual teeth during the wartime labour mobilization looked at the real world labour markets and compared them with the textbook version.[2] They concluded that the textbook version just didn't measure up to reality. One noted labour economist, Clark Kerr, described the real labour markets as "Balkanized," comparing them to the fragmented and divisive political states in Europe's Balkan Peninsula. Others developed the ideas of vertical labour markets and horizontal labour markets. In vertical markets workers were hired at the bottom of a job ladder and moved upward over time within a single employer. In horizontal markets skilled workers moved from employer to employer as jobs came and went. These various labour markets were linked by structures of job clusters (groups of workers whose wages were related), wage contours (groups of employers who maintained consistent patterns of wage differentials between them) and job queues (queues or lineups of workers ranked by personal characteristics waiting for available job opportunities) operating within "orbits of coercive comparison" (power structures in the labour market determined by unions, collective bargaining institutions and corporate power relations.)[3]

This was a far cry from the orthodox version of the labour market but one that is far more compatible with the ongoing conflict between workers and employers for control of the workplace and for shares of income.

One of the main ways employers respond to competition or to an economic downturn is to attempt to cut labour costs. The most significant ways of cutting labour costs include job fragmentation and de-skilling; incentive schemes to tie workers' compensation to output; segmentation of labour markets (discussed below); and welfarism and paternalism (this ties workers to individual employers so that they are not free to take advantage of higher wages offered by other employers). All these strategies imply that workers are not identical and compet-

Table 5.1: Characteristics of the Dual Labour Market

Type I / Primary	Type II / Secondary
Job Characteristics	
• relatively good pay	• relatively low pay
• reasonable job stability	• job instability
• promotion opportunities	• dead-end jobs
• stable work rules	• arbitrary management
• unionized	• non-unionized
Labour Force Characteristics	
• majority group	• minorities
• prime age	• youth, older workers
• male	• female

ing for the same jobs. In the idealized world of neoliberal economist, employers are all similar and competing for the same workers. In the real world they are not.

Some political economists describe the labour market as being **segmented** into two different markets: the **primary labour market** composed of "good" jobs and the **secondary labour market** made up of "bad" jobs. There is considerable evidence in support of this **dual labour market** interpretation. However, the labour market is in fact far more complex than this simple "good jobs/bad jobs" division suggests.

The concept of a highly structured and segmented labour market is not new. Labour economists in the 1940s were well aware of how fragmented the labour market was. However, segmentation was rediscovered in the 1960s when U.S. researchers asked why poverty continued to persist despite the massive amounts of money spent on educating and training the poor and unemployed. The researchers found that when education projects were complete, poor, unemployed, poorly-educated blacks had become poor, unemployed, well-educated blacks.

Researchers identified two distinct jobs types: Type I jobs became known as the primary labour market, Type II jobs as the secondary labour market. Typical characteristics of the primary and secondary labour markets are described in Table 5.1.

Though these characteristics were noted and described, they were not explained. The point of this chapter is to explain why and how the market is divided up in this manner. This analysis is summed up at the end of this chapter in Tables A5.1 and A5.2.

Further research also found differences between primary and secondary labour market employers. Large monopoly sector firms and the public sector employers tended to be primary labour market employers, and small competitive sector employers tended to be secondary labour market employers.

However, there were significant exceptions. Within a large monopoly sector firm would be occupational groups with secondary labour market characteristics and many small firms in very competitive industries would have stable, primary

Table 5.2: Monopoly Sector Characteristics

Business Structure
- high capital intensity
- specialized capital
- high technology
- relative stability of prices
- markup pricing
- responds to demand by quantity adjustment
- high proportion of non-productive (clerical, advertising, sales) workers
- strategic and tactical planning

Labour Process
- high division of labour/skill fragmentation
- separation of conception (organization) from execution (doing)
- centralization of knowledge and planning
- institutional segmentation, bureaucratic and machine control

Table 5.3: Competitive Sector Characteristics

Business Structure
- low capital intensity
- general purpose, non-specialized capital
- low technology
- prices subject to competitive fluctuation [competitive pricing]
- low proportion of non-productive workers except in the exchange (sales) sector
- limited tactical planning, almost no strategic planning

Labour Process
- limited division of labour or skill fragmentation
- limited division between conception, (organization) and execution (doing)
- direct (some machine) control

market characteristics. While there was mobility between the two markets, that mobility was restricted and very dependent on the level of unemployment. With all these complications it was apparent that labour markets could not be fully explained by a simple good job/bad job labour market theory.

To understand the structuring of the labour market we must go back to look at the structure of business enterprises and the organization of work. There are, of course, exceptions to these two types of firms. These are the (usually small) firms that produce a more or less identical product with limited specialized capital and that do not advertise. This class of firm seems to meet the description of the competitive sector, yet have other characteristics of the monopoly sector. They have high price stability, sophisticated technology and strategic planning. Included in this class are the professional and quasi-profession firms (from law and medicine to real estate and public relations firms) to the heavy construction

Table 5.4: Knowledge/Human Capital Sector Characteristics

Business Structure
- high human capital intensity
- sophisticated technology/technique
- price and firm stability/markup pricing
- low proportion of non-productive workers (except among quasi-professions)
- strategic planning

Labour Process
- division of labour but little skill fragmentation
- very limited division between conception, planning, organizing, execution and doing
- autonomous (some bureaucratic) control

---

outfits, machine tools, computer software and other advanced technology firms. What is common to these firms? It is the need for specialized knowledge or skill, and/or restrictions of entry to the industry by credentials such as professional degrees, regulations of professional associations or other means such as university enrolment limits, immigration or migration barriers. For simplicity we can call this the **knowledge sector** or, to use the fashionable economic term, the human capital sector, where people are paid for what they know, not for what they do (see Table 5.4). These people inhabit the same labour market as do the salaried upper professionals and managers in the large monopoly sector.

One can put all these market segments together and, following the tradition that has developed, still refer to it as the primary segment of a "dual" labour market. Here the primary market is itself segmented into three tiers. The top tier is the managerial/professional tier, employees "paid for what they know, not for what they do."[4] That means that they are paid for their investment in professional and managerial knowledge skills, their human capital. Wages and salaries are generally determined more like prices in a capital goods market than wages in a labour market.

The primary labour market also contains a middle tier and a lower tier. The middle tier, also known as the "independent primary market," is the market for craft, technical and lower professional workers—nurses, teachers, lab technologists and journeyman building trades. (Some analysts combine the top and middle tiers into what they refer to as the upper tier.) These workers are also rewarded for their human capital but they face a horizontal labour market rather than an internal (or vertical) labour market. Though they do receive "human capital income," that income is frequently determined institutionally through collective bargaining or by job evaluation. This is a quite different process of wage determination from that of the managerial/professional group.

The lower tier of the primary market, or the "subordinate primary market," is the market for work-skilled employees. They have specific skills, primarily learned on the job. They face an internal labour market, a job ladder that they climb by being loyal and productive employees willing to learn new skills. Many of these job and promotion ladders are negotiated by unions, and the worker's right to

5.3 The Labour Process and the Fast Food Industry

In the fast-food industry, the machines, or the instruments of labour, assume a central place. Instead of assisting workers in the production of the meal, the machines tended by workers are dominant; we now have an objective organization of machines confronting the worker. Marx described this as the transition form "manufacture" to "large-scale industry." Since the motion of the factory proceeds from the machinery and not from the worker, working personnel can continually be replaced. Frequent change in workers will not disrupt the labour process.... [T]his new model is intended to replace the "humanistic concept of service" with the kind of technocratic thinking that in other fields has replaced "the high cost and erratic elegance of the artisan with the low-cost munificence of the manufacturer." McDonald's is a "supreme" example of this kind of thinking.

–Ester Reiter, "Life in a Fast-Food Factory," in On the Job, Craig Heron and Robert Storey, eds. (Kingston and Montreal: McGill-Queens University Press, 1986), pp. 311–31

climb that ladder is, in fact, a property right established by collective bargaining. Unions are extremely important in this sector in establishing both the wage levels and the promotion ladder.

This leaves the important, and growing, secondary labour market. For the most part jobs within this labour market fit the characteristics of the competitive sector in Table 5.3, though many monopoly sector corporations, such as those in the fast food and retail industries, create secondary labour market jobs. Perhaps around forty percent of the Canadian labour force work in the secondary labour market. These jobs are primarily low wage, usually near or below the poverty wage, "dead end" with little chance of job promotion, insecure, subject to arbitrary management and, almost by definition, with no union protection. Jobs in this category include chambermaids, fast food attendants, security agents, department store sales clerks, vegetable pickers, delivery swampers and other forms of casual labour. The labour force that fills the jobs in the secondary labour market is disproportionately composed of women, particularly those from immigrant, visible minority and disadvantaged backgrounds, young people and the aged who can't find permanent jobs.

Discrimination

One conclusion of segmented labour market theory is that discrimination pays.[5] If a job can be de-skilled and routinized and does not require extensive work experience or stable employment characteristics, it can be relegated to the secondary market tapping the lowest wage sector and/or the reserve army of the unemployed—women, children, immigrants and minorities.

The strategy of employers is to convert as many jobs as possible from the primary market to the secondary market. A monopoly sector firm can use a non-unionized subsidiary firm or department to do some of its work. Alternatively, it can subcontract to a separate non-union firm or maintain separate full-time and part-time staff. Increasingly, global firms have contracted with Third World subcontractors to produce brand name products for North American distribution.

Because men are much less willing to work part-time than women or students, for instance, low-wage part-time work becomes "women's work" or, in the case of the hamburger chains, "youth's work." Because immigrants and women are perceived to have less industrial work experience, less experience with machines, or less stable work histories, high-paying, stable industrial employment is denied them and becomes "men's work," and so on.

Discrimination of this sort tends to be self-reinforcing. Poorly paid, casual workers are not rewarded for hard, stable work effort and hence develop patterns of irregular and unstable work. They then tend to become "tagged" and are only employed in low productivity jobs where worker stability is much less necessary. Where this pattern is associated with specific, easily identifiable groups such as Aboriginal people, women and youth, employers practice **statistical discrimination**—that is, they discriminate against the individual because of the real or imagined behaviour of a group. Employers discriminate, not because they have any personal animosity to any particular group, but because discrimination increases profits if the firm can hire low wage workers from the secondary labour market pool rather than employ higher paid primary sector workers.

Notes

1. Many religions, particularly those in the early period before the development of modern science, give human will and emotions to animals, the forces of nature and other natural resources such as trees or rocks. One has to think no further than Prometheus, the Greek god of fire or Neptune, the Roman god of the sea. Animals and the land have human-like will in North American Aboriginal spirituality.

2. For elaboration on the model see Richard Edwards, *Contested Terrain* (New York: Basic Books, 1979), chs. 9–10; David Gordon, Richard Edwards and Michael Reich, *Segmented Work, Divided Workers* (Cambridge: Cambridge University Press, 1982); and Paul Phillips and Erin Phillips, *Women and Work*, 3rd ed. (Toronto: Lorimer, 2000).

3. See Clark Kerr, "The Balkanization of Labour Markets," in Lloyd Reynolds et al., eds., *Readings in Labor Economics and Labor Relations*, Fifth edition (Englewood Cliffs, NJ: Prentice-Hall, 1991); Robert Livernash, "Job Clusters," in Michael Piore, ed., *Unemployment and Inflation* (White Plains, NY: M.E. Sharpe, 1979); John Dunlop, "Wage Contours," in Michael Piore, ed., *Unemployment and Inflation* (White Plains, NY: M.E. Sharpe, 1979); Arthur Ross, "Orbits of Coercive Comparison," in Michael Piore, ed., *Unemployment and Inflation* (White Plains, NY: M.E. Sharpe, 1979). Job competition theory was developed later; for a discussion see Lister Thurow, "A Job Competition Model," in Michael Piore, ed., *Unemployment and Inflation* (White Plains, NY: M.E. Sharpe, 1979).

4. Managers are increasingly recruited from among university graduates, either directly from management schools, or indirectly by promoting other professionals—such as engineers and accountants—from technical work into management. The average engineer, for example, spends only around five years doing purely engineering work before entering into the management stream.

5. For a description of the types and extent of discrimination in the Canadian labour market see Harish Jain, "Employment and Pay Discrimination in Canada," in John Anderson and Morley Gunderson, eds., *Union-Management Relations in Canada* (Don Mills: Addison-Wesley, 1982).

Table A5.1: Inputs and Outputs of Labour Market Segmentation and the Labour Process

Labour Market Segment	Characteristics of Capital (Employer)			Characteristics of the Labour Process	Characteristics of Labour Supply		
	Intensity	Labour Needs	Output Pricing	Dominant Form of Control	Labour Force (Disproportionately)	Education/Training Productivity	Potential
Primary/Upper Tier (Professional/Managerial)	High "Human Capital"	Knowledge; Specialized Skills	Markup	Autonomous; Incentive	Majority; Prime Age; Male	General (transferable) Knowledge and Skills; Post-secondary Institutional Education (Certification)	High
Primary/Craft-Technical-Lower-Professional Tier	Moderately High "Human Capital; Specialized Tools, Equipment	Specialized Skills and Knowledge	Markup	Autonomous; Bureaucratic	Majority; Prime Age Male (Female in Certain Specialized Occupations)	Specialized Skill training; Apprenticeship; Post-secondary Institutional Training (Certification)	Moderately High
Primary/Lower Tier	High Fixed and Specialized Capital	Stability; Regularity; Work Experience (Industrial Discipline)	Markup	Bureaucratic; Machine; Incentive	Majority, Prime Age; Male (Female in White Collar Occupations)	Work Skills; On-the-Job Training; Specific, Work-acquired Skills; Secondary Education	Medium to Moderately High
Secondary	Low Fixed Capital; Non-specialized Capital, Tools; Labour Intensive	Availability; Flexibility; Low Cost	Competitive	Direct; Incentive; Machine	Minority; Immigrant; Youth, Older Workers; Women Women	Ubiquitous, General Skills, Unskilled; Minimal Literacy and Numeracy	Low

In Table A5.1, under Capital characteristics, Intensity refers to the amount and type of capital associated with the employer. Labour Needs refers to the characteristics of labour needed by employers, and Output Pricing refers to the predominant method by which output prices are determined. Labour Process, Dominant Forms of Control refers to the predominant method by which the employer controls work effort.

Under Labour Supply characteristics, Labour Force reflects the primary recruitment ground by age, sex, race or ethnicity. Education–Training reflects the primary recruitment ground in terms of formal education and training; and Potential Productivity refers to the potential value of labour productivity as determined by intensity of labour, and fixed and human capital.

Table A5.2

Labour Market Segment	Characteristics of the Labour Market			Types of Employees	Labour Market Results
	Structure of the Market	Wage Determination Mechanism	Safety Net	Typical Occupations and Industries	Wages, Job Security, Union Potential, and Status
Primary/Upper Tier (Professional/Managerial)	Primarily Horizontal; Non-competitive; Non-Union; Limited Promotion Ladders	Supply and Demand (for Scarce "Human Capital"); Availability of Qualified Labour	Low Unemployment; Personal Contracts; Tenure, Unemployment Insurance	Professionals, Professional Employees in Finance, Insurance, Public Services; Education, Health and Welfare; Scientists, Engineers, Middle Management	High Wages; High Horizontal Mobility; Non-Unionized; Generally Job Security; Tendency to Small Firms; High Status
Primary/Craft-Technical-Lower-Professional Tier	Horizontal with Limited Promotion Ladders; Highly Unionized in Some Sectors; Requires Certification to Enter Market	Institutional Determination; Collective Bargaining; Job Evaluation	Unemployment Insurance; Seniority; Horizontal Mobility	Skilled Crafts; Technicians and Technology Workers; Nurses, Therapists, and Related Health Professionals; Teachers, Culture Workers	Usually Good Wages; Job Security or Union Protection though Subject to Frequent Layoffs in some Crafts; Moderately High Status
Primary/Lower Tier	Vertical, Internal Labour Markets, High Unionization; Entry at Limited Job Ports	Institutional Determination; Collective Bargaining; Job Evaluation	Unemployment Insurance; Seniority	Production Workers in Heavy Manufacturing, Mining, Forestry, Transportation, Communications and Utilities; Clerical Workers in Large Firms and the Public Sector	Moderate to Good Wages; Job Security (though Subject to Layoffs); Limited Horizontal Mobility; High Union Potential; Medium Status
Secondary	Horizontal; Competitive; Non-union; Non-structured	Subsistence ("Reserve Army of the Unemployed") or Alternative Subsistence; Minimum Wages; Community Standards; Welfare	Welfare; Unemployment Insurance; Food Banks	Production Workers in Light and Seasonal Manufacturing; Agricultural Workers; Personal Service Workers; Many Clerical and Sales Workers	Low Wages, Insecure Employment; High Horizontal Mobility; Tendency to Small Firms although also in Large Sales and Service Firms; Low Status

In Table A5.2, under Labour Market characteristics, Structure indicates whether jobs are structured in a vertical manner (e.g., job ladders, internal labour markets) or in an horizontal manner (e.g., relative job equality among skilled electricians or tool-and-die makers within and between employers); Wage Determination refers to the major forces determining the level and structure of wages. The Safety Net column lists the major provisions, public or private, providing job security or minimum income security in the event of a job loss; and Employee Types... indicates the characteristic types of employees by typical occupation or industry found in the corresponding labour market. When multiple classifications are given in Table A5.2, the rank order implies the degree of importance.

Chapter 6

The Labour Market
Part Two

The Dimensions of the Canadian Labour Market

To understand the Canadian labour market, it is necessary to have some idea of its dimensions, how many people work, in what occupations and industries, and where they are located in the country. The Canadian labour market can be divided by geography and by occupation. Generally, one thinks of a geographic labour market as being bounded by the distance within which it is feasible to commute. But when a symphony orchestra is looking for a new conductor, it may well search the whole world. Because of the short supply of medical doctors, Canadian health officials have been recruiting in Europe, South Africa, India and wherever medical training standards are considered comparable to those in Canada. In contrast, a local merchant looking for a janitor is unlikely to look beyond his own town or city.

Obviously, the geographic limits of the labour market are at least in part determined by skill, knowledge and regulation—the occupational boundaries of labour markets. The market for electricians is limited by the number of people who are certified as journeymen electricians. For biologists it may be the number of people who possess a university degree in biology, while for lawyers it is only those who have membership in the bar association of a particular province.

The dimensions of the labour market depend also on time. Is labour needed tomorrow, next month or next year? If it is tomorrow, it is unlikely the employer can search beyond the local market, nor can the worker migrate or retrain. If it is next month, the possibilities widen. If it is next year, the market might expand to the whole world and to anyone who can be trained for the available job within a year. Studies of the labour market for college graduates in the United States show that the supply of labour takes about four years to adjust to a change in demand.[1] In short, the dimensions of particular labour markets depend on the **mobility of labour**— how willing and able people are to move geographically (to another city, province or country) and from one occupation or employer to another.

Before looking at the statistics that describe the Canadian labour market (many of which will be out of date in a year or two), it is important to have an understanding of how Statistics Canada measures and defines our productive labour force. The following are the official definitions.

The Labour Force: "That portion of the civilian, non-institutional population, 15 years of age and over who, during the reference week in which the labour force survey was taken, were employed or unemployed." This needs a little bit of explanation. "Civilian, non-institutional population," excludes the military and those

6.1 Credentialism

Formal schooling was of little significance even for the professions through the mid-nineteenth century; by the 1930s post-secondary education had become an important criterion for entry into most professions; by the 1960s this requirement had become almost universal....The most dramatic recent increases in entry requirements have been among manual workers. In the1930s hardly any manual labour jobs required a high school diploma. By the early 1980s, the majority of skilled manual jobs required a diploma for entry, and about a quarter called for some post-secondary certification. Since the early 1980s, there has been a rapid increase in the use of high school graduation as a screen for entry into most unskilled manual jobs. [One set of] recent surveys of the array of possible hiring criteria and activities finds that about three-quarters of all non-college jobs now use high school diplomas as an initial screen. Even to push a broom in a steel mill, you now need to have a diploma. The "credential society" has definitely arrived.

–David Livingstone, *The Education–Jobs Gap* (Toronto: Garamond, 1999), pp 72–73

in prison or in mental institutions (though it includes university students). It also excludes Indians on reserves, the Yukon, the Northwest Territories and Nunavut, not for the reason that they are not part of the civilian labour force, but because their numbers are too small to be statistically significant.

Employed: "All persons who worked, full- or part-time (even one hour a week), and those who would have been at work were it not for illness, disability, family responsibilities, bad weather, labour disputes or vacations."

Unemployed: "Persons without work but seeking work, those who have not sought work in the previous four weeks but were either laid off for less than six months and are available for work or who have a job to go to within four weeks." The people who are excluded by this official definition of unemployment are those workers so discouraged that they have stopped looking for work (discouraged workers); and also workers who are employed part-time and would like to work full-time (involuntary part-time workers).

Participation Rate: "The proportion of people in the potential labour force—those people who could work; that is, are 15 years of age or older—who are actually working or are officially unemployed." There is another measure that is sometimes used and that is the **Employment Rate**, the proportion of the total working age population that is actually employed. It has the advantage of telling us, indirectly, how many disabled and retired people are out of the labour force. It also gives us some indication of how many are actually unemployed including discouraged workers.

Mobility

Labour markets are not static. There is a great deal of mobility in and out of specific markets. They vary from day to day, season to season, year to year. Part of what determines labour market activity, in particular how many people are available, includes mobility. There are several dimensions to mobility. First there is physical (or geographic) mobility. People move between cities and provinces and to and from rural and urban areas. This we call **internal migration**. People also move between countries. This we call **immigration** or **emigration**.

Second, there is **occupational mobility**. Moving into occupations depends upon the availability of education and training programs, on-the-job training within firms, and what some call "credentialism." This means that to get into some jobs you have to have the credentials—journeyman papers, university degrees, college diplomas or membership in professional associations. Some firms may have **internal labour markets** that allow employees to retrain and move up the occupational ladder within the firm. Companies have to be big enough and be motivated to promote, for example, servers to maître'd and to restaurant manager— and to provide for the necessary training to equip the person to take on the new responsibilities.

A third dimension of mobility is the degree of **inter-employer mobility**. Can people move from one firm or employer to another? Even highly qualified people may have difficulty changing employers. Often, for example, a hospital lab technician would find it difficult to get a job in the lab of an agricultural-chemical plant. As well, firms are often reluctant to hire people away from another firm in the same industry because they don't want to lose their own employees. Many union contracts also require an employer to fill job openings by promotion of existing employees rather than hiring from outside the firm.

> ### 6.2 The "Brain Drain:" Canada's "Brain Gain" 400% Larger than the "Brain Drain"
>
> There is at the moment a small net outflow of university-educated people moving from Canada to the United States. However, according to an October 1998 Statistics Canada study, international immigration of university-educated people into Canada— a "brain gain"—is at least four times larger than the "brain drain" to the U.S.
>
> The StatsCan study found that, between 1990 and 1996, approximately 8,500 university-educated people per year moved from Canada to the U.S. During the same period, approximately 32,800 university-educated people per year moved to Canada....
>
> Nevertheless, why are some university-educated people moving to the U.S.? Even if this brain drain is only a trickle and not, as many perceive, a flood, the question remains important.
>
> Most are leaving either because they cannot find work in their chosen fields, or because they can earn more money in the U.S.
>
> ... the health care sector represents the only area where international immigration does not currently outstrip emigration to the U.S.... In large measure, it has been public sector cutbacks, not high taxes, that have forced these young university-educated people to leave.
>
> –Seth Klein, "Loss of Professions to U.S. Exaggerated," CCPA *Monitor*, March 1999

Finally, we have mobility in and out of the labour force. This dimension depends very importantly on who and how many people are in the reserve army of the unemployed. People move in and out of the labour force depending on the type of jobs available and the personal situation of potential workers, such as the number of dependent children in the family of the potential worker and the availability of daycare centres and schools. The availability of short-term and on-the-job training that permits new workers to respond to employment opportunities is also important.

Canadians are renowned for their tendency to move within Canada, usually in search of a job or, less frequently, a better job. This rate of movement is tied to both the existence of job opportunities in the receiving area and the unemployment rate where they currently reside. When unemployment is present in all regions, movement tends to be at a minimum. Indeed, during these periods unemployed workers often return to their depressed home regions, despite the absence of job opportunities, in order to have the support of friends and relatives.

Immigration has been a major contributor to Canada's labour force at certain periods in our history. After the Second World War many people fled the economic and political problems of postwar Europe for new opportunities in Canada. More recently high unemployment in Canada has resulted in a decline in the country's attractiveness (the "pull" effect) while improved economic conditions in Europe have reduced the desire of migrants to leave (the "push" effect).

Recent high unemployment has led Canada to adopt increasingly restrictive immigration legislation. Even bona fide refugees facing persecution from right-wing, military regimes in Latin and South America have faced difficulty in being accepted as immigrants. Nevertheless, there has been a steady stream of applicants for immigration into Canada from the less developed parts of the world, particularly from Asia and Latin America, and from the countries of Central and Eastern Europe, whose economies have deteriorated with the abandonment of their state socialist systems. Whatever the labour market conditions in Canada, they are immensely better than in these countries.

While immigration has played a significant role in supplying labour to Canada, there has also been significant emigration out of the country. During the second half of the nineteenth century just as many emigrants left Canada as immigrated into the country. Recently, emigration to the United States has been particularly pronounced among university-trained professionals, leading to complaints of a "brain drain." However, while Canada has undoubtedly suffered a net loss of Canadian-educated labour to the United States, it has been the net beneficiary of educated labour from other parts of the world.

In summary, the supply of labour to a local labour market depends in part on the mobility of labour into (in-migration) or out of (out-migration) the local area or region. In-migration minus out-migration is defined as "net migration." Net migration, therefore, is an important variable in changes in the supply of labour to a local or the national market, particularly in the short run. In the longer run, the major source of new labour is natural increase in the population, the excess of births over deaths. However, because of falling birth rates in Canada, labour force growth has been increasingly dependent on net-migration.

6.3 Internal Labour Markets

The central concept ... is that of the *internal labor market*, an administrative unit, such as a manufacturing plant, within which the pricing and allocation of labor is governed by a set of administrative rules and procedures. The internal labor market, governed by administrative rules, is to be distinguished from the *external labor market* of conventional economic theory where pricing, allocating, and training decisions are controlled directly by economic variables. These two markets are interconnected, however, and movement between them occurs at certain job classifications which constitute *ports of entry and exit* to and from the internal labor market. The remainder of the jobs within the internal market are filled by the promotion or transfer of workers who have already gained entry. Consequently, these jobs are shielded from the *direct* influences of competitive forces in the external market.

–Peter Doeringer and Michael Piore, *Internal Labor Markets and Manpower Analysis*, 2nd. ed. (New York: M.E. Sharpe, 1985), pp. 1–2

Occupational Labour Markets

The supply of labour to a specific occupational labour market, either local or national, depends on two factors. One is the number of workers with the particular skills or credentials who are already in the market. This is normally very large compared with the second source of supply, the flow of new workers with the required skills or credentials into the market. Take, for instance, nurses in Manitoba. In 2002 there were around 11,000 nurses, but the number of new nurses in any one year may be only a few hundred. This flow of newly trained workers is influenced by migration and net immigration. Given the current continent-wide shortage of nurses, many provinces have been scouring other provinces, the United States and even as far afield as the Philippines for nurses while American hospitals have been poaching for nurses in Canadian waters.

More important, however, is occupational mobility and inter-generational mobility. **Occupational mobility** is where workers retrain to acquire new skills. The supply of such new sources of labour for specific occupational labour markets is, in turn, largely determined by the availability of schools and programs for obtaining the necessary skills, training, knowledge, experience or credentials. **Inter-generational mobility** is the entry of children into occupations that are different from their parents'. They are able to enter different occupations by acquiring skills, training or specialized knowledge that is required to enter a specific occupational labour market.

> ### 6.4 The Concept of the "Cost of Job Loss"
>
> The aggregate unemployment rate is a widely-used measure of labour market "tightness" or "the power of the sack" and, in general of capital's ability to subordinate labour.... There are several reasons, however, for questioning the adequacy of this measure of relative class power. Not only does the unemployment rate exclude "discouraged workers" who have abandoned job searches for want of employment prospects, but it also fails to consider properly the economic hardship resulting from unemployment.... The "cost of job loss"—defined as the percentage of annual income that a "representative worker" would lose upon being dismissed or laid off—is a more appropriate measure of the balance of power. Rising real wages, internal labour markets, and social welfare programs weaken the link between unemployment rates and relative class power. Therefore, the monetary cost of job loss is more significant than the aggregate unemployment rate in the "decision calculus" of individual firms and workers, and in class "behaviour" as well.... Measuring the cost of job loss thus involves four separate considerations: the level of previous employment earnings; the duration of unemployment; the availability of alternative forms of income while unemployed; and the "in-kind" income provided by government health and education expenditures.
>
> —Hugh Grant and Frank Strain, "'The Power of the Sack': The Cost of Job Loss in Canada, 1953–1985," Labour/Le Travail, 25, (Spring 1990), pp. 144–145

These skills, knowledge and credentials may be obtained in a number of ways. Most of us will think first of formal education and training programs in schools, universities, community colleges, technical schools, government training programs, apprenticeship programs, correspondence courses and private training agencies. But in fact more labour and work skills are learned "on-the-job." This can be through formal or informal on-the-job (OJT) training. Much on-the-job training, particularly in firms that provide for promotion up the job ladder, involves little more than workers observing and imitating more experienced co-workers. Specific training in this case is usually accomplished by a combination of work experience and either, or both, formal OJT and informal tutelage. Indeed, probably the most important source of occupational mobility (60 to 80 percent) comes from informal, on-the-job work experience.

On-the-job experience and training is frequently not sufficient to acquire the skills and knowledge required for many skilled and technical occupations. In these cases, work experience and on-the-job training need to be supplemented by formal education and training programs. These vocational or occupational programs provide not only the theoretical and practical knowledge required for specific occupations but also "credential" workers, certifying their occupational competency.

The determinants of inter-employer mobility are more difficult to specify because they depend greatly on the behaviour of employers and the state of the labour market (i.e., the rate of unemployment). Employers might tacitly agree not to raid each other for experienced workers because this would have the effect of bidding up wages. However, sometimes it may be cheaper for an employer to bid a worker away from a competitor than to train an inexperienced worker. Workers tend to be reluctant to quit a job when unemployment is high because of the risk of not finding another one or because they may lack job security with a new employer.

Horizontal (Inter-firm) and Vertical (Intra-firm) Labour Markets

In general, there are two types of labour market based on inter-employer mobility: horizontal and vertical. In **horizontal labour markets** workers have high inter-employer mobility. A plumber in the construction industry can, and usually does, move easily from one employer to another. Longshoremen may have a different employer almost every other day. Many, if not most, specialized skilled, technical and professional workers are willing and able to seek work with any firm that employs that particular type of skilled worker. Workers in many secondary labour market jobs such as farm labourers and general labourers also confront a horizontal labour market.

Vertical (or internal) labour markets are those that have low inter-employer mobility. That is, an employee of General Motors does not normally look to other companies for new or better jobs. This employee will look first for a promotion or transfer within GM. Most of these kinds of firms have well-defined job ladders (described above as internal labour markets) within the firm. Recruitment is by promotion within the firm, a characteristic of the lower tier of the primary labour market described in the previous chapter.

The supply of labour to any specific labour market will be determined in part by the ease with which people can move in and out of the market. The most important determinant of this is the size and characteristics of the reserve army of unemployed and underemployed. The underemployed include those who can only find part-time or part-year work and those who cannot find jobs that utilize their skills, knowledge and training.

Two examples will suffice. In an agricultural area there may be large

6.5 Underemployment

The idea that some people are denied the opportunity to use their full capability at work has been around as long as there have been class societies in which rewarded work has been hierarchically organized and gifted children have been born into the lower ranks. Conversely, the existence of mediocrity among the higher ranks has frequently been recognized by those beneath them; a recent expression of this is the "Peter Principle," which identifies a tendency for managers to be promoted until they reach a level beyond their actual competency. Of course, in any market-driven economy, paid workplaces are continually changing and there are always mismatches between employers' aggregate demand and requirements for employees on the one hand, and the aggregate supply and qualifications of job seekers on the other.

–David Livingstone, *The Education–Jobs Gap* (Toronto: Garamond, 1999), p. 53

numbers of farmers and their families who are available for part- or full-time work and who want to work, either seasonally or regularly throughout the year in order to supplement their farm income. They can only do so, however, if there is such work available in their area. There are many housewives who are available for work, particularly seasonal and part-time work. However, they will only take a job if the right types of jobs are available and affordable alternatives are provided for child care, house cleaning, laundry, food preparation and other necessary domestic work.

Furthermore, when unemployment is high and chronic, many workers become discouraged and leave the labour market (that is, they stop looking for work). These discouraged workers are available to the labour market when job opportunities increase.

Mobility makes it very difficult to specify the dimensions of any labour market, particularly over time. However, at any point in time one can approximate the overall dimensions of the Canadian labour market by measuring labour supply.

Labour Supply

The total potential supply of labour in Canada depends on the size and age composition of the population. The larger the population (other things remaining the same) the more potential

> ### 6.6 Men Work from Sun to Sun: A Woman's Work is Never Done
>
> Traditionally, the sexual division of labour within the family has been on the basis of men working outside, frequently distant from, the home while women have worked within, or around, the household, producing for the family, cleaning, washing and mending, caring for and nurturing the children. This has meant that "women's work" has been 7 days a week, 14 to 16 hours a day while men have tended to do very limited work around the home such that their working hours have gradually been reduced to not much more than their 40 hours or so a week spent at their place of employment. This is confirmed by recent studies by Statistics Canada:
>
> > The latest information on household work is contained in the 1992 *General Social Survey* and reported in Ronald Bodkin's 1999 paper "Gender Differences in the Canadian Economy." Married women with children and who are also working were reported to spend an average of between 23 and 32 hours a week in combined domestic work and child care depending on the age of the child. When no children are present, housework drops to just under 20 hours per week. Women who are not working but who have spouses typically reported time spent in domestic work and child care at from half to two-thirds more than women working outside the home—that is from 32 hours for women without children to 38 hours with children over 5; and 50 hours for women with children under 5 years. For men, the comparable figures are 7, 13 and 18 hours per week or one-third of the time spent by women.
>
> –Paul Phillips and Erin Phillips, *Women and Work*, 3rd. ed. (Toronto: Lorimer, 2000), pp. 48–49

workers there will be. The size of the Canadian labour supply is limited by the fact that child labour is illegal in Canada. This may seem obvious, but it is worth recognizing that there are still many less-developed agricultural societies in which child labour is common.

The actual supply—defined as the **labour force**—depends not only on the available "bodies," but also on age and sex. For example, as more students go on to higher education, their participation in the labour force tends to drop, at least during the school year. Older people participate less in the labour force because they may no longer want to work or because they have health problems. This is particularly the case as social security systems such as pension schemes become

6.7 Discouraged Workers

Discouraged workers are those who are unemployed but do not look for work because they believe there is no work available. As a result, they are not included in the unemployment statistics. However, Statistics Canada in recent years has included a question on discouraged workers in its labour force survey. As might be expected, the number of discouraged workers rises dramatically when unemployment rises, and falls as unemployment falls. The rates of discouraged workers by sex and year for the most recent years when Statistics Canada reported them are given in the following table. Inclusion of discouraged workers in the unemployed would raise the official unemployment rate by 0.6 % in 1997 and by 0.3 % in 2000.

Year	Rate of Unemployment	Rate of Discouraged Workers		
		Male	Female	Total
1997	9.1	0.7	0.7	0.6
1998	8.3	0.4	0.6	0.5
1999	7.6	0.4	0.4	0.4
2000	6.8	0.3	0.3	0.3

–Statistics Canada, *Labour Force Historical Review* (71-F0004XCB) 2001

available. Women tend to participate less because of family responsibilities, social attitudes and, in some regions or areas, the shortage of "socially acceptable women's work," such as in isolated mining, lumbering and construction communities. In fact, women probably represent the most significant proportion of the reserve army of unemployed in Canada.

The percentage of the potential labour force that actually participates in the labour force is termed the **participation rate** (see Table 6.1). It is calculated by dividing the number of people employed and unemployed by the total potential working population; that is, the total population 15 years of age and older. It should be noted that female participation rates have been rising quite rapidly since the 1960s (adding to women's double workload), at least up until the 1990s. In the early 1960s less than 30 percent of adult women were in the labour market. By 1980 that figure had risen to just over half. Women's participation continued to increase rapidly in the 1980s, reaching 58.5 percent by 1990. The recession of the early nineties and the impact of technological change, the trade deals and government cutbacks severely restricted the growth of what have traditionally been considered women's jobs through most of the nineties. As a result, the participation rate for women rose by a mere 1 percent over the past decade. At the same time, participation rates for men have remained relatively constant or declined slightly.

What are the reasons for the rising rate of female participation? The most obvious reason is economic need. On the one hand the market has invaded the household—prepared foods, inexpensive synthetic, perma-press clothing, automatic washers and dryers have changed the nature of housework. In the process the "value" of housework has declined, while the cost of raising children has risen. There has also been an increase in the number of female-headed, single parent families who need income to raise their children.

Economic need in general has been

6.8 The Cost of Raising Children

The Manitoba Department of Agriculture, *Family Resource Management Guide* for 1998 estimates the cost of raising a child to age 18 at around $160,000. Of course, if children remain dependent on their parents while getting a post-secondary education, this cost would rise to over $200,000. This means that children who, in an earlier age, were an economic asset to the family through both paid and unpaid labour, have now become a major financial liability.

Table 6.1: Labour Force and Participation Rates by Age, Sex and Region 2000

Labour Force by Age

TotalParticipation			15-24	25-44	45-64	65+
		Rate	Yrs.	Yrs.	Yrs.	Yrs.
	(000s)	(%)		(000s)		
Total	15,999	64.9	2,621	8,197	4,964	218
Male	8,649	70.7	1,368	4,392	2,740	150
Female	7,350	59.2	1,253	3,805	2,225	68

Labour Force by Region
(000s and percentage of total Canadian labour force)

	Atlantic	Quebec	Ontario	Prairies	B.C.
Total	1,152	3,753	6,228	2,766	2,100
	(7.2)	(23.5)	(38.9)	(17.3)	(13.1)
Male	615	2,062	3,330	1,516	1,127
	(7.1)	(23.8)	(38.5)	(17.5)	(13.0)
Female	538	1,691	2,898	1,250	973
	(7.3)	(23.0)	(39.4)	(17.0)	(13.2)

Source: Statistics Canada, Labour Force Historical Review *(71-F0004XCB) 2001*

rising in the last two decades. The real disposable income of families has stagnated because of declining male wages and rising personal taxes for the average Canadian. The increased tax burden was the result of the Conservative Mulroney government's decision to bring in the Goods and Services Tax and the increasing portion of tax revenue that came from individuals.

But even if the cost of running the household hadn't risen and the real wages of men had not fallen, Canadians had come to expect a gradual increase in their standard of living. This was part of what has been termed the **"postwar accord"** between government, labour and capital. Under this informal understanding organized labour would not contest business's right to manage their corporations and the economy as long as workers received a fair share of rising economic productivity. For its part government was expected to provide an adequate level of social and economic security. This unspoken agreement allowed the labour market to operate relatively efficiently without workers being forced to bear an inequitable share of the cost of market fluctuations. Under these circumstances, income expectations rose. Women also wanted to participate more fully in society and use their talents and their education to raise their families' levels of consumption. Thus more and more women entered the labour market, at least until the 1990s. By then, however, the postwar accord had effectively been abandoned by employers and by government.

On the other hand, all the willingness of women to enter the labour market would have been of little effect if it were not for the increasing numbers of "acceptable" female jobs. The postwar boom saw a large increase in clerical, sales and service jobs. Many of these jobs reflected the market's extension into the household. Work that women had done at home for free they now did for pay as nurses, cleaners, cooks and waitresses, teachers, child care workers and in related personal services. These jobs had been increasing since the administrative revolution that accompanied the transition to monopoly capitalism at the turn of the century.[2] For the most part, these were not particularly good jobs. Women workers were often treated poorly and paid badly. Nevertheless, they allowed women the opportunity to earn an income, an important opportunity in an increasingly market society.

There are many problems when we attempt to get a handle on the actual supply of labour to any particular labour market. We have no real measure of the supply of labour by occupation. Many workers do not actually work at the specific occupation for which they were trained, and the majority of occupational training is on-the-job or informal. As well, the potential supply of labour to lesser skilled jobs includes all the people who have superior qualifications. That is, an unemployed space scientist can compete for jobs as a taxi driver, but most taxi drivers cannot compete in the market for space scientists.

The best we can do is measure the occupation distribution of the experienced labour force—those who are employed now in an occupation or those unemployed but who were recently employed in an occupation. These numbers really only tell us how many people employers want to hire for particular occupations (that is, labour demand), not how many people want to work in these occupations. They also exclude the unemployed who have never worked or who last worked more than one year ago (see Table 6.2).

Table 6.2 shows that service, sales, clerical and managerial occupations account for around three-quarters of the labour force. Sales and service occupations alone account for a quarter of the total labour supply. Occupations in traditional goods production, in the primary industries, manufacturing and processing and in construction, account for a mere 14 percent of workers. The table also demonstrates the very marked difference between the occupational distribution of women and of men. Women are three times as likely as men to be in administrative and clerical occupations, 65 percent more likely to be in sales and service occupations, four times as likely to be in health occupations, but only a third as likely to be in primary occupations and half as likely in processing and manufacturing jobs. In short, for most major occupational groups, labour supply is decidedly gender-related.

Labour Demand

The demand for labour is ultimately determined by the demand for goods and services that labour produces. These demands are constantly changing and differ from one place to another. Also, since different regions have different resource endowments industries are not distributed evenly across the country. Alberta has oil but Quebec has none. The population distribution in Canada is uneven with population concentrated in central Canada, Ontario and Quebec. This means that demand for labour for consumer services is likewise concentrated in these provinces.

Table 6.2: Employment by Occupation 2000

Occupation	Total (000s)	%	Male (000s)	%	Female (000s)	%
All Occupations	14,910	100.0	8049	100.0	6,860	100.0
Managerial	1,432	9.6	926	11.5	506	7.4
Business and Admin	2,646	17.7	761	9.5	1,885	27.5
(of which Clerical)	(1,468)	(9.8)	(432)	(5.4)	(1,036)	(15.1)
Health Occupations	780	5.2	152	1.9	629	9.2
Teachers and Professors	559	3.7	207	2.6	353	5.1
Sales and Service	3,723	25.0	1,548	19.2	2,175	31.7
Trades, Transportation, Equipment Operators	2,130	14.3	1,995	24.8	135	2.0
(of which Construction Trades)	(300)	(2.0)	(292)	(3.6)	(9)	(0.1)
Primary Occupations	578	3.9	461	5.7	117	1.7
Processing and Mfg	1,222	8.2	858	10.7	364	5.3
Other (Natural and Social Science, Recreation and Culture)	1,840	12.3	1,143	14.2	697	10.2

Source: Statistics Canada, Labour Force Historical Review *(71-F0004XCB) 2001*

Historical patterns of development also played a role in allocating demand. In the nineteenth century, many light manufacturing industries set up shop in Quebec to take advantage of that province's concentration of low-wage labour. The garment industry was also attracted to Quebec by its low wages and a large supply of female labour. The availability of large numbers of low-wage, immigrant women was also significant in the development of the garment industries in Toronto and Winnipeg in subsequent years.

Government policies play an important role in determining the demand for labour. In the mid-1980s the Conservative Government of Brian Mulroney created a political controversy when it awarded the maintenance contract for the CF-18 fighter jet to a Quebec-based firm, in the face of technical recommendations that it should give the contract to a Winnipeg company. Critics of the decision said the government had acted for political rather than economic reasons. On other occasions Manitoba has benefited from federal policy. The railways that gave Winnipeg its start were financed by the federal government, while government decisions to centre the grain trade and regulatory bodies in that city ensured it had a continuing economic function.

But demand for labour is not just a function of the distribution of resources, of population and of industrial structure. Technological change can have quite revolutionary effects on the structure and location of the demand for labour. The revolution in computing and electronic transmission and communication technology that we now collectively call information technology (IT) dramatically illustrates this point. Whole new industries have developed, whole communities

6.9 The Social and Economic Costs of Unemployment

Unemployment inflicts high social as well as financial costs.

The financial costs of unemployment are generally well known. A CCPA study ("What is the real cost of unemployment?" by D. Bellemare and L. Poulin-Simon) has calculated that unemployment in 1993 cost the unemployed over $13 billion, business firms over $33 billion, and all levels of government over $47 billion.

Even the federal government calculates that the annual financial cost to the economy could be as high as $77 billion in lost wages, lost profits, and lost government tax revenues. The social costs—the impact on people's physical and mental health—are even more damaging. Applying [the] methods [developed by Harvey Brenner in the U.S.] to ... lowering our unemployment rate from 10% to 6% ... would have these effects:

1. It would lower our mortality rate by 3.6%.
2. It would lower our homicide rate by 5.7%.
3. It would lower our suicide rate by 2.1%.
4. It would lower our admissions to psychiatric hospitals by 12.6%.
5. It would lower the number of arrests by 12%.
6. It would lower the number of prisoners in our jails by 18%.

–CCPA Monitor, March 1997

created or expanded. Older industries, technologies, occupations and communities have disappeared or been radically reduced.

Nor is it just technological change that has played its part in restructuring the demand for labour. Government policy has played a major, if not equivalent, role. Deregulating, privatizing and downsizing of industries, in particular, social services, has resulted in major shifts in the demand for certain types of labour. Cutbacks in the healthcare sector in the 1990s, for instance, resulted in a sharp decline in demand for nurses and other hospital workers. At the same time, free trade and investment agreements—the process we call globalization—changed labour demand worldwide. Jobs in labour intensive manufacturing such as toy production, clothing and textiles, shoe manufacture and electronic assembly moved to the low-wage countries of the Third World.

So far we have talked only about the changing structure and location of industry and occupations on the demand for workers. Also important, perhaps even more important, is how well the economy is doing in providing employment for all who want to work. This question will be dealt with later in much more detail but suffice it to say here, the failure to maintain the overall demand for labour (what economists call the "aggregate" demand for labour) has had disastrous effects for working—or not-working—Canadians. It is called **unemployment**, the most important cause of poverty, disease and despair in modern economies.

Unemployment

Demand for labour has only rarely matched available supply. Except for brief periods such as during the Second World War and during the immediate postwar expansion, the Korean War and the Vietnam War, high unemployment has been the rule and not the exception. Even when demand for labour has been high overall, the kinds of people, their skills, their ages and locations have not matched the job opportunities available. This has resulted in unemployment that has disadvantaged certain regions, certain occupations and certain groups. Some of the regional and gender dimensions of this structure of unemployment are given in Table 6.3.

We can identify four types of unemployment. They are frictional, seasonal,

Table 6.3: The Structure and Level of Unemployment in Canada

Unemployment Rates by Region and Sex: 2000

Region	Total	Male	Female
Atlantic	11.2	12.2	10.1
Quebec	8.4	8.6	8.2
Ontario	5.7	5.5	5.9
Prairies	5.0	5.2	4.9
B.C.	7.2	7.6	6.7
Canada	6.8	6.9	6.7

Source: Statistics Canada, Labour Force Historical Review (71-F0004XCB) 2001

Unemployment Rates: 1946–2000
(percent averages)

1946–50	2.2
1951–55	2.8
1956–60	4.7
1961–65	5.4
1966–70	4.4
1971–75	6.0
1976–80	7.7
1981–85	10.4
1986–90	8.4
1991–95	10.5
1996–2000	8.3

Source: M.C. Urquhart and K.A.H. Buckley, eds., Historical Statistics of Canada, (Cambridge: Cambridge University Press, 1965); Statistics Canada, Labour Force Historical Review (71-F0004XCB) 2001

---

cyclical (or deficient demand) and structural (or technological) unemployment. **Frictional unemployment** (also called **job search unemployment**) is by and large unavoidable, though it can be minimized by having a good network of (public) employment agencies. It is caused by "friction" in the market—the time taken to match unemployed workers to existing job vacancies.

When a construction worker finishes a job he or she might experience a short period of unemployment until he or she finds another job. When a student graduates, she or he spends several weeks looking over the market, making applications and having interviews before landing a job. With frictional unemployment, workers are available and employers want to hire them, and it is merely a question of matching them up. In other words, the number and structure of the unemployed equal the number and structure of job vacancies. The problem in matching those looking for work and employers looking for

6.10 Human Resource Development Canada (HRDC) and the Labour Market

When Unemployment Insurance was first established in Canada in 1940, one of the major tasks of the new federal agency created was the provision of employment exchanges. These were offices where the unemployed could go to in order to find out what jobs were available, and where employers could find workers available for employment. This labour exchange function was designed to reduce "frictional unemployment."

These labour exchanges were somewhat limited in their effectiveness because employers tended to list only low skilled, often casual, jobs that required minimal qualifications and used other methods such as newspaper ads or informal employee networks to recruit for more skilled positions. However, these centres provided an additional function in bringing the unemployed to "manpower" or "employment centers" where they could also receive counseling and, in some cases, access to training.

During the 1990s, HRDC, which now administers unemployment insurance and the labour exchanges, converted much of its labour exchange function to information and services delivered on-line via the Internet or through call centres. In 2001, Jane Stewart, the Minister responsible for HRDC reported:

> Our Department's delivery network has 100 main Human Resource Centres of Canada (HRCCs) and 220 satellite offices for a total of 320 points of service in communities. The delivery network includes 21 call centres (11 Employment Insurance call centres, and 10 Income Security Programs call centres), four regional Information Technology Centres with two satellites (sic) sites and more than 5,000 interactive kiosks. Through our Internet website, the Department provides extensive information on HRDC programs and services. HRDC's electronic Job Bank is by far the most popular government website. [HRDC, Departmental Performance Report (Ottawa: HRDC, 2001), p. 6]

This development has increased both in speed and in scope access to information on job vacancies for the unemployed and made it possible to access the electronic labour exchange from Internet-connected homes. However, critics have pointed out that most of the unskilled and poorer unemployed do not have home Internet connections nor do they have the knowledge and experience to navigate the HRDC website from the kiosks that have largely replaced the information officers at the resource centres.

qualified labour is a temporary and generally low-cost one. In the early sixties, frictional unemployment in Canada was estimated at 2 to 3 percent. It may be somewhat higher now because of the increased rates of layoffs and turnover and the trend toward the creation of contingent jobs (temporary, contract and sub-contract, part-time and part-year jobs).

Seasonal unemployment arises from seasonal differences in the demand for, or supply of, labour. This can be the result of weather. Construction and recreation industries such as ski resorts or golf courses are obvious examples. Other seasonal demands for labour are tied to natural life cycles, as in agriculture and what is left of the fishing industry. Social, cultural and community institutions also play a role. Toy manufacturers, book publishers and recording companies time production for the Christmas rush, and florists for Mother's Day and Valentine's Day. Many tourist and recreation industries target school holidays and vacations.

Cyclical (or, more accurately, **deficient demand**) **unemployment** arises from the inability, or unwillingness, of consumers, businesses, foreigners and governments to buy up all of the goods and services produced. We live in what economists call a "demand constrained" economy. What this means is that in the normal course of events, business, governments and consumers cannot purchase what the economy and its workers are able to produce. As a result, some workers (and some capital equipment) will remain idle—a polite name for unemployed. Why this should be is explored in detail in chapter 9.

Structural (technological) unemployment arises when the structure of demand for labour (i.e., by occupation or location) does not match that of available workers. If the only unemployment was structural unemployment, the number of job vacancies would equal the number of unemployed, but the unemployed would not be able to fill the job vacancies. It is often associated with technological change because such change destroys old skills and creates demands for new ones. A classic case occurred when the automobile destroyed the demand for harness makers and teamsters while creating demands for mechanics, and truck and bus drivers. A more contemporary example is that of information technology destroying demand for secretaries and telephone operators but creating demands for computer engineers and programmers.

Full employment is generally conceived of as the absence of seasonal, structural and deficient demand unemployment and the minimization of frictional unemployment through labour market information systems such as Human Resource Development Canada's electronic job market and employment centres.

Alternatively, full employment means that anyone who wants to work can find a job in a reasonable period of time and at the prevailing wage or salary level for their qualifications. Several conditions must be met. First, workers who want to work must be able to find work. Second, they must be able to find work in a reasonable period of time. Third, the jobs available must provide reasonable wages for the skills required and in comparison to prevailing wage rates in similar types of work. (Full employment is discussed in further detail in chapter 9.)

There is a major difficulty in the official measure of unemployment. It

---

6.11 Unemployment Adds $1 Billion to Canada's Health Care Costs

"Unemployment is increasing Canada's health care costs by at least $1 billion a year."

That's the conclusion of a study—*The Health Impact of Unemployment*—conducted by Robert L. Jin, M.D.; Chandrakant P. Shah, M.D.; and Tomislavj Svoboda, B.Sc.; supported by the Public Health Committee of the Ontario Medical Association.

"Unemployment is an important determinant of ill-health," the study declares, "having detrimental impacts on mental, physical and social (family and community) well-being. Health is affected by both the stress of job loss and the deleterious effects of chronic joblessness."

The authors found strong evidence of the various adverse health effects of unemployment, including higher mortality rates from heart disease and suicide. "[There is] a generally increased risk of morbidity among the unemployed," they stated, "including mental and physical symptoms, health disorders, and greater utilization of health care services ... (including) higher rates of hospitalization, visits to doctors, use of medications, and other services."

–CCPA *Monitor*, June 1994

6.12 "Chipping" away at Clerical Workers

Through much of the postwar period, clerical work was the most significant employment destination of the swelling ranks of female workers. By the 1990s, however, computers and new information technology had seriously eroded the demand for clerical workers. Between 1988 and 1998, there was a drop of almost 7 percent in the number of clerical jobs in the Canadian economy when professional occupations in business and finance are excluded. Between the 1991 and 1995 censuses, the number of legal secretaries dropped by as much as 17.3 percent, the number of medical secretaries by 2.1 percent.

–Paul Phillips and Erin Phillips, *Women and Work* (Toronto: Lorimer, 2000), pp. 118–119

6.13 Involuntary Part-Time Workers

As the following table indicates, there are a sizeable number of workers, particularly women, who want to work full-time but are only able to find part-time work. If it is assumed that on average these involuntary part-timers are working half-time, this would bump the *real* unemployment rate up by over 2 percent, over 3 percent for women.

Involuntary Part-Time Employment: 2000

	Total	Men	Women
Part-time as % of Total Labour Force	16.9	9.6	25.5
Involuntary Part-time as % of Part-time	25.3	27.5	24.3
Involuntary Part-time as % of Total Labour Force	4.3	2.6	6.2

–Statistics Canada, *Labour Force Historical Review* (71-F0004 XCB) 2001

6.14 National Poverty* Rates—Before and After the Impact of Transfers**

International Comparisons (1998)

	All Households		% of Two-Adult Working Families With Children	
	Before	After	Before	After
Canada	22.9	11.2	12.6	6.4
United States	25.3	17.1	15.4	12.7
Germany	22.1	5.5	3.1	1.5
France	34.5	8.2	18.7	2.1
Sweden	33.9	6.5	8.6	1.4

* Income of less than one half the median income.
** Transfers involve government payments to individuals and families and not market earned income. In Canada this would include pensions, child tax credits, social assistance, unemployment insurance benefits, maternity leave benefits, workers' compensation payments, etc.

–OECD (1998) as reported in Andrew Jackson and David Robinson, *Falling Behind: The State of Working Canada 2000* (Ottawa: CCPA, 2000), p. 43

Note that not only does the United States have high rates of market poverty, but it has a very poorly developed social welfare state in that transfers do very little to bring down the rate of poverty compared with European states and even with Canada. In Canada, for instance, transfers reduce the poverty rates by half; in the U.S. by a quarter to a third. In Sweden, by contrast, transfers reduce the rates of poverty by up to 80 percent with similar results in France and Germany.

does not include involuntary part-time and other underemployed workers. By underemployed, we mean workers who have a job but either do not work full time even though they want to, or the job does not utilize the full skills of the worker. The stereotype of the second type of underemployed worker is the Ph.D. graduate in physics who is driving a taxi. In both cases, the worker is underutilized: in the first case the worker's time is underutilized, in the second, the worker's skill is not fully used. Official unemployment figures measure neither. Information on the numbers of involuntary part-time workers is, however, collected and published.

Wages

As noted in chapter 5, wages reflect different institutional, power and market forces in the various segments of the labour market. The result is wide variances in wages between regions, occupations, industries and genders. Selected examples are given in Tables 6.4 and 6.5. Even these figures underestimate wage differences because they do not include the economic value of most fringe benefits.

Moreover, these differentials are getting wider. In the United States the soaring wages, salaries and stock options of senior management in major corporations now averages close to *five hundred times* the wages of the average production or office worker. At the same time the wages of low-income earners have been stagnant or falling. Furthermore, the social safety net, including unemployment insurance and so-

Table 6.4: Average Earnings and Wages in Canada by Occupation, Sex and Union Status, 1994

Occupation	Non-Union As % Of Unionized			Non-Unionized			Union Wages
	Total	Male	Female	Total	Male	Female	All Workers
	(dollars per hour)						(%)
Manag, Admin	19.89	21.24	18.40	17.65	19.79	15.30	89
Teaching	21.83	23.44	20.84	14.87	18.91	13.33	68
Medical	19.06	17.78	19.26	14.46	16.69	14.21	76
Clerical	14.21	16.60	13.52	10.51	12.28	10.23	74
Sales	11.29	13.55	10.50	9.86	12.25	8.13	87
Services	14.37	15.37	12.91	7.94	9.06	7.38	55
Processing	14.18	17.02	10.49	12.59	15.47	7.12	89
Machining	20.14	20.37	8.39	12.29	12.46	9.17	61
Fabricating	18.37	19.06	14.39	12.84	13.45	9.56	70
Trans, Comm	17.72	17.82	15.59	11.92	11.97	11.52	67
Materials Handling	16.79	17.26	12.70	9.04	9.20	8.16	54
All Occu- pations	18.38	19.15	17.51	13.29	15.02	11.62	72
Lowest as % of Highest	52	58	40	45	46	47	

Source: Statistics Canada, Survey of Labour and Income Dynamics, *1994*

Table 6.5: Average Weekly Earnings by Province and Industry, 1997

Province	Average Earnings	% of Cdn Avg.	Industry	Earnings	% of Indust. Avg.
Nfld.	527.38	88	Forestry	797.46	133
P.E.I.	475.13	79	Mines	1,054.65	176
Nova Scotia	501.47	84	Manuf.	737.45	123
New Bruns.	522.72	87	Constr.	709.20	119
Quebec	584.98	98	Trans., Comm.	755.09	126
Ontario	638.97	107	Trade,		
Manitoba	524.37	88	Wholesale	653.35	109
Saskatchewan	527.14	88	Retail	355.20	59
Alberta	600.47	100	Fin., Ins.	742.13	124
B.C.	614.17	103	Services	506.89	85
			Pub. Admin.	740.35	124
Canada	598.26	100	Ind. Agg.	598.26	100
Lowest as % of Highest	74			34	

Source: Statistics Canada, Employment, Earnings and Hours *(SC 72-002), January 1998*

6.15 Earnings Differentials

Ratio of the Average Weekly Earnings of the Top 10 Percent to the Bottom 10 percent of Adult ("Prime Age") Men and Women, 1981–93

	1981	1984	1989	1993
Men (aged 25-54)	4.3	4.9	5.2	5.1
Women (aged 25-54)	6.3	6.6	6.5	6.2

–Garnett Picot, cited in Andrew Jackson and David Robinson, *Falling Behind: The State of Working Canada 2000* (Ottawa: CCPA, 2000), p. 31

cial assistance, has been gutted by neoliberal government cutbacks. As a result, the United States and Canada have the highest poverty levels of any countries in the industrial world. Falling real wages for young people and for men generally in the last decade reflect the effects of unemployment, the decline of private sector unionism and the "levelling down" impact of the trade agreements.

The Labour Market in Action

This chapter has outlined the dynamics and complexity of the Canadian labour market. The supply of labour is constantly changing as people enter and leave the labour force, as people migrate between local labour markets, between employers and between occupations. The structure of supply has changed markedly as more and more women have entered the labour market and as the education system has produced new types and higher levels of skills. Demand has also been changing in response to technological and structural changes in the economy, high interest rates, the impact of trade agreements, and government policies of privatization and downsizing of social programs and the social safety net. The effect on the job market and on incomes has been dramatic. The nineties were a pretty dismal decade for workers, at least until around 1997, as a result of what some have called the policy of permanent recession and the consequent high unemployment.[3]

Such has not been the case for corporations and the elite. There has been a significant increase in inequality during the last two decades. In terms of family incomes, economist Andrew Jackson and the co-authors of a study on income distribution conclude:

> Lower-income and middle-income families today have a smaller share of the income pie than in the past. In 1970 ... families in the three lowest deciles [the bottom 30 percent] received about 10.7% of all family income before income tax. By 1995, their share dropped to 9.9 %. The share of income going to families in the middle four deciles [middle 40 percent] dropped from 35.6 % in 1970 to 34.5 % in 1995. Meanwhile, families in the top three deciles [top 30 percent] increased their share of family income from 53.6 % in 1970 to 55.4 % in 1995.[4]

Corporate profits, although they have risen substantially from the low levels of the 1970s, have still not recovered to the heights of their glory days in the 1950s and '60s and were particularly badly hit by the recessions in the early 1980s and again in the early '90s. Their recovery, however, has come in part at the expense of labour's share of national income.

If workers have fallen back since the 1970s and profits have only partially recovered, where has all the money gone? Economist Jim Stanford has presented part of the answer. It has gone to the owners of financial wealth—paper assets in the form of bonds, mortgages, bills, debentures and other forms of financial capital. Stanford has calculated the difference in the distribution of capital income between the 1950s and the 1990s. Over that period corporate and small business profits as a percentage of GDP fell by 8.6 points. Over half of that decrease, 4.5 percentage points, went to financial capital in the form of higher interest and investment income (which economists call *rentier* income). This was primarily the result of the regime of high interest rates set by the Bank of Canada that prevailed until almost the end of the twentieth century. But the major cause of labour's woes was not the shift of wages to profits but changes in the labour market that hollowed out the middle of the labour market and produced both unemployment and underemployment.

> ### 6.16 Income Polarization and the Labour Market
>
> - Overall [among the middle 5th of income earners] incomes rose somewhat from 1973 to 1984 and 1984 to 1990, but fell in the 1990s. In 1996, real incomes were only slightly higher than in 1984.
> - The bottom fifth of working families experienced a major decline in income from 1973 to 1984, some recovery from 1984 to 1990, and then a huge income decline in the 1990s. The poorest 10% of families had very low market incomes throughout the entire period, and these shrank dramatically to just $435 per family in 1996, indicating almost complete marginalization from the job market....
> - The story for the top 20% of families is different again. Their market incomes rose by about one-quarter from 1973 to 1990. However, even this top group did not fare well in the 1990s. Only the very top 10% experienced a market income gain in the 1990s, and this was just 2% (1990–96).
>
> –Andrew Jackson and David Robinson, *Falling Behind: The State of Working Canada 2000* (Ottawa: CCPA, 2000), pp. 27–29

Notes

1. Richard Freeman, "The College Labor Market," *Labor Markets in Action* (Cambridge, Mass.: Harvard University Press, 1989).
2. See in particular Graham Lowe, *Women in the Administrative Revolution* (Toronto: University of Toronto Press, 1987).
3. For a detailed account of this dismal decade, see Andrew Jackson et al.., *Falling Behind: The State of Working Canada, 2000* (Ottawa: Canadian Centre for Policy Alternatives, 2000).
4. Andrew Jackson and David Robinson, *Falling Behind*, p. 117.

Chapter 7

Investment
Closing the Circle

Reading the Report On Business

One would expect that the business sections of our daily newspapers would provide a great deal of information about investment. After all, investment is key to ongoing economic growth. And the papers often report at great length on the buying and selling of corporate assets. At times, it appears that these assets are tangible. For example, there might be a story about a bankrupt steel firm having to liquidate its assets. That is a gentle way of saying it must sell off its equipment and buildings at fire sale prices to pay off as many of its creditors as it can. In the next article you read about Long Term Capital Management, an investment fund that is on the verge of bankruptcy because it was speculating in derivatives (whatever they are) that have gone bad, and it has to be "rescued" by the international banking system to prevent a financial crisis. This all sounds much more ephemeral. It is not clear what sort of capital goods Long Term Capital has that it could dispose of in the here and now.

The underlying problem, which keeps cropping up every time we talk about capital, capital investment or capital markets, is that the term capital is used to refer to two different, but related, things. In one breath it can mean the equipment, machinery, buildings, bricks and mortar, inventory of raw materials and unsold output; the physical means of production, or capital goods. That is **real capital**. But it can also be used to refer to the money and credit used to finance the means of production. This sort of capital ought to be referred to as **financial capital.** And in the same way there can be two types of investment.

Real investment is the act of acquiring capital goods for the production of other goods and services. It is important to distinguish between investment, as defined by economists, and financial investment, which is what most people think of when they hear the word investment.

Financial investment means buying an income earning paper asset (deposit, stock, bill, bond, debenture, mortage). Real investment involves expenditure on capital goods or inventory. Financial markets are just a "veil of money" hiding the real economy.

If I have $100,000 I can invest it in buying an apartment block, a *real* bricks and mortar asset. Or I can buy bonds (say Government of Canada Savings Bonds or a bond of the Canadian Pacific Railway), a *financial* asset. So when a broker says, "I would love to buy that townhouse, but I don't have the capital," what is really meant is, "I don't have the *money*." Thus "financial capital" is really money paid, or

7.1 The Two Faces of the Canadian Economy

The financial economy (also called the "paper economy") represents the huge industry that has developed around the creation, purchase, and sale of money and other financial (or paper) assets: stocks, bonds, loans, mortgages, mutual funds, derivatives, foreign currency, annuities. The wheelings and dealings of the paper economy have an incredibly high profile. Daily fluctuations in stock markets, bond prices, interest rates, and exchange rates are followed extremely closely by economists, journalists, and politicians, and are often held to be a barometer of the general well-being of the economy.

Yet, despite the apparent importance of finance, in a fundamental sense its operations are *tangential* to the economic life of a country. This is because the activity of the financial sector—its "output"—does not directly contribute to the material well-being or productivity of Canadians. It is the *real economy* that produces the products and services that contribute concretely to our material standard of living.

–Jim Stanford, *Paper Boom* (Ottawa and Toronto: CCPA/ Lorimer, 1999), p. 23

about to be paid, to purchase a piece of paper that says somebody, some firm or some government, owes you money, or that you own part of their business assets.

There is no single market for capital goods. There are markets for buildings, for machinery, for raw materials, for equipment, for research and development and so on. Each will have its own market with its own supplies and demands and sets of prices. The only thing that is common to all these capital goods markets is that purchases of capital goods must be financed. This means that firms must go to a market to purchase credit to finance their purchases of capital goods, and that market—the market where financing is purchased— is called the capital market, though it should probably more accurately be called the market for financing the purchase of capital goods, and the price paid for that financing is the interest rate(s). When we talk about investing in real capital, we cannot add up trucks, milling machines, factories, stockpiles of ore and computers but we can add up the amount of money spent on them and the cost of borrowing the money to finance their purchase. And that's what the business pages are all about, the financing of the purchase of capital goods.

The money that is traded, speculated with or used to buy stocks, shares, bonds, mortgages, futures and derivatives is referred to in the business pages as "capital"—meaning the money necessary to buy these pieces of paper. There are many different kinds of paper—stocks, shares, bonds, debentures, mortgages, money, foreign exchange and commodity futures, derivatives—but they have one thing in common. They are IOUs, claims on companies, individuals, or governments that may be purchased on stock, money or "over the counter"[1] markets that exist all around the world. People buying these pieces of paper are called "investors," when in fact they are not investing at all but just putting someone's savings into a piece of paper. The difference is that the piece of paper either says it will be worth more in a year's time (that is, pay an interest premium), entitle the owner of the piece of paper to a share in the profits of a business (that is, pay a dividend) or entitle the owner to sell the paper for a higher value at some later date (that is, pay a capital gain).

What are those assets? That can become very complicated. I can own a share in a company. Many of us may already do so through our pension plans. I can own an IOU from the City of Windsor because I loaned it some money by buying a city bond to build a water treatment plant. But I can also own a share in an expected profit if I own the right to buy wheat at $4 a bushel and expect to sell it at $6 a bushel six months from now. That is what is known as a **future.** Maybe I pooled my money with a bunch of others to loan to an international exchange dealer to buy a share of an expected increase in the price of the Canadian dollar versus the Euro. That means I am buying a **derivative**. In most respects this is nothing but a big gambling game, what many observers have come to call **casino capitalism**.

Why then should we be concerned about financial capital markets? Aren't they just like other speculative or gambling markets? Unfortunately no. Instabilities and interest rate fluctuations affect everybody, something that Keynes, for example, was well aware of.

Characteristics of the Real Capital Market

In mainstream economics, the capital market is treated just like any other market for commodities.[2] A firm that is thinking about investing in a new plant or equipment (or a government thinking about investing in a new school or hospital) looks at what it is going to

> ### 7.2 Financial Fragility
>
> The general concept of "financial fragility" can be described as follows: The rise (and fall) of asset market valuations can become detached from the market's real economic underpinnings, yet also can have important real economic consequences. Stock markets and other asset markets alternate between booms inspired by hope, faith, and greed on the part of investors betting on a continued rise in asset prices, and subsequent crises of confidence on the part of those same investors when it appears that asset prices might fall.
>
> This boom-and-bust process can occur independently of the underlying economic fundamentals of the particular companies involved, yet ironically the cycle can have important effects that extend beyond the paper economy to the investment of real capital and the real production of goods and services....Economic growth itself becomes subject to the whims of markets.
>
> –Jim Stanford, *Paper Boom* (Ottawa and Toronto: CCPA/ Lorimer, 1999), p. 285
>
> Classic recent examples of financial fragility crises being followed by economic recessions in the real economy are the decade-long recession in Japan that followed the collapse of the inflated Tokyo land market in the early 1990s and the recession in the United States that began in March 2001, following the collapse in the inflated value of technology stocks, in particular the "dot-coms."

cost. First of all, over a period of time that new plant and equipment will be "used up" or become obsolete. If you buy a computer that is good for five years then one fifth of the computer is used up each year. If the computer cost $2,000 to buy then the cost of that equipment will be $400 each year. This "using up" is what we call **depreciation**. However, depreciation is not the only cost of investing in capital goods. The firm must often borrow the money to make the original purchase. If it borrows the $2,000 from a bank or other financial institution, sells stocks or bonds to raise the money, or borrows from itself money that it could otherwise have loaned to someone else, it either pays the interest rate or loses the income from loaning out its own funds.

Borrowing money costs money in the form of interest. The cost of investment in real capital, therefore, is the cost of the capital depreciation in any period (which is, of course, directly related to the purchase price of the capital good) plus the cost of financing the investment (interest paid or interest forgone by not loaning out the firm's savings, or what the economist calls opportunity cost).[3] That is, the cost of capital investment over its life is the cost of the original

7.3 Capacity, Profits and Investment

It is common for economists—left, right and centre—to assume that it is rising profits and lower interest rates that are the spur for business investment. However, the empirical evidence is that the real incentive for investment is rising capacity utilization of existing machinery and equipment.

When companies have capacity utilization rates of less than 80 to 85 percent, they believe they can meet foreseeable increases in demand by hiring a few more workers and using existing but un- or under-utilized equipment. However, when utilization rates rise above the 80 to 85 percent level, firms (realizing that it takes time to bring new plant and equipment into production) begin to invest in additional capacity. This is supported by the econometric evidence that Jim Stanford found of the strong relationship between growth and investment and the relatively much weaker relationships between profits and interest rates and investment. He found that:

- An increase of 1 percentage point in GDP spurs an increase in investment of two-thirds of one point of GDP with the effect felt not only in the year of the increase but also in the following year.
- An increase of 1 percentage point in the real long-run interest rate spurs a decrease in investment of one-third of one point of GDP also with effects over two years.
- An increase in business profits of 1 percentage point of GDP spurs an increase in investment of one-quarter of one point of GDP, though in this case, the effect is not fully felt until two years after the profit increase occurred.

He concluded from these results that growth in output (an increase in capacity utilization) was twice as important as interest rates in affecting investment and between three and four times as important as increased profits in spurring investment.

–Jim Stanford, *Paper Boom* (Ottawa and Toronto: CCPA/ Lorimer, 1999), pp. 164–5

investment plus the cost of financing it. The cost of the computer is $2,000 plus the interest paid on funds to finance its purchase. The original purchase cost equals the depreciation on the computer itself over its lifetime.

How does a firm know whether it is worth its while to invest in building a particular plant or purchasing a specific piece of equipment? Quite simply it looks to see how much extra revenue that investment is going to generate. If it will generate enough revenue to pay the total cost of the investment plus a target rate of profit, the firm will invest. The demand for investment goods is directly related therefore to the net value of extra output that the investment returns to the firm and the expected rate of profit that the firm wants to achieve. Thus, according to the conventional economic interpretation, supply and demand in the real investment market is determined by the cost price of the investment good, the interest rate in financial markets, the expected demand and price of the final product, and the technical productivity of the capital investment.

Unfortunately, there are many problems with this description of how markets for capital goods work. Some of these problems are quite technical. For one thing, the price of capital goods depends, in part, on the expected profitability of the investment—but the expected profitability of capital investment, in turn, depends on the price of the capital. It gets even more complicated. The expected price of the product in the monopoly sector, as demonstrated in chapter 3, is determined by cost markup—but the cost is in part determined by the cost of capital, which in turn is dependent on the expected price of the product. We keep running in circles.

These technical glitches in the theory of how capital markets work are of more concern to economists than they are to the real world of workers, businesses and consumers. What is of more concern is that the expected profitability of investment also depends on business confidence. Businesses attempt to anticipate what the market for their products is going to be in the future when the investment must be paid off. This sense of the future is what is known as business confidence. It is subject to wild fluctuations that are based on emotion and instinct as much as research and science, leading British economist John Maynard Keynes to comment on the "animal spirits" of businesspeople. If suddenly business grows fearful about the economy's future and cuts back its investment, the whole economy becomes depressed, often bringing about the very outcome the investors feared.

Keynes pointed out that this **fundamental uncertainty** about future markets was precisely the reason that government must be prepared to step in. He argued that government spending needs to increase when business is cutting its investment spending. Furthermore, technological change is an additional uncertainty. With technology changing quickly and unpredictably, there is more uncertainty about how long the capital equipment that the firm has invested in will remain economically useful. This makes business very leery of long-run investment.

Finally, we have the problem of interest rates. In the short run, interest rates are set by policy, not by the demand for and supply of loans in capital markets. The Bank of Canada sets short-term rates when it announces changes in its target rate for overnight loans made between banks to cover their reserve requirements. However, these short-term rates may change frequently and are designed to achieve specific

---

7.4 Keynes on Instability and Animal Spirits

Even apart from the instability due to speculation, there is the instability due to the characteristic of human nature that a large proportion of our positive activities depend on spontaneous optimism rather than on a mathematical expectation, whether moral or hedonistic or economic. Most, probably, of our decisions to do something positive, the full consequences of which will be drawn out over many days to come, can only be taken as a result of animal spirits—of a spontaneous urge to action rather than inaction, and not as the outcome of a weighted average of quantitative benefits multiplied by quantitative probabilities. Enterprise only pretends to itself to be mainly actuated by the statements of its own prospectus, however candid and sincere. Only a little more than an expedition to the South Pole, is it based on an exact calculation of benefits to come. Thus if the animal spirits are dimmed and the spontaneous optimism falters, leaving us to depend on nothing but a mathematical expectation, enterprise will fade and die—though fears of loss may have a basis no more reasonable than hopes of profit had before.

It is safe to say that enterprise that depends on hopes stretching into the future benefits the community as a whole. But individual initiative will only be adequate when reasonable calculation is supplemented and supported by animal spirits, so that the thought of ultimate loss that often overtakes pioneers, as experience undoubtedly tells us and them, is put aside as a healthy man puts aside the expectation of death.

This means, unfortunately, not only that slumps and depressions are exaggerated in degree, but that economic prosperity is excessively dependent on a political and social atmosphere that is congenial to the average business man.... In estimating the prospects of investment, we must have regard, therefore, to the nerves and hysteria and even the digestions and reactions to the weather of those upon whose spontaneous activity it largely depends.

–J.M. Keynes, *The General Theory of Employment, Interest and Money* (London: Macmillan, 1961 (c. 1936)), pp. 161–162

---

inflation and exchange rate goals. They are not very suitable for regulating long-term capital investment.

This is particularly true when speculators create a "bubble" in something like real estate prices. This is what happened to an Alberta bank that "borrowed" money from depositors (at low interest rates), which it then loaned out at much

7.5 *The Thrift Disaster*

No book on modern finance would be complete without a look at one of the greatest monetary disasters of all time, the savings and loan (S&L) debacle of the 1980s. While hotshot S&Ls were among the most enthusiastic makers of the great boom, they collapsed at a cost of $200 billion to the U.S. government, to be paid for well into the next century.... S&Ls, also known as thrifts [and akin to Canadian credit unions], prospered during the housing boom that followed World War II. Deposits and mortgage loans soared, though capital ratios sank as profits lagged growth. ... Worse, the inflation and high interest rates of the later 1970s exposed the S&Ls' tragic flaw, borrowing short to lend long: depositors tempted by higher rates in the unregulated world were free to withdraw on a whim, but their funds had been committed by thrift managers to 30-year mortgages. As rates rose, the value of outstanding mortgages sank.

–Doug Henwood, *Wall Street: How It Works and for Whom* (New York: Verso, 1997), pp. 86–88

higher interest rates. However, when the real estate bubble burst and land prices tumbled, many people and firms walked away from their mortgages resulting in the failure of the bank. In East Asia in 1997 banks were borrowing short and lending long to finance land developers (that is, borrowing money with short-term loans and then lending the borrowed money as long-term loans and mortgages). The East Asian economic crisis began when the real estate bubble burst. The resulting losses by financial institutions played havoc with economies around the world. The failures of the savings and loans institutions in the United States in the 1980s cost American taxpayers hundreds of billions of dollars. If, for all these reasons, we reject the mainstream description of how capital markets really work, what can we put in its place?

More realistic are strategic and tactical competition models of investment, which are based on market share and capacity utilization.

Strategic and Tactical Models of Investment

Aside from investment undertaken to replace broken or depreciated equipment, most investment is done for market rivalry reasons. Some of this investment is **tactical** (a shorter-run response) to meet the competition of rivals. For instance, a restaurant chain may invest in cappuccino makers for all its outlets because a competing chain has begun offering specialty coffees as part of its standard menu. Other investment is **strategic:** it is meant to gain an advantage over rivals (a longer run response). By investing in minivans before the other auto manufacturers, Chrysler effectively cornered the market for the new type of vehicle for two or three years. By making such a long-term investment, business hopes to significantly reduce costs to gain a price advantage; to develop a new product, process or market (a "breakthrough"); or to increase the firm's market control (i.e., market share or monopoly power).

In the competitive sector, investment is almost exclusively devoted to replacing aging equipment or machinery. Alternatively, and perhaps to a much lesser extent, it may be tactical. A small producer may attempt to compete with a new fad or consumer taste. In these cases, the neoclassical market explanation is relatively accurate. Take a shoe repair shop—when the shop's sewing machine wears out, the owner will look at the price of a new one and the interest rate required to borrow the necessary money, and whether this is affordable given the shop's normal revenue. If the cash return is equal to or greater than the cost over the foreseeable future, the owner will probably invest in a new machine. If it is not, the business may fold. If the competitor down the street buys a new type of re-soling machine that cuts the time and cost of such repairs, the shoe repair shop owner will face the decision of whether or not to follow suit. Again, a calculation of benefits and costs will determine whether the owner will purchase a new machine, remain with the present machine (and perhaps take a lower personal income) or go out of business.

In the monopoly sector, however, the investment decision is much more complex. It takes on the multiple dimensions of a battle plan involving both tactical diversions and responses and strategic thrusts with long-term planning. Indeed, **investment is the primary mechanism of competition in the monopoly sector**.[4] Investment decisions may be taken to pre-empt a move by a competitor (e.g., the establishment of a supermarket in an area prior to the development of housing in order to secure the market before a competitor can establish). Businesses also view investment in automation, robots or similar technology as a way to reduce the bargaining power of labour. Alternatively, investment can be used to acquire a new technology or to prevent a competitor from acquiring it first.

Perhaps the most visible form of buying equipment, buildings and technology in the monopoly sector is the corporate takeover. This kind of investment is really not true investment at all since no new capital goods, buildings or equipment results; all that happens is a transfer of capital goods from one owner to another. Takeovers may be an alternative to new investment by companies since big corporations often find it cheaper to buy out a smaller company than to invest in comparable capital equipment, particularly if the smaller firm is in financial difficulty. This is particularly true in depressed economic times when the stock prices of firms with deflated profits or losses decline, leaving them vulnerable for takeovers. For the corporation buying a troubled company, a takeover often has the dual advantage of providing under-priced capital and eliminating existing or potential competition.

A takeover may eventually produce real investment. If the shareholders of the firm taken over are paid in shares or stocks of the amalgamated firm, no investment takes place. If they are paid in money that they then use to purchase government bonds, existing stocks or mortgages, etc. (i.e., to save), no investment takes place. If they use all or part of the cash to develop a new firm or to invest in new facilities and equipment, investment does take place. However, this is more the exception than the rule.

A Cash Flow Model

Consider a strategic investment by a pulp and paper corporation facing a decision about whether or not to build a new mill. Given the fluctuations in the market and the rate of technological change, it sets its planning horizon at eight years. Assuming three years for planning and construction, this means cash flow from sales by the new mill in years four to eight must cover all costs of capital, financing and operating and return a target rate of profit to the firm. In other words, once the plant starts operating, it must generate sufficient income to cover the costs of building the mill plus generate a target rate of profit within the next five years. Planning estimates will be made of all costs and revenues including tax advantages such as capital cost allowances (allowable deductions from income to cover depreciation of capital) that reduce effective interest costs. If the balance is positive, the mill will be built.

Even if the cash flow balance is negative, the mill may still be built. Why? Because, if it is not built, timber rights might be lost to another corporation. This loss of timber rights could reduce the profitability of the firm's other mills through increased competition for markets or loss of rights to raw materials in the long run.

These kinds of considerations, rather than the cost price of the investment good, the interest rate, the expected demand and the technical productivity of the capital investment determine the strategic investment plans of monopoly sector firms. They are not, however, the kinds of considerations found in most orthodox economics textbooks, which look only at the static market supplies and demands of firms.

Investment and the Labour Market

The traditional argument of economists and employers is that workers should welcome investment because it creates jobs and raises productivity, particularly investment that embodies new technology. This higher productivity allows the firm to pay higher wages and/or hire more workers.

In the real world, the connection between investment and the welfare of workers is fraught with problems. There are several ways investment can be quite detrimental to workers, particularly in the absence of unions to protect workers' interests. Investment in new equipment and machinery may improve productivity and better working conditions, but it can also destroy jobs and, in fact, reduce wages. Let us look at the potential negative impacts of investment on workers.

- Investment can improve productivity such that a smaller number of workers can produce the same or more output than before. Unless demand for the output increases proportionately, which is rare, the result is layoff of workers. Investment, in this case, does not create jobs but, rather, destroys jobs. Workers are replaced by machines, creating unemployment and thereby exerting a downward pressure on wage rates. Mechanization and automation are prime examples. Numerically controlled machine tools replaced skilled machinists in the metal manufacturing industries in the 1960s and 1970s. A decade later, welders were being replaced by welding robots. As a result, the number of metal trades in manufacturing declined markedly over this period. In the 1980s and 1990s, computers replaced secretaries in many office occupations and jobs. Generally, a woman with a computer could do as much work as one and a half women could do with typewriters. As a result, the number of women employed in clerical work in the 1990s declined markedly.

- Investment in new machinery may result in the de-skilling of existing jobs such that skilled, highly paid, workers can be replaced by unskilled, low-paid, workers. This was the major result of the industrial revolution of the late nineteenth century when, for instance, skilled coopers (barrel makers) were replaced by barrel making machines, and the skilled coopers were reduced to poverty. Generally, investment that embodies technology tends to de-skill many workers. This results in the expropriation of the workers' investment in their skills. An example of this is the numerical, or computer, machine control that replaced the skills of the craft worker machinist.[5] This means that a worker's investment in education, training and skill development is expropriated *without compensation* by employers.

- Given the imbalance in market power between employers and labour in the last couple of decades, the increase in productivity has gone almost entirely to the employers in the form of profits and not to labour in the form of wages. (For a discussion of the disconnection of productivity to wages see chapter 10, box 10.20.)

- Certain types of investment give management more control over the labour process. Computer monitoring, for instance, gives supermarket supervisors immensely increased powers to control and monitor the output of checkout clerks. It also reduces the bargaining power of workers and unions in industries that employ computer monitored flow technology. Such technology allows extended operation of continuous operations by supervisory staffs in the event workers go on strike in defence of bargaining demands. Furthermore, investment tends to create wider divisions within the work force by de-skilling some workers while increasing the skill requirement of others. This

7.7 Co-determination in Germany and Slovenia

Co-determination is a system of management developed in postwar Germany and involves two levels of worker participation in management of enterprises. At the "shop floor" level, workers' councils are established which have the power to control, or share control, of a number of local matters such as working conditions, social matters (such as holiday scheduling), health and safety, discipline, transfers and discharge, and work organization, but not of basic wages and conditions established in the collective agreement. At the top end of management, workers elect at least one third, in some cases one half, of the Board of Supervisors and have veto power over the appointment of the Labour Director, the human resource and personnel manager on the Board of Management. Industry-wide trade unions, however, bargain wage rates, hours and major benefits.

Slovenia, one of the now independent republics of the former Yugoslavia, from the 1950s up until the 1990s shared the Yugoslav system of "socialist self-management" in which the workers had total management control (at least in theory) of socially owned enterprises, including the hiring and appointment of managers. When Yugoslavia broke up and Slovenia began the transition to a capitalist, market economy, the country adopted co-determination patterned on the German model but with even more worker influence. For one thing, privatization of enterprises in Slovenia took the form of the distribution of shares to workers combined with extensive "worker-buyouts." Thus, employees share in management both as workers and as owners. But perhaps more important, wages and benefits are negotiated at the national level through a 'social contract' between the unions' and employers' central organizations that covers all workers. Supplemental, and generally more favourable, contracts are negotiated between specific industrial unions and industry employers' organizations, while a third level of contracts are negotiated between the industrial union and some, but not all, of the individual firms.

–Paul Phillips and Bogomil Ferfila, "The Legacy of Socialist Self-Management: Worker Ownership and Worker Participation in Management in Slovenia," *Socialist Studies Bulletin*, no. 61, July–September 2000

has the effect of allowing increased discrimination by employers among ethnic, gender and age groups in their employ. Analysts of the labour market call this strategy one of "divide and conquer," dividing the labour force into groups forced to compete with each other for positions and wages.

On the other hand, it is true that investment can work to the advantage of workers in some cases. Investment can increase workers' productivity, allowing for wage increases. It can also eliminate or ease heavy, dirty and tedious work. In some cases it can increase the bargaining power of workers and unions. Where specifically trained workers are essential to the operation, where an interruption of labour services would be extremely costly, technology can give labour increased bargaining clout.

This kind of tit-for-tat debating about who has the advantage or disadvantage with the introduction of technology is, however, beside the point. The real question is who decides? Do workers and their unions have any say in how investment effects their livelihood or the quality of their jobs? In contemporary North America the answer is no. There is no reason why this need be the case.

Studies have shown that where workers participate in investment and work organization decisions, the efficiency of production is enhanced. Why then is there so much opposition by capitalists to sharing decision-making with labour? The answer is simple: power. Business makes investment decisions for their own reasons, mostly profit but also prestige, keeping up or ahead of their competitors, or simply maximizing growth. Sometimes these decisions have results that coincide with the needs and desires of workers. But that is not why such decisions are made. Capital is simply not willing to share economic power with labour unless forced to do so. And Liberal and Conservative governments are unwilling to pressure their capitalist allies to extend democracy to the industrial arena.

The impact of investment on labour depends on who gets what share of the returns for increased productivity. Who gets what depends on the balance of power in both the labour market and in the labour process. It also depends on the extent to which government is willing to intervene to ensure that investment decisions benefit all Canadians. That means that it also depends on the political power of capital versus that of labour. Unfortunately, recent trade agreements that Canadian governments have entered into limit their ability to intervene in the market to maintain the interests of working Canadians. The fact of the matter is, Canadian workers and their families have been sold out by both Liberal and Conservative governments with respect to the protection of working class interests.

Notes

1. "Over the counter" refers to stocks and bonds sold directly by brokers to investors and not through the stock or bond market.
2. The most recent and comprehensive analysis of Canadian capital markets is Jim Stanford, *Paper Boom* (Ottawa/Toronto: CCPA/Lorimer, 1999). An exhaustive and stimulating analysis of the American market is Doug Henwood, *Wall Street* (New York: Verso, 1997). Earlier discussion and evidence of the investment behaviour of firms in the modern economy can be found in Robert Averitt, *The Dual Economy* (New York: Norton, 1968); Samuel Bowles and Richard Edwards, *Understanding Capitalism*, ch.11;

and John Kenneth Galbraith, *The New Industrial State* (Boston: Houghton Mifflin, 1967), chs. 3–4.

3. Opportunity cost is the cost of an income earning opportunity foregone because of one's own use of a resource. For example, the opportunity cost of using one's own savings to finance investment in capital is the interest foregone by not using that money to purchase Canada Savings Bonds or some other interest earning asset. Likewise, the opportunity cost of a farmer's labour is the wages lost by the farmer not taking a job working for someone else.

4. The investment decisions of monopoly firms are also influenced by the fact that a very significant part of investment funds comes from retained earnings (profits that are retained by corporations and not distributed as dividends to shareholders) and not from borrowing or the sale of stocks or shares. As a result, market interest rates are less important to the firm than long-term strategic plans. This makes the investment decision unlike that of more competitive, small firms.

5. These were technological advances in machine tools, first using numerical tapes and, more recently, computer programs to control and operate machines and equipment that previously were controlled by skilled workers.

Chapter 8

Growth and Crisis

The Aggregate Economy

Up to this point, we have been dealing with various components of the economy—individual markets, factors, firms, consumers, workers, governments. The activity of all these taken together makes up the whole economy, known as the **aggregate economy** or **macro-economy**. Two major concerns at the aggregate level are what determines the growth of the economy and what determines whether the economy will be operating at, or near, potential. Failure to reach potential, of course, means unemployment and misery. Overreaching potential—what is usually referred to overheating the economy—on the other hand, means rapid increases in the cost of living, referred to as inflation. If inflation gets out of control, there are serious problems for those on fixed incomes. It is obviously important, therefore, to know what determines the growth and level of economic activity if we are to avoid the miseries of unemployment and/or of inflation.

Sources of Economic Growth

Economic growth can be defined simply as the growth in the amount of goods and services produced or the amount of income in an economy. That, however, does not give us a meaningful measure of well-being. If population is changing, we don't know what is happening to per person output or income. Therefore the most common measure of economic growth is the increase in income and output per capita. However, these figures may also be misleading for reasons discussed in chapter 1 (they do not consider real income created in the informal economy, the distribution of income between low and high income groups in the economy, or several other indications of real well-being).

Despite these qualifications, the elements contributing to total growth in national income are easily identified. The first is perhaps the easiest to see, growth

8.1 The Bank of Canada's Harmful Quest

In the early 1990s Bank of Canada Governor John Crow sought to achieve a policy of zero inflation by raising interest rates. Basic economic reasoning, however, tells us that the pursuit of zero inflation is bound to have negative consequences for the economy. The reason is simple. Companies increasing productivity must share it with their workers in the form of higher wages if these workers, as consumers, are to be able to purchase the increased output. If they cannot, the firms' inventories will increase, employers will lay off workers and unemployment will rise. Workers in firms that do not have the same increase in productivity, however, will normally get comparable wage increases. This means that the firms will, in many cases, have to raise prices to break even. If they do not, they will go bankrupt, again throwing workers into unemployment. Therefore, the acceptance of low levels of inflation—2 to 4 percent—has been recognized by most economists, including 2001 Nobel Prize winner Joseph Stiglitz, as not only acceptable but also desirable to "lubricate" the economy and maintain healthy economic growth.

8.2 Resources and the Limits to Growth

The global ecosystem's source and sink functions have large but limited capacity to support the economic subsystem. The imperative, therefore, is to maintain the size of the global economy to within the capacity of the ecosystem to sustain it. It took all of human history to grow to the $600 billion/yr scale of the economy of 1900. Today [1997], the world economy grows by this amount every two years. Unchecked, today's $16 trillion/yr global economy may be five times bigger only one generation or so hence....

While it now looks inevitable that the next century will be occupied by double the number of people in the human economy consuming resources and burdening sinks with their wastes, it seems doubtful that these people can be supported sustainably at anything like current Western levels of material consumption.

–Robert Costanza et al., *An Introduction to Ecological Economics* (Boca Raton, Florida: St. Lucie Press, 1997), pp. 6–7.

in the number of people working in the economy or—more formally, an increases in the labour force. However, a worker with a front-end loader is much more productive than the same worker with a shovel. This points to a second source of economic growth, an increase in the amount of capital goods used in production.

A third factor of production is natural resources and energy. The number of workers can increase through immigration, natural increase or simply by more people participating in the labour force. It is equally clear that the stock of capital equipment can increase through more investment. While the total supply of natural resources is limited by what the classical economists called the "original bounties of nature," the *effective* supply can increase by searching for new resources and for new sources or new ways of accessing known resources. Exploration is constantly underway for new fields of oil and natural gas. "Off-shore" and non-conventional (oil sands and shales) sources are being used more and more. Alternatives such as wind- or hydroelectric-power are being developed. Pipelines and long-distance electric transmission lines give access to increasingly distant energy sources. Still, it must be recognized that, with the exception of solar and wind power, energy resources are finite as are supplies of all other

8.3 The Cost of Sickness and Injury

In 1997, excluding women on maternity leave, an estimated 5.5% (489,000) of full-time employees missed some work each week for personal reasons: 4.1% for illness or disability and 1.4% for personal or family responsibilities. As a result of these absences and their durations, 3.0% of full-time employees' usual work time was lost each week in 1997; about 2.5% due to illness or disability and 0.5% to personal or family obligations. On average, each full-time employee lost 7.4 days over the year for personal reasons (about 6.2 for illness or disability and 1.2 for personal or family demands). In total, full-time employees lost an estimated 66 million workdays in 1997. [At $12 an hour for an 8-hour day, that is $6.34 billion loss in 1997.]

Work Days lost per year

	Total	Illness or Disability	Personal or Family Responsibilities
All employees (15+)	7.4	6.2	1.2
Men	6.3	5.3	0.9
Women	9.1	7.6	1.5

–Ernest Akyeampong, "Work Absences: New Data, New Insights," *Perspectives* (Statistics Canada no. 75-001-XPE), Spring 1998, p. 16–17.

resources. We cannot expand our use of resources indefinitely.

What about the *quality* of these same factors? Improving the quality of labour has been one of the most important sources of increased productivity and of output over the last two centuries. This improvement takes the form of education, training, on-the-job instruction, work experience and any other activities that improve a worker's skills, knowledge and capacity to learn, adapt and be creative. But improvement is not restricted to education and training. Quality is also improved when workers have better health, nutrition and physical and mental fitness. Similarly, productivity will be better where working conditions are safer and the working environment cleaner.

New technologies, both in production and in new products and services, are also extremely important. They contribute not only to increasing economic output but also to changing our patterns of consumption. The information technology (IT) revolution, for instance, has not only drastically changed how we produce our goods and services but also what we produce and consume. Computers greatly enhance the secretary's and the architect's productivity while at the same time shifting many of us from buying stamps to purchasing Internet access for e-mail. Productivity-enhancing technological change, however, almost always requires new investment. A secretary's productivity will not increase until the boss junks the old electric typewriter and buys an office computer. Furthermore, the secretary's productivity will not increase to its potential until the boss or the worker invests in training, either formal or trial-and-error, on the software packages required to use the computer. Even with the most advanced equipment in the world, productivity will only rise if labour has the skill and training to take advantage of it. In short, technological change normally requires complementary investment in both physical and human capital to promote economic growth.

Finally, not all growth-enhancing changes are technological. Many are organizational and motivational. They depend on improvements in working conditions, on how work is organized and goods and services distributed, and on the quality of management. This element in growth is considered sufficiently important that economists have given it a special name, x-efficiency. Henry Ford is legendary in the history of American manufacturing for implementing a new organization of production, the "production line," which proved to be a much more efficient (at least from the capitalist's point of view) way of making cars.

In summary, economic growth is determined by increases in the quantities of factors of production (labour, capital and natural resources) and by increases in the productivity of these agents of production through investment in human and physical capital, and technological change, or improvements in organizational and management efficiency.

Economic growth, even per capita growth, should not be equated with improvements in human welfare. In fact, average welfare levels can decline even when it looks like the economy is growing. If income inequality increases, economic and political power becomes concentrated in the hands of the corporate elite. Despite the growth of national income in the eighties and nineties, the average real earnings of male workers in Canada actually declined. While average earnings of women rose, average family incomes stagnated or rose only modestly over the period.

8.4 Participation, Productivity and Power

The management of modern corporations through segmented labour markets, hierarchical job ladders and bureaucratic controls have brought their own problems. Richard Edwards describes one problem. Bureaucratic control has resulted in a great deal of "discontent, dissatisfaction, resentment, frustration and boredom with their work" he notes. Attempts by capitalists to counter this alienation from work have taken the form of job enrichment and enlargement and the transfer of limited self-management or co-management rights to the their employees. However, this has had limited success.

> Polaroid, in an experiment in the 1960s, had discovered other problems for management. The company set up a special worker-participation project involving some 120 machine operators. The production requirements did not seem especially promising for the experiment; making the new film packs called for the skillful operation of complex machinery in the face of a pressing deadline.... According to Polaroid's organizational development consultant, the film was brought into production on time, and "most people think we would never have gotten it out otherwise." Nonetheless, the experiment was liquidated, not for efficiency reasons but because democracy got out of hand. Ray Ferris, the company's training director, explained: "[The experiment] was too successful. What were we going to do with the supervisors—the managers? We didn't need them anymore. Management decided it just didn't want operators that qualified."

–Richard Edwards, *Contested Terrain* (New York: Basic Books, 1979), pp. 154–156

As discussed in chapter 1, a major problem with the way we measure national income is the fact that "externalities"—negative byproducts of economic growth, that impose "non-market costs" on the population—are not subtracted from the positive additions to income. So income may rise while well-being falls. Growth can be accompanied by more pollution-induced lung and heart disease and cancers and more urban congestion resulting in longer commuting times and gasoline usage. In reality this means the public welfare has declined. But because the money spent on treating these illnesses, building more freeways and buying more gasoline is counted as part of the gross national product, economists have traditionally treated this as growth.

Finally, a great deal of the increase in *measured* income in the twentieth century is merely the measurement of productive activity that has moved to the market sector from the home or the informal sector.

Expansion, Depression and Accumulation Crises

However much we should be wary of our simple measures of economic growth, it is still true that, in Canada, average human welfare has improved quite considerably over the past century. This improvement, however, has been very unsteady. Periods of expansion have alternated with prolonged periods of recession and depression. In fact, the source of these economic crises lies in the growth process itself. To understand both growth and crises we have to delve more deeply into the "laws of motion of capitalism" (to use Marx's descriptive terminology).

The process of economic growth, by its very nature, produces reoccurring crises. The underlying reason is that there is no automatic mechanism for equating the increase in the supply of commodities with the increase in demand for those commodities. In other words, there is no reason to believe, as the nineteenth-century economist J.B. Say did, that "supply creates its own demand," that is, there is no necessary reason why the aggregate demand—the total demand for goods and services purchased in Canada—need be equal to the

8.5 Earnings of Men, Women and Families

Average Real Annual Earnings ($1997) of Men and Women 1975–1997
Full-Year, Full-Time Workers

	Men $s	Women $s	Women as % of Men
1975	42,635	25,664	60.2
1980	42,586	27,405	64.4
1989	42,328	27,928	66.0
1997	42,626	30,915	72.5

Average Family Income ($1996) Before Transfers, 1973–1996 (Families with Children)

	1973 $s	1984 $s	1990 $s	1996 $s	% Change 1973–90 %	1990–96 %
Bottom 5th						
Decile 1*	5,204	2,062	2,760	476	-47	-84
Decile 2	19,562	14,930	16,599	11,535	-15	-31
Middle 5th						
Decile 5	40,343	42,495	46,477	42,929	+15	-8
Decile 6	46,136	49,664	54,561	51,494	+18	-6
Top 5th						
Decile 9	71,611	79,628	88,426	86,497	+23	-2
Decile 10	107,253	123,752	134,539	136,737	+25	+2

* A decile is a tenth of the population. Thus, Decile 1 is the bottom tenth of the families in Canada ranked by average income. Decile 10 is the top tenth of families ranked by average income.

–Andrew Jackson and David Robinson, *Falling Behind: The State of Working Canada*, 2000 (Ottawa: CCPA, 2000) pp. 19, 28 (Average Family Income data is credited to Armine Yalnizyan, *The Growing Gap*, Centre for Social Justice, October 1998)

aggregate supply, the amount of goods and services produced by the Canadian economy. Aggregate demand is made up of the private consumption demand of Canadian consumers, investment demand by business, government, community organizations and individuals, government expenditure demand and the net demand by foreigners for Canadian goods and services. Net demand by foreigners is export demand minus that part of consumption, investment and government spending that is fulfiled by imports. Aggregate supply is the total amount of commodities supplied in the economy. This is illustrated in Figure 8.1, which shows that aggregate supply must, at the end of the year, equal aggregate demand—but there is no guarantee that this will be at a level of national output that will produce full employment.

There is no reason to believe that workers will want to consume exactly the amount of consumer goods that firms produce; that foreign countries will want exactly the amount of commodities that are produced for export and are surplus to our domestic demands; that firms will want to purchase exactly that quantity of

8.6 What is a Recession?

The term *recession* was adopted to refer to milder downturns than the Depression of the 1930s in the aftermath of the Second World War. Although no formal definition of an *economic recession* has ever been adopted, the most generally accepted definition is a period of at least two consecutive quarters (6 months) of negative economic growth; that is, two quarters where the gross domestic product of the country is actually declining. (In the United States, a committee of the National Bureau of Economic Research looks at the "entrails"—statistics of the last couple of quarters—of the American economy and comes to a decision if, and when, a recession has commenced.) How long a recession must persist before it becomes a depression is not clear. The HarperCollins *Dictionary of Economics*, for instance, merely refers to a depression as a "severe" decline in economic activity.

Some economists also now distinguish between an "economic recession," as defined above, and a "growth (or workers') recession." In a growth (workers') recession, GDP does not actually decline and continues to grow—but at a rate that is insufficient to employ increasing numbers of workers—with the result that unemployment rises or fails to fall significantly from economic recession levels.

investment goods that are produced; or that government will want to purchase exactly the surplus of commodities that nobody else wants. Yet if they do not there will be a glut of commodities. Such a glut leads to falling prices and profits and/or unemployment as firms lay off workers to reduce production in order to sell their surplus goods. If these gluts are widespread enough, the result will be a general slowdown in the economy, even negative economic growth, falling profits and rising unemployment. Such downturns in the economy, if major and prolonged, are known as **depressions**, but if they are relatively mild or of short duration, as **recessions.**

There is another way of thinking about aggregate supply. It is the total amount of income generated in the process of creating this supply—wages paid to the workers, profits to the capitalists and rents, the economists' name for the income paid to owners of natural resources. What can be done with this income? It can be spent on **consumption**; it can be **saved**; or it can be paid to the government for **taxes** [see Figure 8.1]. Again, there is no reason to expect that the desired collective savings of everyone should be exactly equal to what businesses collectively want to invest, that taxes should be exactly equal to what governments want to spend, or that foreigners will want to buy from us exactly what we want to buy from them.

Indeed, it makes more sense to say that aggregate supply and aggregate demand will fluctuate unequally in the process of growth, producing crises of production, employment and prices.[1] Some of these crises will be relatively small and short, a process known popularly as "boom and bust" or, more formally, as the **business cycle** (called a **disequilibrium crisis**). Others are prolonged periods of growth and of relative stagnation known as **long waves**. The stagnant phase of the long wave is called an **accumulation crisis**. Prior to the Second World War, these long waves were reflected in extended periods of rising world prices followed by similar periods of falling prices. The general price pattern on a world scale is shown in Figure 8.2. The periods of rising prices were generally periods of prolonged growth and expansion, while periods of falling prices were marked by low or no growth and frequent depressions.

Since the Second World War, this pattern has been somewhat different. The great postwar expansion saw moderate inflation, but since around 1970 there began what has been termed a **structural crisis**. It is caused by the growth of

Figure 8.1: The Keynesian Cross

aggregate demand = $C + I + G + [X - M]$
where C = consumption demand
I = investment demand
G = government demand
$X - M$ = net export demand (export demand minus import supply)

aggregate supply = $C + S + T$
where C = consumption
S = savings
T^* = taxes and other government levies

The economy will expand (contract) until the aggregate supply is equal to the aggregate demand; that is, where: $C + S + T = C + I + G + [X-M]$

*Note: Taxes include payroll taxes such as unemployment insurance and workers' compensation premiums.

Figure 8.2: Long Waves in the Capitalist World Economy

1789 rise 1814 fall 1849 rise 1873 fall 1896 rise 1919 fall 1939

imbalances between supplies of, and demands for, raw materials and natural resources; and between the power of corporations and that of workers and consumers. During this later period prices did not fall but actually rose, in some periods in a rapid and uncontrolled fashion. The 1970s were called a decade of **stagflation** because there was economic stagnation (relatively low but still positive economic and productivity growth combined with high rates of inflation). One of the reasons for inflation in the face of slow growth was the consolidation of market power by large corporations and their use of markup pricing. The actions of the Organization of Oil Exporting Countries (OPEC) constitute the most notable example of the exercise of market power to raise prices. In the 1970s OPEC, an oil cartel established by the oil exporting countries, announced a reduction in its combined production of crude oil. As a result the price of oil quadrupled in 1973–4 from around $4 to $16 a barrel. In 1978 a second OPEC production cutback more than doubled the price of oil, which at one point reached $40 dollars a barrel. Other natural resource and food prices were also increasing due to rising world demand following over two decades of rapid economic growth.

The rise in government employment and expenditures after the Second World War reduced the tendency for demand and for prices to collapse into depression when investment faltered. This, combined with the increasing reliance on credit-based money (rather than on gold-based money),[2] accommodated price increases, allowing inflation to occur. Put in simpler terms, the rise in personal, corporate, government and international debt was a significant part of the inflation story.

8.7 The Paradox of Thrift

One of the conclusions that is drawn from Keynesian economics is that, quite contrary to the pithy little sayings of Benjamin Franklin and the Protestant Ethic—such as "a penny saved is a penny earned"— saving can be dangerous to your financial health. The negative result of saving is called the *paradox of thrift*. Jim Stanford explains this result.

> In a demand-constrained economy, employment, production, and hence incomes all depend on the amount of purchasing power coursing through the economy. Suppose that individuals decide they want to save more, perhaps to accumulate more financial wealth for retirement. Those individuals all must spend less from their current incomes in order to save more. Less spending, however, means less demand for the products of the companies which were supplying those now-miserly consumers. Those companies lay off workers, who in turn spend even less, and the whole economy slides into recession. Incomes fall, and hence so does personal saving—despite the well-intentioned efforts of households to save *more*, not less.

> –Jim Stanford, *Paper Boom* (Ottawa and Toronto: CCPA/Lorimer, 1999), p. 226

Governments and central banks, led by the United States Federal Reserve System, attempted to control inflation by restricting the growth of the amount of money in the economy. This policy of restricting the supply of money in the economy, called **monetarism,** had the effect of raising interest rates to extremely high levels. The result was the severe recession of 1981–83 and the Third World debt crises from which many countries, particularly in sub-Saharan Africa and South America, have yet to recover.

Inflation began to increase again in the later 1980s as the world recovered from the earlier recession. But again central banks increased interest rates. The result was another severe recession in 1990–93. In Canada the 1990-93 recession was particularly severe. The imposition of the GST and Canada's entry, first into the Canada–U.S. Free Trade Agreement and subsequently into the North American Free Trade Agreement (NAFTA), contributed to the destruction of around three hundred thousand or more jobs. This job loss was primarily in manufacturing, traditionally a sector of fairly good, well-paid jobs. As a result, recovery was not only slow but was also marked for the first time by what became known as "jobless growth."

Long Waves in Canadian Economic Development

Economic development in Canada has taken place in a series of long waves. From the 1840s to 1873 the economy expanded with massive investment in canals and railways and growing international demand for the products of our forests and shipyards. But falling international commodity prices and a general slowdown in the British economy in the following quarter–century brought uncertain times into Canada. There were many years of high unemployment and low or negative growth interspersed with a few more prosperous years.

Then around 1897 the economy began to expand rapidly again. This was fuelled in part by western agricultural expansion, in part by new mining frontiers in Ontario and British Columbia producing coal and base and precious metals. The development of these frontiers arose in response to rising international markets and petered out by the end of the First World War. A very serious depression wracked the economy in the early years of the 1920s and was followed by a moderate recovery by 1929. Then came the worst economic calamity in the nation's history, the Great Depression of the 1930s.

The expenditures associated with fighting the Second World War overcame the Depression. This paved the way for the great postwar expansion based on the export of raw materials to the United States and the production of consumer durables (cars, appliances, housing) for the domestic market. By the end of the 1960s, the boom had played itself out and stagflation set in. By the late 1970s and early 1980s, real wages of workers were also stagnant or falling, and unemployment had reached the highest rates since the Depression. Despite a renewal in moderate economic growth after the 1981–82 and 1990–93 recessions, unemployment persisted at rates between 7 and 10 percent, high by historical standards. After the turndown in the early 1990s, unemployment only began to fall significantly after 1997. At the time of writing (summer of 2002) it is still not yet clear whether Canada will again fall into recession as the U.S. economy is threatened by a second recession in two years (a so-called "double-dip" recession). Given the continuing decade-long recession in Japan and the economic slowdowns in the European Union countries, this could have serious consequences for the Canadian and world economies.

In short, Canada has witnessed a series of sustained economic expansions of roughly twenty to thirty years, followed by similar periods of relative stagnation. Such long waves in the expansion of capitalist economies were first identified by the Russian economist Nicolai Kondratieff in the 1920s.[3]

8.8 Stagflation, Monetarism and the Birth of NAIRU

In response to stagflation in the 1970s, Canada's Department of Finance and the Bank of Canada adopted policies based on monetarist economic theories. This also led to the development of what became known at the Non-Accelerating Inflation Rate of Unemployment (NAIRU).

The strange theory goes something like this. The wage increases that result when unemployment falls "too low" are the primary or even the sole source of inflation. This is harmful to financial investors. It also cuts into the profit margins of employers in the real economy. If the labour market is "too tight," inflation will accelerate continuously. It is not simply a matter of tolerating a slightly higher rate of inflation in return for a slightly lower rate of unemployment, rather once the economy steps across the minimum acceptable level of unemployment, then the inflation rate will begin to soar without limit.

Unless government and the central bank act to pull the economy back from the abyss (through higher interest rates to slow down investment and overall economic growth) hyperinflation and financial chaos will be the ultimate result. That minimum level of unemployment is called, in one of the most bizarre acronyms ever invented, the NAIRU". It is also known, more pejoratively [and inaccurately] as the "natural" rate of unemployment.

–Jim Stanford, *Paper Boom* (Ottawa and Toronto: CCPA/Lorimer, 1999), pp. 194–5.

During the second half of the 1990s as unemployment rates dropped in the United States to levels unseen for decades, talk of NAIRU and the "natural rate" quietly disappeared in that country as the "strange theory" was discredited. Unfortunately, it remained well ensconced, and generally unfazed by the facts, in Canada's governing circles.

However, renewed interest in "Kondratieff waves" was prompted by the recent reappearance of stagflation in western capitalist countries.[4]

What are the causes of these reappearing and sustained crises? Economists from various perspectives tend to stress different elements.[5] One is the appearance and adoption of a new generation of production or consumption technology. This technology first fuels and then extinguishes a wave of investment. This

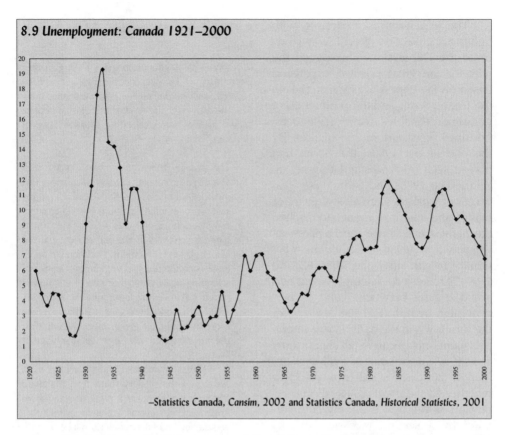

8.9 Unemployment: Canada 1921–2000

–Statistics Canada, *Cansim*, 2002 and Statistics Canada, *Historical Statistics*, 2001

explanation is stressed by many of the followers of the Austrian economist, Joseph Schumpeter.

Orthodox followers of Marx have argued that long periods of downturn are related to the accumulation of stocks of real capital in the form of plants and equipment after a period of steady investment. Given these accumulated stocks of productive capital, firms must compete by increasing price competition in order to sell their increased supply of commodities or leave some of their machinery and equipment idle. As a result of falling prices, excess capacity or a combination of both, there is a tendency for the rate of profit to fall (the rate of profit is the rate of return on investment)—unless this tendency is continually offset by comparable increases in productivity. If profits fall and unused capacity increases, this is a signal to capitalists to reduce investment.

Other economists, particularly those of the institutional and Keynesian schools, stress a decline in demand for the new generation of goods. Demand falls because a market becomes saturated with a good. Consumers become unable or unwilling to buy more new products. Once a family has one, or possibly two, SUVs in the driveway, they have little interest in purchasing another vehicle. This reluctance to purchase more and more, particularly of consumer durables such as cars and appliances, is compounded by the rise in consumer debt. People's credit becomes, in the popular language, "maxed out." When this is combined with an increasing maldistribution of income, which means that working-class and middle-income earners are increasingly unable to purchase the growing output of the economy, an **underconsumption crisis** becomes inevitable.

A more recent and comprehensive explanation contains many of these elements. It ties downturns to a deterioration, from the viewpoint of business, in the environment for investment (or to use the classical term, the environment for the accumulation of capital). By environment we mean the whole structure of economic power as it impinges on the freedom of business to make profits. This environment is referred to as the **social structure of accumulation**. These economists argue that as a long-wave expansion takes place, wages increase as does union militancy and workers' political power. Workers demand a greater share of the economic pie, greater job satisfaction, greater workplace health and safety provisions, and shorter hours. Governments respond to workers' and consumers' demands by increasing the regulation of markets and of business practices. All of these demands erode profit rates and reduce business's willingness to invest.[6] When this happens growth slows, unemployment rises, unions lose economic and political power and worker militancy evaporates, though this may take a generation or two. When profits begin to rise along with the economic and political power of capitalists, the environment for capitalist accumulation, for investment, improves. The stage is set for another long-wave expansion.

The life cycle of a long wave, whichever explanation you care to accept, can be described as follows. There are a number of events that can trigger a long wave—the discovery of a new technology, a new labour process, a new market or even a war. Each of these involves the destruction of the value of the stock of accumulated capital equipment. Technological change brings technological obsolescence, bankruptcy, mergers or acquisitions. A change in labour process may trigger a significant decline in unit labour costs for innovating firms. A war can open up a huge market for weapons and for disposable labour. A significant expansion of credit may produce an upward shift in the profitability of investment, initiating a new cycle of investment, or an accumulation cycle.

Whatever triggers the investment by the initial business or businesses, rival (or "follower") firms must also invest in order to remain competitive. At the same time, "imitator" firms spring up to share in the profits. The investment wave creates the demand for more labour, thereby increasing wages and employment, which, in turn, increases demand for consumption goods. Also, increased wages and employment and the accompanying "boom mentality" encourages consumers to increase their use of debt to finance consumption and for financial institutions to accommodate this increased demand for credit.

As accumulation proceeds and unemployment recedes, labour begins to flex its muscle, demanding not only higher wages but also, on the political front, an increase in the **social wage**. The social wage is made up of the goods and services such as medicare, unemployment insurance and education that are provided by the government, funded by taxes and distributed independent of labour market work.

Profits from accumulation tend to be monopolized by a small portion of businesses and of the population, primarily large corporations and the economic

8.10 The Social Wage

The social wage is the net income the working class and others receive from the state for being a citizen, rather than for any labour, service or good that the worker tenders to the government. Economist Isa Bakker defines it this way.

> In economics the net social wage can be defined as the net outcome after taking into account the taxes paid and benefits received by a worker or the working population at an aggregate level. The way it is derived here takes into account both government expenditures and taxes which are based on the traditional categories employed when estimating aggregate social spending levels.
>
> The conventional method divides the population into groups with different incomes and calculates the welfare type benefits received by each of these income categories. A progressive distribution of after-tax income (a positive social wage) is said to result if the lower income brackets receive relatively larger amounts of government benefits. Taxes are usually taken into account to show that higher income brackets pay more taxes.
> –Isa Bakker, "Canada's Social Wage in an Open Economy," in Daniel Drache and Meric Gertler, eds., The New Era of Global Competition (Montreal and Kingston: McGill-Queen's University Press, 1991), pp. 271, 284

Included in the benefits are social services, labour and employment benefits, housing assistance, transportation, health, education, recreation and culture and environment services provided by the government. Subtracted are social security taxes, direct taxes, health care premiums, and motor vehicle licences and property taxes paid by working people.

elite. This leads to an ever increasing concentration of wealth and of the income that is claimed by the wealthy— interest, dividends and profits (what economists call property income). Consumers, having purchased considerable consumer durables and fearful of further debt, cut back on their buying. Firms having bought the new generation of technology, cease to buy new machinery and equipment. At the same time, the entry of new firms or the competitive expansion of old firms lowers margins and profitability unless prices begin an inflationary rise. If inflation rises, interest rates also rise. This can trigger a debt crisis for firms, consumers and even governments who have borrowed in the expansion and now find they must use more and more of their income to pay the increased interest. Some are simply unable to do so and are forced into bankruptcy.[7] Governments also cut back on expenditures and the social wage to deal with rising debt.

These various forces produce a **crisis of accumulation**. The decline in consumption and investment produces a surplus in the marketplace. Firms must either sell fewer goods or lower prices. As a result, they cannot actually make, or realize, the potential profits the businesses had anticipated. In other words, they experience a **realization crisis**. This fall in profits brings a halt to investment. But this only adds to the problem. Not only is there surplus production of consumer goods, but now there is increased overproduction of capital goods. Firms in both sectors respond by laying off workers. Unemployment rises, leading to less worker income and reduced consumption. Now, the problem of overproduction of consumer goods gets even worse. The problem of insufficient aggregate demand simply escalates. The economy spirals downward and stagnates until a new set of conditions, as enumerated above, occur and allow for a new wave of expansion.

Some of the classical economists of the nineteenth century, notably Malthus and Marx, recognized that the economy was prone to these long-term crises, and

8.11 The Rise and Fall of the Keynesian Welfare State and the Social Wage

Early in the twentieth century Canadian governments began to weave the social security net that we know as the social (welfare) state and that makes up the components of the social wage. These programs were introduced to provide working Canadians with some protection from the economic devastation that can flow from the normal but unstable workings of the market economy—sickness or injury, unemployment, and simply aging. A chronicle of some of the more important measures includes:

1914	First Worker's Compensation (Ontario)
1927	Old Age Pensions Act
1940	Unemployment Insurance
1944	Family Allowance Act
1947	First Hospital Insurance Plan (Saskatchewan)
1951	Old Age Security
1956	Unemployment Assistance Act
1957	Federal Hospital Insurance
1962	First Medical Insurance Act (Saskatchewan)
1965	Canada and Quebec Pension Plans
1966	Canada Assistance Plan and the Guaranteed Income Supplement
1967	Federal Education Grants
1968	Medicare
1971	Major improvement and expansion in Unemployment Insurance
1984	Canada Health Act

But even before the net of social programs was in place, it was under attack. Ever since the mid-1970s, the business-led neoliberal attack has been hacking away at the Keynesian social state. This was heralded by the abandonment of Keynesian economic stabilization policies and the official adoption of monetarism by the Bank of Canada in 1975. As a result, Canada has been in what some economists call a "permanent workers' recession" over most of the last two decades.

Major cuts to the social safety net include:

1984	Reductions in scheduled increases in funding for health care and post-secondary education (Established Program Funding or EPF)
1985	Partial de-indexing of family allowances
1986	Further reductions in EPF funding; de-indexing of personal tax exemptions
1987	Increased patent protection for drug companies
1989	Canada–U.S. Free Trade Agreement comes into effect; cuts to social housing funding; reductions in regional development and EPF funding; clawback of family allowance and old age security; federal government withdrawal from UI funding and reduction of UI benefits
1990	Freeze on EPF payments to the provinces; limits placed on the Canadian Assistance Plan (CAP); funding reduced to Aboriginal programs
1991	Further limitation of CAP increases; 24% increase in UI premiums
1992	Further increase of 7% in UI premiums
1993	Further extension of monopoly protection of drug companies; further cuts in social housing funding; EPF cash transfers phased out; family allowances eliminated; cuts to UI
1994	NAFTA implemented; UI benefits cut and two-tier system introduced
1995	Canada Health and Social Transfer eliminates EPF and CAP and reduces spending on health and education; Crow rates for prairie farmers eliminated; further cuts to UI
1996	Cuts in CPP benefits, increase in contributions and partial privatization of the plan; federal contribution to social housing eliminated; federal cuts to job training
1997	Further reduction in health and social transfer funding; major reduction in eligibility and benefits for unemployment insurance (misleadingly renamed "Employment Insurance"; by 1998, the proportion of the unemployed eligible for benefits had fallen to just over one third).

–CCPA Monitor, March 1999

identified their cause. However, the majority of their successors refused to acknowledge that such crises were even possible. It was not until the Great Depression of the 1930s that John Maynard Keynes re-explained the theoretical cause of sustained crisis.

> In light of the Great Depression, Keynes saw the distinct possibility that economic stagnation was the natural tendency in mature capitalist economies. With consumption occupying a smaller proportion of output, thus generating increasing amounts of savings, and with the existing stock of capital being relatively abundant, thus reducing the likelihood of new investment being profitable, there would be a tendency for the economy to stabilize at a level of output below full employment. The slump in profit rates may become so severe at this point that a solution to stagnant investment through reductions in the rate of interest rates would simply not be available.[8]

Keynes's solution was to "socialize" investment decisions, making investment a "social decision" not a private firm decision. Such socialization was not achieved outside of wartime. In any case, Keynes was never clear on what he meant by socializing investment or exactly how it could or should be achieved. However, he (or rather, his followers) did advance the notion that aggregate demand could be manipulated by government **fiscal policy** (tax and expenditure policy) and **monetary policy** (interest and money supply policy) to greatly reduce the severity of the disequilibrium crises (or business cycle). The notion of using government's ability to spend, tax and set interest rates to regulate aggregate demand, which has become known as **bastard Keynesianism**, however, was picked up by Western governments, including Canada's.[9] As a result the postwar expansion was remarkably devoid of major recessions (or disequilibriums) up to the 1980s. While these same "Keynesian" policies mitigated the unemployment problem in the postwar period, they also contributed to the inflation that accompanied it. There is also little doubt that it was monetary policy that triggered the accumulation crisis, the stagnation phase of the long wave, in the last two decades of the twentieth century. While eventually taming inflation, restrictive monetary and fiscal policies have driven unemployment rates to levels last seen in the depression of the thirties, not only in Canada, but also around the world, in Europe and, to a lesser extent, the United States.[10]

The next chapter will discuss the theory and use of this kind of "Keynesian" demand management policies in the mitigation of short-term business cycles.

Notes

1. The problem is that, at the end of the day, aggregate demand and aggregate supply must be equal. So if aggregate demand begins to rise at a slower rate than aggregate supply, businesses will see their inventories rise. To prevent that from happening, they lay off workers and cut production. This reduces aggregate supply. But it also reduces income and results in rising unemployment. I will give a much fuller discussion of the mechanics of booms and busts in chapter 9.
2. Prior to the depression of the 1930s, all major currencies in the world were tied directly

or indirectly to gold. This was the famous "gold standard." This collapsed during the 1930s because of the depression, but it was reintroduced in a somewhat different form, the "gold-exchange standard," after the war. It was based on the value of the American dollar being tied to gold ($35 USD = 1 oz. of gold). In 1971 President Nixon broke the tie of the American dollar to gold. This meant that, in effect, all countries could now print as much money as they wanted since money became really nothing more than the circulating debt of the government. The money supply in most countries was now at the discretion of governments. And many of the governments were not very discreet!

3. Because his interpretation conflicted with Communist orthodoxy at that time, Kondratieff's discovery brought him only exile to Siberia.

4. Cy Gonick, *Inflation or Depression* (Toronto: Lorimer, 1975), chs. 3–4.

5. Maurice Lamontagne, *Business Cycles in Canada* (Toronto: Lorimer in association with the Canadian Institute for Economic Policy, 1984).

6. Samuel Bowles and Richard Edwards, *Understanding Capitalism* (New York: Harper and Row, 1985), ch. 14.

7. This is exactly what caused the debt crisis in Third World countries after the run up in interest rates in the early 1980s. To this day, many of these countries, particularly in sub-Sahara Africa, are simply unable to finance their debts. Their interest payments are greater than the incomes they can use to pay the interest.

8. Cy Gonick, *The Great Economic Debate* (Toronto: Lorimer, 1987), pp. 75–6.

9. David Wolfe, "The Rise and Demise of the Keynesian Era in Canada: Economic Policy, 1930–1982" in Michael Cross and Gregory Kealey, eds., *Modern Canada* (Toronto: McClelland and Stewart, 1984).

10. Fiscal policy in the United States in the 1980s was very expansionary as the Reagan government ran huge deficits to finance a military buildup. This policy has been labelled "military Keynesianism." In the 1990s, monetary policy in the U.S. was considerably easier (lower interest rates) than it was in Canada or Europe. Indeed, the very tight fiscal and monetary policies called for in the agreement to form the European Union (EU), the Maastritch Agreement and the European Currency Union (ECU) have been blamed for the poor performance of the EU economy in the 1990s. See Tom Palley, "The Role of Institutions and Policies in Creating High European Unemployment: The Evidence," Working Paper No. 336, Levy Institute, August 2001, available at www.levy.org

Chapter 9

Aggregate Economics
Smoothing the Flow

The Circular Flow

In order to figure out in more detail the nature of short-term economic crises, we must have a clear picture of the circular flow of income and its composite parts. A simplified version of this flow was illustrated in Figure 2.1. A more complete version is given in Figure 9.1. Note that money incomes generated in the sphere of production (that part of the economy where goods and services are produced) are paid out in the sphere of distribution (factor markets where the money incomes generated in production are distributed) either as labour income or as property income (interest, rents and profits). Labour income is paid to government as taxes, saved or used for consumption either of domestically produced goods and services or of imports. Labour income is also supplemented by government transfer payments such as child tax benefit, unemployment insurance, old age pensions, social assistance or some other elements of the social wage.

Property income is either saved, paid in taxes, used for capitalists' consumption (the goods and services consumed by capitalists and paid for out of property income) or spent on investment goods. Property income is also supplemented by government subsidies such as regional development grants, research grants or grants for labour training. Firms that require financing for investment find these funds in the **money market**. This is where the savings of labour and property owners are collected in the form of bank deposits, pension funds, investment funds, savings bonds and so on, and loaned to borrowers. These borrowers include firms wishing to invest and also consumers who wish to buy "on time" or borrow through a credit card.[1] Included in the finances available to big business through the money market are their own retained earnings and their depreciation allowances, money put aside to offset depreciation on their capital assets.

Government income comes from indirect taxes such as sales taxes, the Goods and Services Tax, and customs and excise duties; from business taxes such as corporate income tax; and from taxes on labour income, primarily personal income tax. Much, if not all, of this income is spent as government expenditure. If the government's expenditure is greater than its revenue, it runs a deficit financed by also borrowing on the money market. If government expenditure is less than revenue, it runs a surplus and loans money on the money market or pays down its debt.

Finally, income comes into the Canadian market to pay for goods and services that we export to other countries, while income leaves the Canadian market to pay for goods and services imported from other countries. Obviously the income

Figure 9.1: The Complete Aggregate Flow of Income

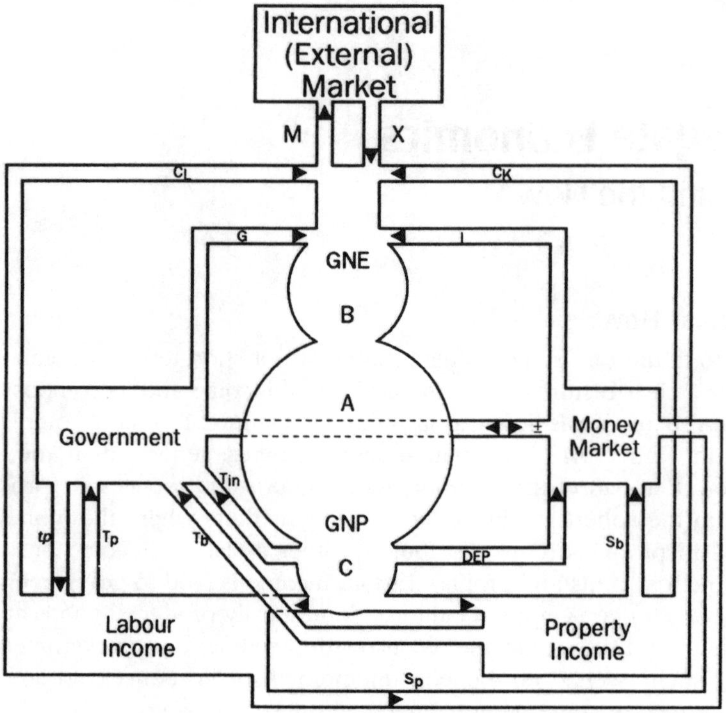

Key to Money Flows

GNP	— Gross National Product	A — Sphere of Production	
GNE	— Gross National Expenditure	B — Sphere of Exchange	
T_{in}	— Indirect Taxes minus Subsidies	C — Sphere of Distribution	
T_b	— Business Taxes		
T_p	— Personal Taxes		
tp	— Transfer Payments	C_L — Labour Consumption (wage goods)	
DEP	— Depreciation	C_K — Capitalist Consumption	
S_b	— Business Saving	G — Government Expenditure	
S_p	— Personal Saving	X — Exports	
–	— Government Deficit	M — Imports	
+	— Government Surplus	I — Investement	

coming into all firms must equal the total income received by labour and property owners. Or put another way, all the income entering the sphere of exchange must exit into the income flow through the sphere of distribution.

At the end of the accounting period, the total expenditure of firms, consumers, governments and foreigners (minus expenditures on imports)[2] must be equal to what is produced. This must be so because when businesses can't sell their commodities to consumers, governments or foreigners, they in effect purchase their own production surpluses by building up their inventories (what is referred to as inventory **investment**).

Statistics Canada measures the circular flow of income at two points. It measures the expenditures of consumers, businesses, governments and foreigners (GDE). It also measures workers', firms' and property owners' incomes and what they do with these incomes (GDP).

The income that all components of society dispose of through consumption, saving or net taxation must equal what they receive in the form of expenditures by society and foreigners for consumption, investment, government expenditures and net exports. This is just another way of saying the aggregate demand must end up being equal to aggregate supply (see Figure 9.2 for a formal expression of this equivalency).

From the above description of the circular flow of income, we can see how disequilibrium crises occur when more is being produced (aggregate sup-

ply) than what consumers, investors, governments and foreigners want to purchase (aggregate demand). Remember, the relationship of expenditure to income is after the fact. Firms producing blue jeans find out they have produced too much when they are left with piles of unsold jeans at the end of the year. When the owner of a barbershop checks his monthly receipts and expenditures he may discover his employees were actually only cutting hair half the time they were employed in the shop. For the blue jean manufacturer this would result in an involuntary investment in unsold goods—that is, an unwanted increase in inventories. The barbershop owner could find that his store is losing money.

In either case, the firms will want to reduce employment and/or wages and prices to try to restore sales and profits. However, if all firms are reducing employment or wages, workers have less money to spend on consumption.

9.1 Sources of Investment Finance

There has been considerable consternation in the last few decades about the failure of Canadians to save and invest in stocks and equities in Canadian industries, about government deficits "crowding out" businesses from the bond market, and similar explanations for Canada's somewhat dismal investment and productivity performance. This is perpetuated by those whose primary concern is reducing government programs in favour of tax cuts for the wealthy.

The fact of the matter is that corporate investment in Canada is not financed out of individual Canadian's 'investments' in the stock market or out of corporate borrowings on the bond markets in competition with government. Indeed the stock market is almost insignificant in providing capital for new investment. The fact of the matter is that 90 percent of investment has come from the internal business savings.

See Jim Stanford, *Paper Boom* (Ottawa: CCPA and Lorimer, 1999), pp. 219–220 [For similar American figures, see Doug Henwood, *Wall Street* (London: Verso, 1997), ch. 2]

Figure 9.2: Aggregate Demand and Aggregate Supply

Aggregate Demand (GDE) = Aggregate Supply (GDP)

$C + I + G + (X - M) = C + S + T$

where   C = consumption
        S = savings
        T = taxes
        I = investment
        G = government expenditure
        X = exports
        M = imports

Firms reducing prices have less profits for investment. As a result aggregate demand tends to fall further, making the crisis worse. Neoclassical economists have argued that such disequilibrium crises are a natural part of the business cycle. Eventually, they say, the fall in prices and wages would lead to increased demand for goods and services and, as old machines wore out and needed replacement, investment would also recover. This would restore demand and with it would come full employment.

A short description of the business cycle will illustrate its dynamics.

1. *Expansion phase.* An initial expansion in aggregate demand occurs, initiated perhaps by a rise in investment or consumption, by an increase in demand for our exports or maybe by increased government expenditures. However it starts, the increased demand reduces inventories, firms up prices and profits, and encourages investment and production. This stimulates employment and wages, which further increases consumption demand. The process accelerates and multiplies as business produces more to meet demand. This can be called an expansionary disequilibrium and it is usually accompanied by price increases.

2. *Crisis phase.* Strategic and tactical competition by individual capitalists who invest more (new firms start, old firms expand) bringing about a major increase in capacity and production. At the same time, wages and costs also tend to rise as workers and unions take advantage of rising demand for workers. Thus, with all this investment and expansion of capacity, businesses get to the point of overproduction, or excess supply of goods and services. This produces a squeeze on profits as prices do not keep up with rising costs.

3. *Recession phase.* Overproduction brings rising inventories and, with lots of unsold goods, pressure to reduce prices. As prices drop, profits are squeezed and firms now have reason to lay off workers and reduce investment. Layoffs and reduced investment by firms contribute to a spiral of reduced demand by consumers and businesses. Monopoly firms may try to raise prices to compensate but this means lower sales, lower output and lower employment, which contribute to a further contraction of aggregate demand and even more unemployment.

   The pressure on prices and reduced sales has two "self-correcting" results. The least efficient firms and those with the smallest financial reserves go bankrupt, reducing aggregate supply. At the same time, such bankruptcies provide "distress, sale-priced capital" to the surviving firms. This reduces costs for surviving firms but at the same time reduces the need of surviving firms to invest in the replacement or expansion of capital equipment. As a result, investment demand further shrinks. Meanwhile, unemployment undermines labour's market power, resulting in a relative decline in wages. The relative decline in wages further reduces consumption demand though it also reduces the real labour costs of the surviving firms.

4. *Recovery phase.* The decline in output resulting from the disappearance of marginal firms and the rise of unemployment, and the consequent decline in wages, have a curative effect. Aggregate supply is reduced and unit labour costs decline, leading to a recovery in profits and therefore in the inducement

to begin investing again. Meanwhile, the wearing out of existing capital necessitates investing in replacement machinery and equipment. At the same time, consumption stops decreasing as incomes approach the subsistence level. This prevents demand from falling further and begins to expand it. As prices and demand stabilize, stocks of unsold goods decline and profits increase. As profits increase, momentum is added to the inducement to invest. This in turn raises investment, productivity, employment and consequently consumption. Aggregate demand again leads supply and a new expansion phase is entered.

> ### 9.2 On the Plight of the Unemployed before Unemployment Insurance
>
> I haven't done any work since June 28, 1930; I have a wife and three girls aged 13 yrs, 11 yrs and 9 yrs ... I've been going and regoing to the City to get work: all I get is We will see what can be done: Our rent is back from Nov. Dec. 1930 and this month God only knows where are [sic] going to get it from: I have asked & asked the City to help, and they say its been turned down for some reason, the reason they won't tell: Today I whent [sic] to get $3 to keep us for a week and Mr. Valcourt of the city Office said I couldn't get it because someone said we had a radio.... Then he says he don't have to give us help if he don't want to; I as you Sir, "who was this money given to and what for?" is if for a man to crawl on his hands and knees to get a loaf for his family? I ask you Sir how do you think we live on $3 a week and cant get that because some people make up a lie: What sort of country have we; I don't want help: I want work; I'll do anything to keep my family.
>
> —Letter to Prime Minister R.B. Bennett from P.W.L. Norton, January 1931, quoted in James Struthers, No Fault of Their Own (Toronto: University of Toronto Press, 1983), p. 50

This is the classic "business cycle" that has been a feature of capitalist economies since the emergence of industrial capitalism in the eighteenth century. When business cycles coincide with a structural crisis the devastating results have threatened the social fabric of society. For the most part however, they are in the long run self-correcting. John Maynard Keynes's comment on this faith in the self-correcting nature of markets was that "in the long run we are all dead." By this he meant that the unemployed and those that suffer the enormous social and personal costs associated with even short-term unemployment were likely to gain little comfort from the knowledge that the economy would eventually self-correct. Keynes believed that the government ought to step in with policies that would counteract the negative swings in the business cycle. To understand these Keynesian policies, it is first necessary to come to terms with the monetary sector and monetary policy.

The Monetary Sector and Monetary Policy

The money market is the market that brings together savers and borrowers. Savers are those who wish to save rather than spend their money income. They include workers and consumers who have savings accounts, firms with undistributed corporate profits) and governments that have budget surpluses. Borrowers include all of those who wish to borrow the use of money to finance investment, consumption or government deficits. "Manufacturing" money is virtually costless and money has no use value in itself—other than to pad mattresses, of course.

What is Money? Economists usually define money as "anything that is used as money." Or as John Kenneth Galbraith put it, money is "what is commonly

9.3 Sources of Bank Income, Five Largest Banks, Fiscal 1998

	Income Source ($ billion)	Share of Total Income (%)
Tradition Lending		
Interest Income	67.0	
Interest expense	46.2	
Loan Loss provision	2.2	
Net interest income	18.5	49.4
Non-Interest Income		
Banking and credit card service charges	4.9	13.1
Investment banking	6.5	17.5
Wealth management	2.4	6.3
Trading and derivatives profits	2.1	5.5
Insurance and other	3.1	8.2
Total non-interest income	19.0	50.6

—Jim Stanford, *Paper Boom* (Ottawa: CCPA and Lorimer, 1999), p. 60

offered or received for the purchase or sale of goods, services or other things."[3] If money is defined by its usage, just what are the uses of money? Its uses are as a medium of exchange, a standard of value, a store of value and a speculative asset. Without getting too technical, the medium of exchange merely means that people can exchange work and goods for money rather than being paid in goods or bartering to obtain desired goods and services. Money is a standard of value that allows people to compare the relative cost or value of goods in the market. Money allows people to "store" their wealth in a relatively costless and non-perishable form, providing of course, there is limited or no inflation. Finally, money can be used as a speculative asset so people can gamble on a rise in interest rates. An increase in interest rates increases the value of the money since it would now "earn" more when loaned out than it did before the increase in interest rates.

Financial institutions such as the Bank of Canada, the chartered banks and a host of non-bank financial intermediaries buy and sell the *use* of money in the money market, often referred to as the **paper economy**. The Bank of Canada is the federal government agency that controls the Canadian monetary system and the availability and price (interest rates) of money in that system. The other banks, which are private institutions chartered by the federal government, receive deposits from individuals and other institutions and firms and make loans to individuals and other borrowers. They make their (substantial) profits from the difference in the interest they pay to deposits and the interest they charge those they loan to, and from charges they levy on depositors for financial services.

Increasingly important in recent years has been an array of non-bank financial intermediaries. They include mainly trust companies, credit unions, caisse populaire, pension plans, savings, mutual, foreign exchange and invest-

9.4 Assets of Banks and Financial Intermediaries

The following table gives the total assets of the Chartered Banks and the other major Financial Intermediaries at the end of the year 2000.

Institutions:	Assets ($ millions)	Percentage of Total Assets of Financial Institutions
Chartered Banks	927,799	52.3
Trust and Mortgage Companies	10,763	0.6
Credit Unions and Caisse Populaire	122,198	6.9
Non Depository Credit Institutions	86,311	4.9
Life Insurance Companies	184,701	10.4
Investment Funds (at market value)	441,307	24.9
Total	1,773,079	100.0

–Bank of Canada, *Banking and Financial Statistics*, September 2001

ment funds, life insurance companies, brokerage houses, bond dealers, mortgage companies, stock and bond dealers and the like. All these institutions convert savings into loans—and, with the exception of the credit unions and caisse populaire, do this at a profit to the financial institution.

Most money in Canada is not held in the form of coin and paper money. People and businesses deposit either cheques or electronic transfers with chartered banks, credit unions and trust companies and then make most of their expenditures using cheques or debit cards. All of these deposits are based on credits with the Bank of Canada, either in the form of paper money or by chartered bank deposits in the Bank of Canada. In effect, the chartered bank deposits in the Bank of Canada are the Bank's "IOUs" to the chartered banks. The money supply, therefore, is just one big structure of credit.

Monetary policy is the policy of the government and the central bank (the Bank of Canada) towards the supply of money, the availability of credit and the level of interest rates in the economy. It is supposed to operate in the following fashion. If the government and the bank deem it prudent to stimulate the economy, they will want to lower interest rates to encourage borrowing for investment and consumption. To lower interest rates, more money must be supplied to the market. In Canada the amount of money that chartered banks can loan is governed by the amount of the reserves they have on deposit with the Bank of Canada. If the Bank of Canada increases these reserves by in effect loaning money to the banks, it increases the money supply. (The Bank of Canada can also increase the money supply by loaning money to the Federal Government.) When there is more money available for loans, the interest rate, which is the price of money, declines.

The Bank can reduce the money supply (or cause it to expand more slowly than the economy), by redeeming its loans thereby reducing the commercial bank reserves. This is called a tight money policy, which raises interest rates. The Bank of Canada follows such a policy if it deems it prudent to restrain the

9.5 Real and Nominal Interest Rates

In the 1970s, interest rates in Canada were running in the 16–17 percent range. In some Latin American countries, interest rates more recently have been 60 or 100 percent. Are these rates extraordinarily high, usurious loan sharking? Not necessarily. These are *nominal* interest rates, the rates paid on money that itself is changing in value.

Consider the case of someone who loans $100 to a borrower for a year at an interest rate of 10 percent when the inflation rate is 40 percent. At the end of the year, our lender gets back $110 principal and interest. Unfortunately, however, because of the inflation that $110 is only worth $66 in buying power. Our lender has, in effect, lost $34.

Let us say that our lender actually wanted to make a *real* return of 5 percent on his loan. Well, if he were to obtain that he would have to have $145 back at the end of the year. In short, he would have to charge a *nominal* rate of 45 percent in order to get a *real* rate of return of 5 percent. In short, the real rate of interest is the nominal rate minus the rate of inflation.

In recent years, Canada's inflation rate has been running around or below 2 percent a year, low by historic standards. But this means that interest rates of 7 and 8 percent (which have been the prevailing rates for prime loans and mortgages) result in real rates of 5 to 6 percent, which are high by historic standards. Indeed, Canada had a "tight money policy" (high real interest rates) through most of the 1990s. Except at the end of 1996 and extending into 1997 when the Bank of Canada's target overnight rate briefly dropped to 3 percent, the Banks target rate has ranged between a low of 4.25 percent and a high of 5.75 percent until August 2001, when it dropped to 4 percent. It has been dropped a further percent in the aftermath of the September terrorist attack on New York. This means that the target real rate has been in the 2.7 percent–3.1 percent range.

Year	Consumer Price Index	Interest Rate (3-month Treasury Bills, end of year)	Real Rate
1990	4.8	11.5	6.7
1991	5.6	7.4	1.8
1992	1.5	7.0	5.5
1993	1.8	3.9	2.1
1994	0.2	7.1	6.9
1995	2.2	5.5	3.3
1996	1.6	2.9	1.3
1997	1.6	4.0	2.4
1998	0.9	4.7	3.8
1999	1.7	4.9	3.2
2000	2.7	5.5	2.8

–Bank of Canada, *Banking and Financial Statistics*, September 2001

The problem for consumers and business is that they can never be certain what the actual rate of inflation is going to be over the following year, or years in the case of long-term loans. Thus, borrowers and lenders have to make their decisions on the basis of nominal rates and what they expect inflation to be.

Some economists who believe that people are expert in forecasting future prices have developed a theory called "rational expectations" that basically says that what people expect, they actually get. Most economists, however, are much more reticent about the accuracy of crystal balls in predicting the future.

economy (for instance, in an attempt to control inflation). This was the disastrous policy that precipitated the severe recession of 1981–82 when interest rates shot up to over 20 percent. This same policy perpetuated and deepened the depression of the early 1990s.

In recent years it has become clear that the central bank cannot really control the supply of money since most businesses and many individuals have automatic access to money loans through lines of credit, such as those provided to consumers by their credit cards. As a result, central banks have largely given up trying to control the money supply and rather resort to controlling the price of money, the interest rate. The Bank of Canada used to do this by changes to the **bank rate**, the rate at which it is willing and able to borrow or loan money on specific markets as a "lender of last resort." More recently, the Bank has switched to relying on its right to control the **overnight rate**, the rate the commercial banks charge for overnight loans between each other to ensure that they have sufficient required reserves. This rate then becomes the benchmark for other interest rates that the banks and other financial institutions charge.

> ### 9.6 Monetary Policy, Interests Rates and Greenspan, 2000–01
>
> The Fed has cut interest rates nine times this year. The Fed funds rate has dropped from 6.5 percent in January to 2.5 percent, the lowest level since 1962. Yet the economy was still deteriorating even before Sept. 11. To state the obvious: even with the usual "lags," the Fed's cuts weren't powerful enough to offset the ill effects of faltering investment, employment and confidence....
>
> The point is that even zero interest rates can't reinvigorate the economy if other conditions are sufficiently unhealthy. Monetary policy is not some magical potion that can erase any disagreeable problem. What we call "the economy" is simply the baffling amalgam of businesses, financial markets, government regulations, cultural attitudes (toward, among other things, work and risk), popular moods and foreign trade. Monetary policy is only one part and influence....
>
> Robert Samuelson, "The Fed: Another Myth on its Way Out?" *Newsweek*, October 22, 2001

Deficient Demand Unemployment

Before we can understand how and why monetary and fiscal policy is used to attempt to stabilize the economy, it is necessary to understand how unemployment and inflation arise in the first case. Unemployment arises when aggregate demand begins to lag behind aggregate supply. What must be emphasized is that aggregate demand must equal aggregate supply at the end of the day. If we simplify this a little by ignoring exports and imports for the moment, this means consumption, investment and government expenditures (demand) must equal consumption, savings and taxes (supply). Since consumption is a component of both supply and demand, it means that investment and government expenditures *must* equal savings and taxes. The importance of this is perhaps easiest to see by illustrating with a number of cases.

Case 1: *A fall in investment.* Profits fall because there has been overinvestment producing excess production capacity, increased competition, increased costs and falling prices. Falling profits and expected profits lead to a decline in investment. Firms producing investment goods, therefore, cannot sell their output at profitable prices and as a result cut back on their production and lay off workers. Laid-off workers have less income to spend and reduce consumption further.

But unemployed workers have less income and therefore save less. In short they consume more and more of their income. Businesses also have less and less profits and therefore also save less. For the moment assume that the government

9.7 Automatic Stabilization

Monetary policy is notoriously unreliable and ineffective in controlling the economy. It takes a long time to add any stimulus, and while it is more effective in constraining an economy that is overheating, the effects are generally perverse—discouraging consumption and investment.

The alternative to monetary policy is fiscal policy, increasing government expenditures and lowering taxes when the economy is languishing, and decreasing government expenditures and increasing taxes when the economy is booming and threatening to overheat. Fiscal policy, however, also takes a long time just to plan and implement, and curtailing existing investment programs when restraint is required may not be feasible, politically or economically.

The answer to both the political and economic problems are *automatic stabilizers*, those measures that require no government action but that increase aggregate demand when expenditures are falling and reduce spending when the economy is booming. The premier automatic stabilizer is unemployment insurance. When the economy is heading downward, unemployment insurance payments rise, helping the unemployed to maintain their consumption and thereby cushioning the economy against a devastating contraction in consumption demand. But as the economy recovers, the transfer of income from the insurance fund to workers declines, thereby dampening potentially inflationary consumer demand.

Progressive income taxes tend to work the same way. When workers become unemployed their taxes fall more than proportionally as their income shrinks. Conversely, as workers come back to work, taxes rise moderating the rise in consumer spending.

Unfortunately, however, successive Canadian governments have reduced the effectiveness of all the automatic stabilizers by reducing the progressivity of taxes and by drastic cuts to unemployment insurance benefits over the last couple of decades.

runs a balanced budget so that, in this case, savings must equal investment for the economy to remain stable. Sooner or later, the decline in saving equals the decline in investment. The economy will cease contracting but only with substantial and continued levels of unemployment. Of course, the degree of unemployment will be much higher in the absence of unemployment insurance schemes that allow workers to maintain consumption demand, though at lower levels, even when they are unemployed.

Case 2: *A fall in consumption*. Perhaps consumers have been buying on credit. Because of a "tight" monetary policy (reduced credit and increased interest rates) or fear of unemployment, consumers reduce their credit buying. This is the same thing as reducing their consumption and increasing their saving "for a rainy day." The proverbial rainy day comes quickly as firms, overstocked with consumer goods, cut production, lay off workers, try to cut wages and reduce investment, or even go bankrupt. Again the result is a downward spiral until equilibrium is reached between aggregate demand and aggregate supply but at a less than full-employment production level.

Case 3: *A reduction in government expenditure*. In this case, the government, responding to the neoliberal political agenda, cuts back on social spending. Again, all other things remaining unchanged, this means a reduction in aggregate demand. Government employees become unemployed. Firms selling social services or related supplies to the government find demand for their goods and services down and lay off employees and reduce intended investment. In turn, this means a reduction in consumption and investment demand and a downward spiral until a new, lower level of employment and income is reached.

As outlined previously, this lower level of income and employment will tend to persist unless, or until, something spurs an increase in consumption, investment, government spending or exports. This spur could be that enough firms go bankrupt and/or equipment wears out and is depreciated to the point that profit rates begin to rise, inducing new investment. Or governments, responding to political pressures, increase spending or decrease taxes thereby increasing aggregate demand. Alternatively, falling input prices, including falling labour costs, could restore profit rates. But falling labour costs can be a two-edged sword if they are achieved by reducing wages. If wages fall, workers' ability to consume is reduced. If workers' consumption falls, this reduces aggregate demand, profits fall, and so on. Keynes, for example, was quite adamant that, because of this effect, reducing wages was *not* the route to go to try to stem unemployment.

We can go through any number of other cases. A possibility is that some external factor—such as a crop failure in the United States—could create a significant increase in the demand for Canadian exports, thereby increasing aggregate demand. This would have the opposite effect as those listed above. Incomes of Canadian farmers would be increased, leading to increased consumption and an expansionary spiral as aggregate demand leads aggregate supply. Similarly, a decline in interest rates initiated by the central bank could prompt an increase in credit buying of consumption goods, particularly hous-

> ### 9.8 Socializing Investment
>
> For my own part I am now somewhat sceptical of the success of ... monetary policy directed towards influencing the rate of interest. I expect to see the State ... taking an ever greater responsibility for directly organising investment....
>
> In conditions of *laissez-faire* the avoidance of wide fluctuations in employment may, therefore, prove impossible without a far-reaching change in the psychology of investment markets such as there is no reason to expect. I conclude that the duty of ordering the current volume of investment cannot safely be left in private hands....
>
> I conceive, therefore, that a somewhat comprehensive socialization of investment will prove the only means of securing an approximation to full employment; though this need not exclude all manner of compromises and of devices by which public authority will cooperate with private initiative. But beyond this no obvious case is made out for a system of State Socialism which would embrace most of the economic life of the community. It is not the ownership of the instruments of production which it is important for the State to assume. If the State is able to determine the aggregate amount of resources devoted to augmenting the instruments and the basic rate of reward to those who own them, it will have accomplished all that is necessary. Moreover, the necessary measures of socialization can be introduced gradually and without a break in the general traditions of society.
>
> –J.M. Keynes, *The General Theory* of Employment, Interest and Money (London: Mcmillan, 1961 (c. 1936)), pp. 164, 320, & 378

ing, and/or an increase in investment, thereby also stimulating aggregate demand and reducing unemployment.

There are many possibilities for expanding the output of an economy operating at less than full employment. But before examining some of these possibilities, we need to consider what full employment really means. During the 1960s the Economic Council of Canada set the goal of full employment as an unemployment rate below 3 to 4 percent. Using the neoliberal concept of the natural rate of unemployment (described in chapter 1), in the 1990s the Bank of Canada defined full employment at around 8 percent unemployment. Many economists today who are working on economic policy programs for full employment follow Keynes and define full employment as a situations where "anyone who wants a job can find work at the current levels of wages for the type of work he or she is qualified to do." What actual level of unemployment is compatible with this definition may be disputed, but it is well below current rates and, if history is to be our judge, is probably below 4 percent. What is clear, however, is that it is possible through increasing aggregate demand to reduce unemployment from its present level.

Policies to do so all involve increasing the aggregate demands on the capacity of the economy through augmenting consumption, investment, government or net foreign expenditures. Anything that reduces any of the demand elements will bring down supply. This will normally come about through falling employment until the new equilibrium level is reached. The unemployment at this new equilibrium level is **deficient demand unemployment**.

Indeed, now one can understand Keynes's solution to the Depression of the 1930s. He recommended taking some of the investment decision out of the hands of businesses, where it depends on expected profits (which Keynes said were determined by the "animal spirits" of business people), and making it at least in part a function of public decision. While Keynes believed in letting private capital run the businesses, he thought investment levels too important to be left to the changing expectations of private business.

Such a policy recommendation was not popular with business interests. In Canada it was partially adopted during the Second World War when government determination of investment was used to rapidly develop our war industries. Beyond that one experiment, in Canada the "socialization" of investment was shelved in favour of what has been termed **bastard Keynesianism**.

The essence of bastard Keynesian policy in the postwar period has been to use fiscal policy and monetary policy to attempt to regulate aggregate demand. **Fiscal policy** is the government's use of taxes, transfer payments (payments to individuals and businesses by the government and not related to sales of factors or of goods and services to the government) and government expenditures intended to add to, or subtract from, aggregate demand. In the case of deficient demand unemployment, there are a number of fiscal and monetary policies that have been advocated to bolster aggregate demand. These include:

- increased government expenditure to directly increase demand such as building roads, schools or hospitals;
- decreased personal taxes to encourage increased consumption by giving people more disposable income;
- decreased business taxes to encourage increased investment, in effect providing business with more undistributed earnings to finance investment;
- increased transfers to individuals to encourage consumption, for example, by raising the child tax benefit, giving lower-income families more disposable income;
- increased transfers to businesses (subsidies) to encourage investment, again providing business with extra resources to finance investment; and
- decreased interest rates and expanded availability of credit to encourage both consumption and investment.

Not all of these are universally accepted as being effective in increasing demand, at least in the short run. Decreased business taxes, increased subsidies to business and lower interest rates to encourage investment are the most controversial. There is little evidence, for instance, that lowering taxes or interest rates on business promotes investment *if there is not sufficient aggregate demand to purchase the additional output*. As many critics point out, "you can't push on a string." Raising taxes may reduce investment and aggregate demand, but lowering them will not directly increase investment or aggregate demand.

In addition, governments have used international trade and exchange rates to try to stimulate demand. The **exchange rate** is the rate at which our money is exchanged on the international currency market. Lowering the value of the loonie, for instance, makes our exports more attractive to foreign buyers and makes imports more expensive and hence less attractive. If our exports go up and our imports go down, the net demand for our output rises. High tariffs (taxes on goods imported into the country) and import quotas (restrictions on what can be imported) can also affect exports and imports, though economists often deride such actions as "beggar thy neighbour" policies, since they have a negative impact on trading partners. In any case, these policies are now strictly regulated (and largely prohibited) by the World Trade Organization (before 1995, the General Agreement on Tariffs and Trade or GATT) and other international trade and capital investment agreements such as the North American Free Trade Agreement.

Inflation

Inflation is commonly thought of an increase in the price we pay for the goods and services we purchase. Un-

> ### 9.9 Production Equations and Inflation: A Technical Explanation
>
> This can be made clearer by returning to our production equations and using them to explain the inflation of the 1970s: $\pi = P \times Q - rm - (w + i + dep + T)$ and $Q = f(K, \text{x-efficiency, worker effort, technology})$ where π = profits;
> P = prices;
> Q = quantity of output;
> rm = raw material and energy costs;
> w = wages and salaries;
> i = interest;
> dep = depreciation;
> T = business taxes;
> K = capital stock; and
> x-efficiency = managerial and organizational efficiency
>
> Growth in the quantity of goods (Q) stagnated because of falling investment in capital (K), increasing inefficiency of management (x-efficiency), producing stagnant or falling productivity due to worker dissatisfaction and falling technological change (related to the falling investment and very low expenditures by firms on research and development). At the same time, raw material prices were rapidly increasing, particularly after the two "oil shocks" in 1974 and 1978. Wages were increasing because of union pressures and rising prices and, perhaps more important, many more unproductive workers were employed in selling, advertising, clerical occupations and in financial manipulation (e.g., lawyers, brokers, financial consultants and accountants involved in the wave of takeovers, mergers and other unproductive financial operations), all adding to the wage bill while producing no commodities of use value. Interest rates began to rise, particularly after the adoption of monetarism in Canada in 1975. Finally, taxes had begun to rise to pay for social expenditures (the social wage), government expenditures designed to maintain and encourage investment ("corporate welfare") and for social control (police, courts and penitentiaries).
>
> It is obvious, therefore, that the only way to maintain profits in the face of stagnating output and productivity and rising costs, was to raise prices (and/or to control wages).

fortunately, it is not quite that simple since not all price increases should be viewed as the products of inflation. It is not an example of inflation when automobile manufacturers pass on the cost of emission control devices they are required to install in new cars to reduce pollution. The nature of the product has changed, and the price increased. Inflation is a raise in price for the same goods or services. It can be the result of an increase in demand for the goods or services: in which case it is called **demand pull** inflation. Or it can result when producers in a monopoly setting increase prices even if there is no increase in demand. The OPEC cartel's decision to use its monopoly power to raise the price of petroleum and gasoline on the world market is an example of this **cost push inflation**.

Aggregate demand can sometimes exceed the capability of the economy to produce to meet the demand. In this case the only way that aggregate supply can be increased to equal demand is by increasing prices. This means that supply is increasing in money terms, not in real terms. In short, prices rise so that the money value of supply reaches the money value of demand. This is demand pull inflation, the opposite of deficient demand unemployment. It occurs when consumers, investors, exporters and governments bid up prices in an attempt to obtain their desired level of purchases of goods and services. During the 1960s the U.S. government dramatically increased spending, largely to pay for the war in Vietnam. At the same time it did not raise taxes. The result was increased consumer demand, which led to an increase in inflation.

In the case of demand pull inflation governments may want to decrease aggregate demand to stop the inflation. Alternatively, governments could strive to increase real aggregate supply. This usually takes some time because increasing industrial capacity involves increasing investment which, unless offset by some other policy such as a tax increase, further increases aggregate demand and inflation in the short run. The appropriate policies for decreasing aggregate demand will be the opposite to those for decreasing unemployment. They include:

- decreased government expenditure;
- increased personal taxes to discourage consumption;
- increased business taxes to reduce investment;
- decreased transfers to individuals to decrease consumption;
- decreased subsidies to business to discourage investment; and
- increased interest rate and credit rationing to discourage both consumption and investment.

Cost push inflation results when firms raise prices in order to restore, maintain or increase profits in the face of rising unit costs. Most firms in the monopoly sector practice a form of markup pricing, in which they set prices at a markup over their costs sufficient to return a target rate of profit. If the cost of any component of the firm's inputs increases, profits must fall unless productivity rises, wages fall or prices are increased. Firms can only continue to increase prices to restore profits if the state is willing to accommodate the inflation by allowing the money supply to increase proportionately and by not increasing interest rates.

Ideally, the state and business prefer to restore profits and investment without resorting to inflation of the money supply and prices. That is, they would rather restore profits by lowering wages and business taxes or shifting taxes from business to labour. Not surprisingly, workers—especially unionized workers—oppose such policies. During inflationary periods they wish to see their wages go up, not down. And they have been prepared to go on strike for these increases. This leads to what some economists have called **class conflict inflation** (or the conflict theory of inflation[4]) but is perhaps more commonly referred to as the **price-wage spiral**. The Canadian economy in the 1970s went through such a spiral as employers increased their prices to restore or maintain profits following rise in petroleum and energy costs. As prices rose, workers demanded compensating increases in wages. This in turn further raised costs, since productivity increases had come virtually to a stop. Firms, therefore, raised prices to regain profits and, with a lag, labour again demanded

> **9.10 The Anti-Inflation Board and the Attack on Labour**
>
> The 1975 Anti-Inflation Board (AIB) legislation was a frontal attack on working Canadians. It was to be amazingly successful. Under the guise of wrestling inflation to the ground for the benefit of all, Canadian workers' attempts at playing catch-up, and perhaps making some real gains, were repressed.
>
> Wages were not the demonstrable cause of inflation. The fact is that prices had begun to increase markedly in Canada before the oil shocks of 1972 had taken effect. Even in 1974, price increases ranged between 38 and 58 percent, whereas wage increases ranged between 8 and 15 percent. Yet the way in which the AIB legislation was implemented amounted to an attack on wages, not on profits. It succeeded. By the end of its operating life, the AIB legislation had enabled employers to make 9.2 percent more profit than they otherwise would have.
>
> –Daniel Drache and Harry Glasbeek, *The Changing Workplace* (Toronto: Lorimer, 1992), p. 113

compensating raises. Thus the inflationary spiral. It should be emphasized that, as a study for the Bank of Canada has found, it was prices that led the spiral while workers were responsible only for defending their real wage levels.[5]

The federal government attempted to lower inflation by controlling wages in the second half of the 1970s. The wage control program took the form of federal government legislation to establish the Anti-Inflation Board (AIB) in 1976. Under the AIB, limits were placed on all contractual wage increases from 1976 through 1978. In each year of the three-year control period, the allowable increase awarded workers was ratcheted down. There were some provisions restricting business from raising prices in order to increase profits but these were largely ineffective. Following the expiry of the AIB, the federal government instituted the "6 and 5" wage-control program for government employees in 1980. This two-year program limited public sector wage increases to 6 percent in the first year of the program and to 5 percent in the second.

Economists still dispute the effectiveness of these controls in controlling inflation. In any case, they were not considered effective enough. Inflation and wage controls created considerable social unrest and a politicization of the conflict between workers and the employers and government. Organized labour tried to maintain real wages by fighting for money wage increases. Businesses responded by raising prices to restore profits.

Thus, Canadian governments were caught in a dilemma. They wanted to restore profits, which could only come through price inflation without compensating wage increases. But they did not wish to appear to be favouring business. This meant they were under pressure to control inflation and maintain real wages and social programs. Most Western capitalist economies were caught in the same dilemma. As a result, inflation continued through the 1970s when the dilemma was resolved, largely in the favour of the business community. In 1981 central banks in Canada and the U.S. instituted a massive increase in interest rates. The result was such high unemployment and widespread bankruptcy that wage rates declined, raw material prices began to collapse and governments began a concerted effort to reduce the social wage and transfer the tax burden to individuals.

Inflation was suppressed, but at the cost of continuing very high levels of unemployment and lost output. Profits also suffered initially but began to recover as wages were held down by unemployment. High interest rates also contributed massively to the growth of government deficits and the public debt. In the U.S. huge government deficits to finance military spending—what critics label "military Keynesianism"—helped restore employment but also re-ignited inflationary pressures until a second monetary crunch in 1990 produced another severe recession. In the Third World, the high interest rates of the early eighties resulted in a debt crisis that has devastated much of Africa and Latin and South America in the two decades since.

Over the past two decades bastard Keynesianism has placed some inflationary pressure on the Canadian economy. During the 1990s high unemployment and stagnant wages, declining government spending and high interest rates kept this pressure under control. Keynes argued that government spending and the creation of money would not be inflationary because, while increasing demand, they also increased the supply of commodities to meet that demand. However, in order not to compete with business, government spending in the United States in the 1980s concentrated on military spending, which produced goods and services without providing goods and services to consumer markets. As a result inflation was again rising in the latter years of the decade, which spilled over into Canada despite there being no comparable expansion of military expenditure in this country.

Business subsidies and tax cuts restore profits without new investment and productivity increases and without a corresponding increase in commodities with consumer use value. Therefore, such policies have only minor effects on aggregate demand or aggregate supply. They may, in fact, decrease inflationary pressures by transferring buying power from individual taxpayers, who have a propensity to spend their income, to businesses, who have a high propensity to hoard their increased profits until a more favourable climate for investment develops.

At the same time that high interest rates have caused unemployment, however, they have also increased the long run costs of financing businesses, costs that will eventually be passed on through price markups. This kind of Keynesianism, therefore, has increased some sources of demand without a corresponding increase in real output. This has produced inflationary pressures that will quickly re-emerge if and when unemployment declines and wages again begin to rise in line with labour productivity growth.

At the same time, Canada is faced with a paradox. It has continuing deficient demand unemployment. This unemployment is largely the result of Canada's monetary and fiscal policies, which are among the most restrictive of any of the

Western industrial countries. The government has adopted these largely out of fear of inflation. They fear that if they adopt Keynesian policies that increase demand, business would not increase investment and output. Instead it would restore profits by higher prices, unleashing more demand pull inflation. This would resurrect the inflationary cycle without significantly reducing unemployment. However, unless such policies are introduced, the chances of Canada improving its dismal employment, productivity and income growth record are poor. Much the same can be said about Europe, where economic policy has also been immobilized by fear of inflation.

The real problem in this period of an accumulation crisis is that a real recovery within a neoliberal policy framework requires the re-establishment of a favourable climate for accumulation. This means that what is needed is a recovery in business's profit expectations that will fuel a new wave of investment. What is required is a solution to the more fundamental crisis, a way to solve the current structural problems—that is, a new long wave of expansion. Bastard Keynesian policies will not be enough.

Deficits: The Fiscal Crisis of the State

The current long wave stagnation has given rise what is called the **fiscal crisis of the state**, namely the "chronic tendency for the revenue of the state to fall short of its expenditures."[6] For over two decades in Canada there were continuous government deficits and a major increase in the public debt. This in turn has provided the rationale for a concerted attack on social spending. Business and banking spokespersons argued that government deficits are a major barrier to renewed growth. Workers ask why recovery must be financed through cuts to services that benefit them and their families. At the same time, Keynesian economists argue that cutting back on government expenditures will only make matters worse by decreasing aggregate demand at a time when unemployment is already a major economic problem.[7] In short, this issue is perhaps the most controversial and misunderstood of contemporary political economy.

If we look back at the postwar expansion and the subsequent stagflation, the origin of the deficit issue and its political implications become clearer. Out of the war, when unions established themselves in most major industries and played an important role in the war effort, came the **postwar labour-management accord.** This accord accepted the legitimacy of the capitalist system, including management's right to determine investment

> ### 9.11 The Fiscal Crisis of the State
>
> The "fiscal crisis of the state" is a manifestation of a pervasive feature of all capitalist political economies. This is the attempt by business to socialize the costs of investment and production while privatizing the benefits. More specifically, there is a fiscal crisis of the state in so far as there is a chronic tendency for the revenues of the state to fall short of its expenditures. The concern is with chronic (structural) deficits, as opposed to the cyclical deficits which John Maynard Keynes in particular argued are, in and of themselves, benign events with which we can all be quite comfortable....
>
> Fiscal crises may in general be understood as the way in which crises of profitability within the private sector since the late 1960s have displayed themselves when they have been transferred successfully onto the shoulders of the public sector.
>
> Gavan Butler, "Fiscal Crisis of the State," *Encyclopedia of Political Economy*, P. A. O'Hara, ed. (London: Routledge, 1999), pp. 354–355

and introduce technological change, in exchange for labour's right to unionize and bargain collectively for a share of the increasing productivity. The state cemented this accommodation with a commitment to full employment and an expansion of the welfare state. While there were no shortages of conflict between business, labour and government between 1945 and the late 1960s all three parties attempted to live with these ground rules.

The stagflation of the 1970s, however, undermined this accord. With falling productivity growth, labour demands for real wage increases were stymied. In fact, in the last quarter of the twentieth century, average real earnings of men (before taxes) in Canada declined though those for women continued to rise moderately. Government tax revenues from labour income dropped severely. This is not surprising given the stagnation in real wages and the rise in unemployment. Not only were there less wages to tax, fewer people were earning wages. In addition profits and resource incomes were being squeezed. This led the government to increase **tax expenditures**, provisions in the tax system exempting corporations and some investors from paying certain types of taxes, further eroding government revenues. Furthermore, high interest rates raised enormously the cost to all governments of financing the debt and deficits. Social expenditures, particularly for health and education, which had expanded in the fifties and sixties as part of the development of the postwar welfare state, did not decline, though they rose only very modestly in the 1970s and '80s before falling substantially in the 1990s. The result was steady or slowly rising expenditures, primarily to pay high interest rates, and falling revenues, primarily due to

---

9.12 Corporate Contributions to Canadian Tax Revenue

Since the Second World War, corporate taxes have declined dramatically as a source of government revenues.

Year	Taxes Collected from Individuals		Taxes Collected from Corporations	
	$ Billions	% of Tax Revenue	$ Billions	% of Tax Revenue
1950	$ 3.3	48%	$ 3.2	46%
1960	7.4	56%	5.2	39%
1970	24.7	70%	9.9	28%
1980	41.6	75%	12.7	23%
1992	87.6	90%	7.4	8%

(Taxes covered in this table include personal income tax, corporate income tax, and the goods and services tax.)

–CCPA Monitor, March 1995

Using the most recent data available at Revenue Canada, there were 77 corporations, each with profits greater than $25 million, which paid zero income tax on total profits of $5.2 billion. There were 1,079 corporations, each with profits between $1 million and $25 million, which paid zero income tax on total profits of $4.3 billion.

Of the 62,480 corporations which had profits but paid no income tax, the top 7,000 of them (with average profits of $1.6 million each) accounted for 92% of all the untaxed profits of corporations (totalling more than $12 billion in 1991).

– George Baker, Liberal MP for Gander-Grand Falls, Newfoundland, quoted in CCPA Monitor, March 1995

9.13 Statistics Canada versus the Neoliberals, the Bank of Canada and the Department of Finance

From the end of the Second World War to 1975 Canada adopted the main pillars of its social security system. Over this 29-year period the government budget was in balance and, in fact, registered a small surplus. The social security system was economically and fiscally sustainable. This, however, did not please those opposed to the expanded role of government at the expense of the private sector. They demanded a return to nineteenth-century laissez-faire and a reduction in social security to the much more parsimonious levels in the United States.

This business neoliberal agenda, however, was rejected until the 1970s, when stagflation began to rock the economy. To combat inflation, the Bank of Canada officially adopted a monetarist policy in 1975 and abandoned the previously successful Keynesian approach. One result of monetarism and recession was growing government deficits and a rising public debt, a debt that had fallen steadily as a percentage of GDP in the pre-monetarist period after the war.

The cry went up from the pro-business media and think tanks, the Business Council on National Issues (BCNI) and other business organizations that we were "living beyond our means" and that the cause of these deficits and the rising debt was runaway spending on social programs.

At this point Statistics Canada stepped in. A study, dated June of 1990, contradicted the business and neoliberal contention that social programs contributed significantly to the debt/deficit problem. The study found that over the period from 1975–1989, declining tax revenues, primarily from business and higher income people, accounted for 50 percent of the deficits, while 44 percent was attributed to the high interest rates introduced by the Bank of Canada. Only 6 percent was attributable to government spending. In fact, excluding the cost of unemployment insurance, which varies directly with the unemployment rate, "social program spending has not increased relative to GDP over the last 16 years." [Quoted by Bruce Campbell in "StatsCan study on our debt/deficit 'crisis,'" CCPA Monitor, April 1995.]

Such a message, however, was not compatible with the business and neoliberal government agenda. Despite the fact that the study was favourably peer-reviewed by academic and business economists, intervention by the Department of Finance and the business media was successful in preventing the study from being publicly released for a year. It was finally published in a slightly watered-down version in StatCan's flagship publication, the Canadian Economic Observer in June of 1991. But the message was the same. The critics of Canada's social services system were simply wrong and were pushing an ideological agenda.

Simulations that I have done on the debt and deficits for the first half of the 1990s show that if the level of taxes and the interest rates that prevailed before 1975 were in effect, the government would have run a surplus throughout this period without cutting social programs. Nevertheless, social expenditures were cut quite extensively in the 1990s. This is shown in the following table.

Decline in Social Spending by Government 1989/90–1998/99: Selected Categories of Spending

Federal Cash Transfers to Other Levels of Government		-23.0%
Public Health Care Expenditures (1990–1998)		- 5.1%
Hospitals	-14.5%	
Physicians	- 5.5%	
Capital	-23.9%	
Post Secondary Education		-12.2%
Social Housing Completions		-64.9%

–Andrew Jackson and David Robinson, Falling Behind: The State of Working Canada, 2000 (Ottawa: CCPA, 2000), ch. 6

cuts in taxes to business and upper income earners—in short, rising deficits.

The issue is whether or not deficits are a problem. Are they, as neoliberals and conservatives claim, a burden on future generations? Do they crowd private

9.14 Endogenous Money

The traditional theory of money held by neoliberal and monetarist economists is based on the belief that the supply of money could be controlled by central banks by controlling the reserves of the commercial bank system. This was the theory behind the monetarist policies of the late 1970s and 1980s that tried to control inflation by restricting the growth in the *supply* of money. Central banks, however, found that they were unable to control the supply and that their efforts only resulted in wide and destabilizing gyrations in interest rates which produced the recessions of the early 1980s and '90s.

This led many economists, particularly post-Keynesians, to reconsider the theory of money. They turned the theory on its head and argued that the supply of money was *endogenous*—that is, it was determined by how much money was demanded by consumers and businesses. In short, central banks could not control the supply of money. That was determined by the demand for loans. This new theory, called *the theory of endogenous money*, simply says that, given interest rates, the supply of money will rise (or fall) to meet the demand.

The explanation is actually very obvious. Most businesses and many consumers have "lines of credit"—that is, sources (or supplies) of money that they can borrow at any time. Perhaps the most obvious source of consumer "money on demand" is the credit card, but innovation by the financial sector has created many such ways for consumers and businesses to borrow which cannot be controlled by the central bank, or can only be controlled by destabilizing the whole system.

Central banks have realized they have little or no control over the supply of money and have backed off the monetarist "control money supply" strategy, opting rather for controlling short-term interest rates, which they have more success in doing.

borrowers out of the market and undermine business confidence, thereby discouraging investment? Or do they, as Keynesians claim, maintain aggregate demand, thereby warding off unemployment and preventing business failures? The answer is not a simple yes or no. As long as deficits are financed by domestic borrowing, that is, borrowing by the government from Canadians, repayment of interest and principal is merely a transfer between Canadians like any other transfer (e.g., old age pensions, child tax benefits). However, it is a problem in that the people the government owes money to tend to be the wealthy elite, whereas the highest proportion of taxes are paid by the middle income classes. Thus, interest transfers tend to be from lower income groups to higher income groups, the opposite of most of our social transfers.

One way a government can finance its deficits without making the rich richer is to sell its debts to (which is the same as borrowing money from) the Bank of Canada. That means the government pays interest to the Bank of Canada, owned by the government. Money goes from one pocket in the government's pants to another and the effective cost to the government is zero. However, this method of financing government deficits is the same as increasing the money supply, and governments must be very careful about how much money they can borrow in this manner without risk of igniting severe inflation.

There is no evidence that government deficits have crowded private business out of the bond market; that is, no evidence that government borrowing left little in the bond market for business to borrow. The deficits have come at a time when there has been an unprecedented wave of private borrowing to finance corporate takeovers. Central banks and some economists have come to realize that businesses can always borrow as much money as they want providing they are willing to pay the going interest rates. Rather than government borrowing "crowding out" private business from borrowing on bond markets, central banks "push" private business out of the bond market by holding up interest rates. This simply means that if the Bank of Canada raises interest rates, some businesses will no longer find it profitable to borrow on the money market whereas they would have done so at lower interest rates.

Second, much of the concern with deficits is based on a false analogy to the individual or family. If a person consistently borrows for consumption, eventually he or she will become bankrupt. This is not necessarily the case if the person is borrowing for investment—for example for a house or an education. In these cases, the borrowing is offset, at least in part, by assets (the house or the knowledge acquired through education), which may have a greater value than the debt created to make the investment. The same is true of the federal debt. Since some, though

> ### 9.15 Fifteen Fatal Fallacies of Financial Fundamentalism
>
> Much of the conventional economic wisdom prevailing in financial circles, largely subscribed to as a basis for governmental policy, and widely accepted by the media and the public, is based on incomplete analysis, contrafactual assumptions, and false analogy. For instance, encouragement to saving is advocated without attention to the fact that for most people encouraging saving is equivalent to discouraging consumption and reducing market demand, and a purchase by a consumer or a government is also income to vendors and suppliers, and government debt is also an asset. Equally fallacious are implications that what is possible or desirable for individuals one at a time will be equally possible or desirable for all who might wish to do so or for the economy as a whole.
>
> –William Vickery [Nobel Laureate in Economics], "Fifteen Fatal Fallacies of Financial Fundamentalism: A Disquisition on Demand Side Economics," http://www.columbia.edu/dlc/wp/econ/vickrey.html

a small portion, of the recent deficit in Canada has been incurred to maintain investment in humans through spending on health and education, it has created a productive asset to offset the debt. Deficits and the debt have also maintained aggregate demand, employment and social expenditures. Failure to maintain these services would have undermined the political legitimacy of the government and contributed to a rise in social unrest and perhaps, ultimately, to open conflict in the form of street protests and riots.

Of course, debt incurred for non-productive purposes that do not add to aggregate supply, such as military expenditures, constitutes an inflationary force and a redistributive burden on future workers. Interest paid on such debt will normally be financed by taxes on labour income. And since the debt does not produce any additional supply in future years, workers will have to pay for it out of their existing incomes. Only in this sense is it a burden on the future. However, interest is primarily paid to the holders of wealth, the banks and other financial institutions. Thus, the economic and political implications of government deficits depend not primarily on the size of the deficit but on its causes and composition, how it is financed and the rate of interest.[8] These, in turn, are largely determined by the distribution of political and economic power.[9]

What was the business agenda in the change in economic policies beginning in the 1970s? The interests of the financial elite are easy to see. During the postwar growth period, real interest rates averaged around 2 percent. Because of the inflation of the 1970s, the effective real interest paid to banks and financial institutions fell to as low as *minus* 6 percent. The financiers were desperate that inflation be brought under control and positive interest rates restored. But they were also supported by business in the non-financial sectors in the real economy. Stanford explains this support.

Many real businesses found their activities to be increasingly constrained by tight labour markets, labour militancy, and the economic "incursions" of a confident, growing state (including higher taxes, a larger public sector, and more ambitious and interventionist regulatory structures). The profitability of investment in the real economy, like the paper economy, declined notably as the postwar boom carried on. So financial businesses and real businesses eventually became united in their desire for a fundamental reorientation of macroeconomic policy.

This historic U-turn was engineered at the beginning of the 1980s, and no tool has been more important to its execution than monetary policy. Indeed, the sudden advent of very high real interest rates was like a cannon shot signalling the radical and historic change in macroeconomic direction.[10]

What business wanted, and got, was a complete reversal in economic policy, a reversal that restored the economic and political power of business at the expense, not just of the workers, but of government itself.

Notes

1. This latter flow is not shown in Figure 9.1.
2. This is known as Gross Domestic Expenditure or GDE. Until fairly recently, Canada used the concept of gross national expenditure (GNE) and gross national product (GNP) instead of gross domestic expenditure and gross domestic product to measure the total flows through the economy. To conform to international practice Canada switched measures to GDP and GDE though the United States still uses the old national measures. The differences in the measures are technical and do not make any significant difference to the analysis although the actual difference in the numbers is quite large. Simply put, GNP measures income *received* by Canadians; GDP measures income *produced* by Canadians. This difference is the income produced by Canadians but paid to foreigners in the form of interest, dividends, royalties and other charges paid to foreign-owned firms operating in Canada.
3. J. K. Galbraith, *Money: Whence it Came and Where it Went* (Boston: Houghton Mifflin, 1975), p. 5.
4. Robert Cherry, et al., eds., *The Imperiled Economy, Book I: Macroeconomics from a Left Perspective* (New York: Union for Radical Political Economics, 1987). In this book, see particularly the chapters by David Gordon, Thomas Weisskopf and Samuel Bowles, "Power, Accumulation and Crisis: The Rise and Demise of the Postwar Social Structure of Accumulation"; David Kotz, "Radical Theories of Inflation"; and Part 5: "Macroeconomic Policy."
5. Barry Cozier, "Wage and Price Dynamics in Canada," Bank of Canada Research Department working paper, November 1991. Cozier notes in this paper that, contrary to the conventional explanation, most studies in Canada and the United States show the causation is from price increases to wage increases, not the other way round as is commonly assumed. Work that I did for the B.C. Federation of Labour in the 1960s indicated that prices led wages by a period that averaged about six months.
6. Gavan Butler, "Fiscal Crisis of the State," *Encyclopaedia of Political Economy* (London: Routledge, 1999), p. 354.
7. For a discussion of the early debate in the Canadian context, see Cy Gonick, *The Great Economic Debate* (Toronto: Lorimer, 1987), chs. 4–11.
8. See Ruben Bellan, *The Unnecessary Evil* (Toronto: McClelland and Stewart, 1986).

9. The winner of the Nobel Memorial Prize in Economics in 1996, the late William Vickery, argued strongly that the problem was not that government deficits were too large, but rather that they were *too small*. See his paper "Fifteen Fatal Fallacies of Financial Fundamentalism" which can be found at http://www.columbia.edu/dlc/wp/econ/vickrey.html , July 25, 2001.

10. Jim Stanford, *Paper Boom* (Toronto: Canadian Centre for Policy Alternatives and James Lorimer, 1999), p. 190.

Chapter 10

The International Sector and Globalism

The Basis of International Trade

There is no fundamental difference in the rationale for international trade (trade between say Canada and France) and intra-national trade (between say Manitoba and Nova Scotia). Because of differences in climate, resource endowment, availability and quality of labour, earlier establishment of facilities, government subsidies or one or other of many possible reasons, goods and services can be offered on the market relatively cheaper by some countries, regions or locales than by others. Consumers, businesses and governments who wish only to minimize prices paid will buy in the cheapest market, that is, they will import when foreign commodities are cheaper.

Freer trade between countries has obvious benefits. If there are no barriers to trade, in theory each country can produce and export what it does best and therefore has the least cost to produce and import what it does poorest, which it costs most to produce. This is readily apparent in the case of natural resources such as oil, or climate-dependent products such as bananas. Countries without oil must import it from those that have it. Countries with cold climates must either import bananas or, at prohibitive cost, raise them in greenhouses or go without. For countries to import oil or bananas, of course, they must either export equivalent values of goods or services or else borrow and go increasingly in debt.

The advantages are less obvious when Canada imports computers from the United States and exports communications switching equipment. The reason is that the U.S. has a cost advantage in producing computers, whereas Canada has a similar cost advantage in communications equipment. Reasons for these cost advantages include such factors as specialization, technological head start, size of market, economies of scale, pools of cheap or specialized labour, access to specific technologies, research and development, capital and, in some cases, sheer chance.

While the benefits of trade may seem obvious, governments have intervened with barriers and/or subsidies to trade. The most common form of barrier are **tariffs and customs duties**. These taxes on imports favour domestic production by raising the prices of imports relative to home-produced goods. Much less common are export tariffs, usually designed to make it more expensive to export an unprocessed natural resource out of the country rather than further process it at home. The second major form of restriction on trade includes a whole variety of quotas and **non-tariff barriers**. Some of these involve legitimate health, environmental or cultural concerns, such as border inspections on food products to ensure they meet Canadian standards on pesticide residues, bacteria content or similar sanitary or health standards. Quotas on eggs and milk, for example, have been used in the past to protect Canada's supply-management marketing system for dairy and poultry products from foreign competition. Time-consuming delays or inspection fees at border crossings are sometimes designed deliberately to increase the cost of imports rather than to maintain any legitimate product standards. Some non-tariff barriers include outright bans on imports to maintain some social, economic or cultural goal. An example would be Canada's ban on the import of handguns.

A number of political and economic reasons can be advanced for such intervention, some of which have widespread acceptance even among the most neoliberal of economists. Historically, one of the most important has been to ensure a level of military, political or economic self-sufficiency to defend the political-economic sovereignty of a country. A second reason that is often advanced is to protect **infant industries**, those industries that need time to develop markets, technology, production experience or a sufficient capital base before they become internationally competitive.

A further type of protection that gets general approval from most economists is anti-dumping duties. **Dumping** is the practice of selling products in excess of domestic demand in foreign markets at prices below the cost of production. It is analogous to the clothing retailer left with a stock of unsold inventory at the end of a season who "dumps" it in a sale at "below wholesale prices." When merchandise is sold on the domestic market at below cost in order to drive a competitor from business, this is known as **predatory pricing**, and is illegal. When it is done internationally it is deemed to be dumping. In such a case countries can institute an **anti-dumping duty**—a tax that raises the price of the imported product to what it would have been if it were not being dumped. The same argument has been applied to products that are subsidized, or alleged to be subsidized, by the exporting country, thereby undercutting the prices of competing firms in the importing country.

There are other reasons for advocating tariffs and non-tariff barriers that generally elicit much less support, if not outright opposition, from most orthodox economists. One is the argument for protecting **keystone industries**, those industries that have high spinoff effects for other industries or have important cultural or economic significance such as banking, transportation and communications, publishing and the visual and performing arts. It is especially important to protect primary agriculture where institutions such as the family farm form the basic social structure of rural society. Unfortunately, most economists pay little attention to the social aspects of production and therefore tend to dismiss these arguments for protection.

Labour has tended to support protectionist policies on the grounds that they prevent competition from low-wage, Third World countries or from countries which utilize exploited, underpaid, "sweatshop," child—and even slave or prison—labour. Workers in North America are right to be afraid of such competition since it is the low labour cost in these developing countries that allows them to be competitive. Any attempt by North American labour to compete with this low-wage labour results in a "race to the bottom" with North American standards necessarily falling to Third World levels unless, for other reasons,

North American workers' productivity is significantly higher than that in the developing world. Increasingly that is not the case.

Nevertheless, low wages on their own are not sufficient reason to protect Canada or the United States against imports from developing countries. To do so is to deny workers in the Third World the right to a job and to wages that are better than no wages at all. If real economic development does take place, those wages will ultimately rise as did North American wages over the last century. It also means that North American consumers pay more than they need to for imported or import-competing goods, thereby lowering the standard of living of our own citizens. The argument has weight only if the low wages are maintained by coercion and if labour rights are denied by oppressive governments or by the economic and political power of multinational corporations. It would be more appropriate to ban imports from countries whose labour and human rights policies have been criticized as abusive by the International Labour Organization and the United Nations.

The economic and welfare arguments for "free trade" depend on some very important assumptions that are not

> ## 10.1 The Top 200: The Rise of Corporate Global Power
>
> Of the 100 largest economies in the world, 51 are corporations; only 49 are countries (based on a comparison of corporate sales and country GDPs)....
> General Motors is the 23rd largest economy in the world—larger than Denmark—and DaimlerChrysler is bigger than Poland.
>
> The Top 200 corporations' sales are growing at a faster rate than overall global economic activity. Between 1983 and 1999, their combined sales grew from the equivalent of 25% to 27.5% of World GDP.
>
> The Top 200 corporations' sales in 1999—$30,211,993,000,000—surpassed the combined economies of all countries minus the biggest 10, and amounted to 18 times the combined annual income of the 1.2 billion people (24% of total world population) living in "severe" poverty—on less than $1 a day.
>
> While the sales of the Top 200 are the equivalent of 27.5% of world economic activity they employ only 0.78% of the world's workforce. Of the U.S. corporations on the Top 200 list, 44% did not pay the full standard 35% federal corporate tax rate during the period 1996–1998. Seven of the firms (General Motors, Texaco, Chevron, PepsiCo, Enron, WorldCom, and McKesson) actually paid less than zero in federal income taxes in 1998, because they received rebates.
>
> –Sarah Anderson and John Cavanagh, "The Top 200: Key Findings," CCPA Monitor, March 2001

realized in the real world. The first assumption is that there is full employment in all nations. This is clearly not the case. A second is that labour and resources that become unemployed when imports replace domestic products can be transferred without cost to the production of export goods. From a political economy perspective this is simply not credible.

Further, there must be perfect competition among firms in the various countries so that market prices reflect accurately the relative costs of production, that is, there must be many, many small firms producing essentially identical products. In reality, international trade is dominated by large multinational corporations. In economic terms, these corporations are more powerful than many of the smaller countries in the world, including some highly developed countries. Moreover, at least 40 percent (probably closer to 60 percent for Canada) of what is called international trade never even sees a market but is composed simply of transfers of product within individual multinationals. When

10.2 In Defence of "The Beaver"

Canadians are often confused by the fact that the Canadian dollar is not equal in value to the American dollar. In recent years the Canadian dollar has a value of a little under two-thirds of its American counterpart. After the Second World War, the Canadian dollar was actually worth more than the U.S. dollar. Should not a dollar be a dollar and have the same value? The answer is an emphatic NO.

The fact is that Canada's money should never have been called the dollar. Originally, of course, it wasn't. In the colonial period we utilized both the British pound and the French livre and for a while we had a Canadian pound with a different value from its British counterpart. During the fur trade era, the Aboriginal peoples traded with the Hudson's Bay Company using a monetary unit called the *Made Beaver*—with a value of one prepared beaver skin.

When Canada adopted its own money in the nineteenth century it should have adopted the Beaver as its monetary unit instead of the dollar. This would not only have prevented the confusion that now prevails but would have meant that the money had some relationship with our economic history.

Why did we adopt the dollar instead? Who knows, but we borrowed the name from the Americans. And where did they get it? From the Spanish. What possible connection does the Canadian economy have to the Spanish economy?

Let's bring back the Beaver!

viewed from a political economy perspective, the assumption of perfect competition that underlies the free trade ideology appears absurd.

Therefore, most of the reasons advanced for protection can be defended to some extent. It should be recognized that there may be an economic cost to these restrictions in the form of higher consumer prices, lower quality products and lower real incomes in the short run.

One additional reason why governments intervene in international trade is that this may be the only way they can exert control over a significant sector of the aggregate supply and demand of the economy. In Canada's case, exports and imports each comprise approximately one-third of the total output of the economy. In total, therefore, our external trade accounts for close to two-thirds of our GDP. Keynesian demand-management policies can have little or no effect on the demand for exports nor on the cost prices of imports. Governments, therefore, get blamed for unemployment and inflation over which they may have little or no control unless they influence trade in some fashion.

There are other complications to international trade. International boundaries are quite different from internal geographical divisions in three significant ways. For one, there exist legal barriers to trade between most countries, such as tariffs, quotas and non-tariff barriers (even though these barriers have been declining with the advent of the World Trade Organization and various regional trade agreements).

A second difference between international and internal trade is that the legal, economic, political and tax systems may differ significantly between the two trading countries. This, of course, can also be true in a federal country like Canada.[1] In terms of the legal system, Quebec even has a separate and distinct system of civil law. However, differences within countries, even decentralized federal ones like Canada, are likely to be considerably less than between countries.

Finally, the monetary system and currency in the importing country is different from that of the exporting country. As a result it is necessary to exchange (buy or sell) money in the process of buying or selling commodities. Trade becomes a function not only of the domestic price of the commodities being traded but also of the relative prices of the two monies. Canadian visitors to the United States are well aware that though we call both currencies "dollars," when we exchange Canadian dollars for U.S. dollars, they do not have the same value.

Generally speaking, if the international value of Canada's dollar goes down (depreciates), the prices of Canada's exports go down on international markets, thereby improving Canada's competitive position. If the value of Canada's dollar rises (appreciates), the prices of Canada's exports go up and Canada's competitive position deteriorates. The opposite is true of imports. As Canada's dollar rises, imports become cheaper; as it falls, imports become more expensive. If the value of the Canadian dollar falls, we should sell more exports and purchase fewer imports, thereby increasing domestic aggregate demand and employment. Of course, the improvement in our domestic demand and employment comes at the expense of our trading partners.

A second major complication of the international sector is that commodity trade is not the only economic flow across international boundaries. Money also flows. These flows in money are called **international capital flows**. There are three major streams in this flow.

The first consists of long-term capital flows to finance long-term investment. This can be either in owned real capital (**direct investment**), such as Wal-Mart buying or building stores in Canada; or in loans such as bonds, debentures or minority ownership of stocks (**portfolio investment**), when U.S. banks buy Ontario Government bonds.

The second is short-term capital flows to take advantage of higher interest rates in the receiving country.

The third, and most problematic of money flows between countries, is short-term capital speculation—or to put it more bluntly, gambling on an anticipated change in exchange rates. If you are a speculator you want to hold the money that is rising in international value, not the currency that is falling. The problem is that if all the speculators *think* that the loonie is going to fall in value relative to the American dollar, then they will all go and sell loonies to buy dollars. But if there are enough speculators selling loonies and buying dollars, the value of the loonie will fall and that of the dollar will rise. The value of the Canadian dollar is driven down, not by something that happened in the economy, but by the action of speculators, who thought the dollar would fall. These capital flows help determine the exchange rate independent of trade flows and add a further complication to regulating aggregate demand.

10.3 Keynes on Speculation

It is rare, one is told, for an American to invest, as many Englishmen still do, "for income"; and he will not readily purchase an investment except in the hope of capital appreciation. This is only another way of saying that, when he purchases an investment, the American is attaching his hopes, not so much to its prospective yield, as to a favourable change in the conventional basis of valuation, i.e., that he is, in the above sense, a speculator. Speculators may do no harm as bubbles on a steady stream of enterprise. But the position is serious when enterprise becomes the bubble on a whirlpool of speculation. When the capital development of a country becomes a by-product of the activities of a casino, the job is likely to be ill-done.

–J.M. Keynes, The General Theory of Employment, Interest and Money (London: Macmillan, 1961 (c. 1936)), p. 159

Multinational Corporations and the International Division of Labour

A great deal of international trade is not really trade at all. It involves administrative transfer as one division of a multinational corporation operating in one country is charged costs for goods that it receives from a different division of the corporation operating in a different country. These transfers amount to over one-half of Canada's foreign trade. The prices at which this "trade" takes place are not market prices at all but administrative transfer prices. The basis of exchange within multinational corporations may have little to do with economic efficiency between countries. Instead it is likely to have much more to do with where taxes can be minimized or government subsidies maximized, where environmental protection laws are most lax or non-existent, or where the companies can take advantage of repressive, dictatorial regimes to suppress labour and lower wages.

Thus the multinational corporations have contributed heavily to the emerging pattern of the **international division of labour**. High technology production and the research and development phase of production are concentrated in the developed countries, near the head offices of the multinationals. When the product, its production technology and its market have been fully developed, production is frequently transferred to subsidiaries in low-wage, Third World countries. Factories in these countries, often referred to as export platforms, then manufacture and assemble commodities for export back to the home market. The result is a transfer of jobs, which traditionally formed part of the lower tier of the primary labour market, from the developed countries to the Third World.

Some economists claim that this effect has resulted in a "disappearing middle class" in developed countries. They argue that the majority of new jobs created in the North American economy over the last decade or so have been in the lower wage service sector, resulting in a "tilt to the secondary labour market" in the composition of jobs.[2] In Canada, job creation since the recession of 1981–82 has been primarily at the lowest wage levels and at the top, with a net reduction in the middle ranks.[3] Also, evidence of rising

---

10.4 Multinational Corporations

Definition: Multinational Corporations (sometimes called "multinational enterprises" or "transnationals") are corporations with operations or branches in two or more countries. They may be vertically integrated (branches in one country which produce inputs for other branches, such as American newspapers which have a Canadian newsprint mill subsidiary); horizontally integrated (branches in different countries producing similar products, such as the automobile companies); conglomerates (branches in different countries producing different, unrelated products such as processed food products in one country, luggage in another); or some combination of all three.

Nationality: The nationality of multinationals is generally regarded as the country in which the head office is located, though this can often be misleading where ownership and control is located in another country (e.g., Inco has head offices in Canada but control resides in the U.S., where the majority of shares are owned).

Purposes: The three major goals of multinational expansion are:

1. Strategic expansion (competition) into a new, foreign, market to avoid tariffs and other non-tariff barriers, to take advantage of nationalist buying habits, or to gain any advantage from local knowledge or operating in the local economy;
2. Lowering production costs by establishing production or assembly operations in countries where wages are low (low wage "export platforms"); and
3. Guaranteeing access to and control of sources of raw materials.

inequality in the labour market in Canada and the United States is plentiful.

This movement of economic opportunity from the developed to less developed might be beneficial if it resulted in permanent economic development in the Third World. However, the main attraction of these countries is the low wages paid to workers. The economic returns of the investment in these countries accrue only to the multinationals or to a local ruling class of employers. These local employers are not entrepreneurs in their own right but live off their proceeds as agents for the multinationals exploiting local sweatshop labour. The economic returns that are not paid back to the multinationals are usually not reinvested in Third World development. Instead they find their way to tax havens (such as the Bahamas, the Netherlands Antilles, or the Cayman Islands), to numbered accounts in Switzerland or Liechtenstein, or are used to purchase real estate in the United States.

Trade in Natural Resources

The developed world and the multinationals also have an interest in exploiting the resources of the less developed countries. We have already seen how the multinationals attempt to reduce wages and taxes by locating production in the Third World or moving money into tax havens. They can also maximize profits by reducing the cost of raw materials. This often means developing the raw material supplies within the multinational corporate structure (vertical integration) and playing off one capital-poor country against another in order to procure the most favourable tax and regulatory treatment. The result tends to be that the prices paid by the poor country for capital

10.5 Transfer Pricing

Transfer prices are the prices at which an enterprise transfers physical goods and intangible property or provides services to associated enterprises. Enterprises are said to be associated if one of them participates directly or indirectly in the management, control or capital of both enterprises (OECD 1995). There are two reasons why firms use transfer pricing. The first is to provide managers with the information and incentives necessary to achieve the most profitable (after tax) use of resources within the larger organization. The second reason is that it is necessary for reporting purposes to tax authorities. Policy issues arise because an enterprise may misreport transfer prices with the aim of reducing total taxation liabilities.... [because of] differences in tax and tariff rates between countries. In addition, enterprises may also misreport transfer prices to counter the impacts of investment and exchange rate controls.

–Malcolm Cook and Peter Cribbett, "Transfer Pricing," *Encyclopedia of Political Economy*, Philip O'Hara, ed. (Routledge: 1999), p. 1167

10.6 Nike Export Platforms

The Truth Behind the Nike Label

You shell out $50 for a Nike shirt or $150 for Nike shoes. But Nike never tells you that the young woman who made that shirt or shoes did not earn enough to support herself and her children.

A recent survey of 3,500 Nike workers in Indonesia found that most workers (mainly women) do not earn enough to support their families. And some Nike workers do not even earn enough to support themselves.

Workers [are] forced to work around the clock. The survey found that Nike workers in Indonesia are forced to work as many as 72 hours a week. The Nike code of conduct says that working hours must be limited to 60 hours per week. Through its TV commercial, Nike encourages women to speak up for equal pay but ... when Nike workers in the Dominican Republic speak up for their right to a union, they are fired ... in Thailand ... when Nike workers held a sitdown strike to demand fair pay, Nike pulled the work from their factory.

–Canadian Labour Congress, http://www.clc-ctc.ca/ publications/mag_archive/sweatshop_alert_e.pdf

10.7 Debunking the Myth that Free Trade Benefits the World's Poor

(The view that) misguided (globalization) protesters are ... unwittingly torpedoing the interests of the poorest of the poor ... has been (proclaimed) by advocates of free trade and the WTO....The historical evidence suggests the opposite.

A look at the industrialized countries (Canada, the U.S., the U.K. and other European nations) shows that the path to riches came not from the unilateral opening of borders, but from closing borders in order to protect emerging industries from bigger rivals. Only when these industries became strong did the appetite for free trade gain strength.

The experiment of imposing free trade via the IMF and World Bank in the past two decades, on the other hand, has been an unmitigated disaster for regions like Africa and Latin America. Simply put, no country has gotten rich by leaving the process of development to market forces alone....

Of course, opening up borders may provide benefits to certain segments of the population of a poor country. In every poor country, there is always some 5–10 percent who enjoy very high standards of living.

—CCPA Monitor, May 2000

10.8 Growing Inequality

Here are some key results from a study on Canadian income inequality for the years 1973–1996.

The middle fifth of working families bear out the story of the average person and family told above. Overall, their incomes rose somewhat from 1973 to 1984 and 1984 to 1990, but fell in the 1990s. In 1996, real incomes were only slightly higher than in 1984.

The bottom fifth of working families experienced a major decline in income from 1973 to 1984, some recovery from 1984 to 1990, and then a huge income decline in the 1990s....

The story for the top 20% of families is different again. Their market incomes rose by about one-quarter from 1973 to 1990 However, even this top group did not fare well in the 1990s. Only the very top 10% experienced a market income gain in the 1990s, and this was just 2% (1990-1996)....

–Armine Yalnizyan, The Growing Gap (Centre for Social Justice, 1998), as reported in Andrew Jackson and David Robinson, Falling Behind: The State of Working Canada, 2000 (Ottawa: CCPA, 2000), pp. 27–29

and manufactured commodities from the developed world rise compared with the prices paid by the developed world for the raw materials of the poorer countries. In the language of economics, the **terms of trade** turn against the lesser-developed countries, since they then have to produce more raw materials to get the same amount of manufactured goods.

Multinationals and the Canadian Economy

Multinationalization creates benefits and costs to both the source and host countries.[4] Canada historically has received major benefits from the inflow of foreign capital, particularly in the period before the First World War, when Britain provided most of the investment capital to finance the building of our three transnational railways. Since then, however, the net gain becomes more debatable. Foreign investment is supposed to have provided Canada with increased investment capital, access to advanced technology, guaranteed markets for raw material exports, access to international leverage and expertise in financing, management and marketing. It is easy to overestimate these benefits and even easier to underestimate their costs. Imports of capital must be paid for in the form of interest and dividends. These dividends are paid to foreigners for investment actually provided by Canadian savings, from retained earnings (undistributed profits) of Canadian subsidiaries and from bank loans provided by Canadian banks. In recent years, in excess of 80 percent of all "foreign investment" in Canada has been financed from Canadian sources, while payments of interest and dividends to foreigners considerably exceeded any inflow of foreign funds. Canada's net deficit in 2000 for payments on foreign investment amounted to $27.1 billion. In short, there has been a net outflow of capital as a result of multinationals in Canada.

Multinational operations also drain money from the Canadian economy through business services and payments for management, research and development, and technology. In 2000, Canada had a deficit (primarily with the United States) in payments for royalties and licences of $2.8 billion and in management services of $1.3 billion. This reflects multinational preference to conducting most research and development near their head offices. Another consequence of this is that Canada has the worst record of expenditure on research and development (R&D) of any of the main Western industrial countries, spending only a half or a third of the levels in the United States, Japan, West Germany or Sweden.

The costs of access to foreign management, finance and marketing go beyond the fees charged by multinational corporations. The increasing burden of service costs on Canada's balance of trade is indicated in Table 10.1. Furthermore, the high degree of multinational control of the Canadian economy significantly reduces Canada's sovereignty in economic policy, control over its own fiscal and monetary levers. This is because multinationals can use transfer pricing for management, technology, financial and other business services and for intra-firm movement of goods to avoid Canadian taxes, environmental, research and development and labour regulations and other undesired effects of Canadian domestic policies. This makes it difficult for Canada to have a system of taxes and social expenditures that is different from that in the United States where the head offices of the vast majority of multinational corporations operating in Canada are located. The Canada–United States Free Trade Agreement (FTA), the North American free Trade Agreement (NAFTA) and the proposed Free Trade Agreement of the Americas (FTAA) mean even less Canadian control over investment, ownership and trade.

> ## 10.9 The Terms of Trade and Multinationals
>
> As early as the 1950s, Raul Prebisch of the United Nations agency, the Economic Commission for Latin America, provided statistics showing the price of exports from Latin America were falling relative to the prices for manufactured goods imported from the United States and the developed world. Writing in the early 1970s, Barnett and Muller reported on the findings of Prebisch and his associates at the Commission.
>
> > The industrialized nations ... have used their technological and marketing superiority to obtain terms of trade which, not surprisingly, favor them at the expense of their weaker trading partners in the underdeveloped world. Thus over the past twenty five years ... because of the falling relative price of certain essential raw materials, the countries of the underdeveloped world have had to exchange an ever-increasing amount of such raw materials to get the finished goods and technological expertise they need. This steady worsening of the terms of trade between the rich countries and the poor is an important reason why the "gap" between them has continued to grow.
>
> –Richard Barnet and Ronald Muller, *Gobal Reach* (New York: Simon and Schuster, 1974), pp. 136–37

Hewers of Wood and Drawers of Water?

One highly touted advantage of Canada's ongoing economic integration with the United States has been the promise that it would guarantee access for Canadian natural resources to the U.S. market. That "guarantee" has proved elusive. When

Table 10.1: Balance of Trade in Services

| | (Million Dollars) | | |
	1961	1981	2001
Travel	-214	-1111	-1316
Transportation	-60	-440	-3686
Commercial Services	-517	-2277	-4039
Management	-72	-519	-1626
R & D	-40	-296	1839
Royalties, Patents			
& Trade Marks	-32	-655	3062
Finance & Insurance	*	-276	-1614
Government	-32	-507	659
Total	-771	-3414	-8382

* not available

Source: Statistics Canada, Canada's International Trade in Services (67-203) 2001

it suits their purposes, American politicians have not been afraid to adopt highly protectionist policies.[5] The most recent example of this has been the high tariffs imposed on Canadian softwood lumber. However, even to the extent that such a guarantee exists, it is a mixed blessing. Canada's exports to the American market are concentrated in crude, processed and fabricated natural resources. When we exclude the exchange of cars under the Canada–U.S. Auto Pact,[6] almost two thirds of our exports are basically raw or lightly processed resources. Since the mid-1970s, three-quarters of all Canadian exports were destined for the United States. By 2000, this figure reached over 85 percent. Even excluding automotive trade under the Auto Pact, two-thirds of Canada's exports went to the American market. Despite the inclusion of Mexico, NAFTA has not diminished in any way Canada's growing dependence on the American market or capital.

This dependence on raw material (or "staple") exports, which has long characterized the Canadian economy, has disturbing long-term implications for Canadian workers. Although the re-

10.10 Foreign Ownership and Control in Canada

Foreign control has increased slowly but steadily since 1994. However, who is contributing to this phenomenon? For the most part, it is the larger foreign controlled firms that are raising their share. However, these large foreign firms are only making significant contributions to the increasing foreign share in industries where the foreign share is already dominant, including chemical products and textiles, machinery and equipment and transportation equipment [where foreign control is greater than 50% of both assets and operating revenue]. Most other industries are dominated by large Canadian enterprises....

Looking at the percentage share of Canadian and foreign control within each of the three size groups [small enterprises with operating revenues less than $5 million, medium between $5 and $75 million, and large greater than $75 million] shows that in three other industries ... machinery and equipment, other financial intermediaries, and consumer goods and services industries, foreign enterprises control more than 50% of the assets of the largest firms.

–S. Taylor, *Canadian Economic Observer*, Statistics Canada, June 2001, pp. 3.9–3.10

Table 10.2: Exports by Major Commodity Group: 2001

Commodity Group	All Exports	Non-Auto Pact
	(Percentage)	
Agriculture and Fish	6.34	7.9
Energy	19.21	23.93
Forestry	8.88	11.06
Ores, Metals & other Materials	8.32	10.37
Chemicals	5.12	6.38
Automobiles & related	19.73	---
Total	67.61	59.65

Source: Statistics Canada, Canada's International Merchandise Trade (965-001) 2001

source industries (excluding agriculture) are relatively highly unionized and pay relatively good wages, the potential for job growth or even for the maintenance of existing job levels is bleak. First of all, Canada is reaching, or has surpassed, the limits of sustainable yields in its renewable resources such as forestry, fishing and trapping and, except in some limited areas, hydro power.

Second, accessible non-renewable resources are being exhausted leading to higher cost, less competitive supplies and higher domestic prices. This affects mining, petroleum and natural gas. It was the creation of a continental energy market through the trade agreements and the growth in American demand that "fuelled" the massive increase in natural gas and electricity prices in much of Canada in 2000–01.

Technological change is significantly shifting production to more capital intensive methods, thereby reducing the demand for labour. This has been very pronounced in mining and in logging. Between 1981 and 1987, absolute employment in the resource industries decreased by 4 percent, from 798,000 to 765,000. The decline was particularly pronounced in forestry (9 percent) and mining (10 percent). Given that the Canadian labour force grew 10 percent over the same period, the relative decline was even greater.

The Canada–United States Trade Agreement and the North American Free Trade Agreement

Despite their names, the 1989 Canada–U.S. Free Trade Agreement (FTA) and the 1994 North American Free Trade Agreement (NAFTA) and the Free Trade Agreement of the Americas (FTAA), which is currently under negotiation, are not really free trade treaties.[7] The FTA did provide for the removal of the remaining tariffs on trade between Canada and the United States over a period of ten years and for the elimination of some, mainly Canadian, non-tariff barriers. However, except for the tariff removals and new tribunal machinery for adjudicating disputes, it leaves trade between the two countries and American trade law relatively unchanged. NAFTA by and large just extended the major provisions of the FTA to Mexico.[8] The trade agreements actually extend considerably the protection provided to intellectual property (primarily patents and copyrights), largely for the benefit of American-based multinationals such as the pharmaceutical companies. Rather than being free trade agreements, these are primarily treaties guaranteeing the rights of international capital over the sovereignty rights of the individual nations. They give multinational corporations the ability to block or overturn legislation in most areas of economic development, social services, and environmental and labour standards.

These agreements can more accurately be described as **economic integration treaties** designed to integrate the Canadian, American and Mexican economies into a single continental economy. The proposed FTAA would extend the scope to an integrated hemispheric economy, doing this in a great number of ways. Among the most important are:

1. Creating a continental energy, water and natural resource market guaranteeing the United States privileged access to Canadian and Mexican resources.

2. Integrating the Canadian banking system and capital markets with those of the United States by granting U.S. banks national status (giving them the same status as domestic banks) in Canada, restricting Canada's right to control the inflow of U.S. capital and U.S. takeovers of Canadian firms and resources, and granting all American and Mexican firms national status and the right of operation in Canada. Foreign multinational firms not only have the right to invest in Canada but on doing so they become, in effect, "citizens" of Canada.

3. Granting U.S. firms guaranteed access to Canadian markets for services such as engineering and accounting and, once Canada commercializes its education and health services, also the education and health sectors.

4. Restricting Canadian sover-

10.11 Trade Agreements

There are a number of different types of trade agreements. The largest is the World Trade Organization (WTO), the successor to the General Agreement on Tariffs and Trade (GATT). GATT came out of the Bretton Woods negotiations though it was not signed until 1947. It has been much in the news lately due to the demonstrations of those opposed to the way in which it expands global capitalism both geographically and industrially and extends coverage over services and intellectual property.

The second tier of trade agreements are are restricted to certain regions of the world. In North America the most important, but by no means the first, are the Canada–United States Free Trade Agreement (FTA) and the North American Free Trade Agreement (NAFTA), which, in effect, extended the FTA to include Mexico. Under negotiation is the extension of NAFTA to the whole of North America and South America (excluding Cuba) in the form of the Free Trade Agreement of the Americas (FTAA).

There has been less opposition in most European countries to that region's free trade agreement, the European Union (EU). It is an extension of the European Common Market (ECM) that was established shortly after the Second World War. It originally involved just six countries, but has evolved into an expanded and increasingly more integrated European economy. The EU now has 15 member countries and a waiting list of a number of ex-communistic countries of central Europe which have applied for membership. The EU goes much farther than NAFTA in integrating the economies of the region. It provides for free movement of labour as well as goods and services, common agricultural and social policies and, with the creation of the European Monetary Union (which includes most, but not all of the EU members) a common monetary unit and monetary policy.

Many other local and regional free trade agreements exist in various regions of the world, in South America, Australasia, Asia Pacific, and Western, Central and Eastern Europe though none are as big or as comprehensive, as the EU and NAFTA. (For a description of many of the trade agreements and international trade and finance institutions, see the glossary at the end of this chapter)

eignty over large areas of internal economic policy. For example, economic development programs such as regional subsidies, government procurement preferences, employment, research and development or procurement conditions on multinational investment are restricted or prohibited under the agreements.

5. Restricting the use of the public sector and state aid to promote economic development in Canada.

6. Allowing foreign firms to sue national governments for any restriction on the profit-making potential of the firm through legislation passed by any level of government—this is contained in chapter 11 of NAFTA.

Most of these provisions are reciprocal between all three countries. However, the U.S.'s much more protective trade legislation was permitted to remain in place despite the agreements. This law, which requires the government to protect industries injured by trade, allows the U.S. to invoke countervailing duties against what the U.S. considers to be "unfair subsidies." The multinational grain companies are using this law in an effort to have the Canadian Wheat Board (CWB) disbanded. They claim public ownership of the CWB is an unfair subsidy, even though repeated studies, the most recent by the U.S. government trade office in 2001, have shown that no subsidies are involved. Additionally, the sheer size and power of the American economy distorts the impact of the agreements, allowing the U.S. to contravene the agreements (and the WTO) when it is politically expedient for it to do so.

The most notorious case involves Canada's export of softwood lumber to the United States, where the largest portion of lumber is produced from timber harvested on privately owned land. Lumber companies must purchase their supplies of raw logs by bidding on an open market. Because much of the private and public U.S. land has been deforested and the remaining public forests are protected from logging to preserve parks and threatened wildlife, the price of raw logs has been bid up to the considerable profit of the private owners of forest lands. Simply, the demand has become greater than the supply resulting in rising prices.

In contrast, most forest land in Canada has remained publicly owned, or as it is officially designated, "Crown land." Lumber firms bid for, and purchase, the right to log specified areas of provincially owned Crown land. In exchange for managing the resource (reforestation) and payment of a royalty on the timber extracted, the forestry companies receive a timber licence. The cost of raw timber

---

10.12 Trade Pacts—A Constitution for Capital

Critics of pacts such as NAFTA are correct when they say that the real point of these agreements is to create rules that will allow unelected bureaucrats to overrule the laws of democratically elected governments.

But governments (and Canada's Liberal regime is an exemplar here) have been willing participants in their own hobbling. Why? Because international agreements give elected governments an excuse not to do things that they didn't want to do in the first place.

When asked why it doesn't protect water, or reform the patent laws to reduce skyrocketing pharmaceutical costs, Ottawa can throw up its hands, point to NAFTA, and say it has no choice.

Yet this does not mean that governments are becoming less active. In fact, they are becoming increasingly active—on the side of capital.

–Tomas Walkom, "'Free trade' pacts are really all about making gov'ts subservient to business," *CCPA Monitor*, July/August 2001. [Tom Walkom writes a weekly column for *The Toronto Star*, where a longer version of this article first appeared.]

10.13 Chapter 11 and the Challenge to Democracy

Chapter 11 is the section of NAFTA that allows multinational corporations to sue governments before highly secretive private arbitration panels, if the corporation's "property assets, including the intangible property of expected profits, are damaged by laws or regulations of virtually any kind."

> The most disturbing aspect of Chapter 11 [is] ... its expansive new definition of property rights ... with a potential to override established rights in domestic law. NAFTA's new investor protections actually mimic a radical revision of constitutional law that the American right has been aggressively pushing for years—redefining public regulation as a government "taking" of private property that requires compensation to the owners, just as when government takes private land for a highway or park it has to pay its fair value. Because any new regulation is bound to have some economic impact on private assets, this doctrine is a formula to shrink the reach of modern government and cripple the regulatory state—undermining long-established protections for social welfare and economic justice, environmental values and individual rights. Right-wing advocates frankly state that objective—restoring the primacy of property against society's broader claims.

–William Greider, "The Right and U.S. Trade Law: Invalidating the 20th Century," *The Nation*, October 15, 2001, http://thenation.com

under the Canadian system is less than in the United States primarily because the supply of timber is much greater relative to demand than it is in the U.S. In other words, Canada has a cost advantage due to the relative abundance of its resource base, which has allowed Canada to export large, and increasing, amounts of softwood lumber to the U.S. Because American lumber producers have difficulty competing with Canadian imports they therefore demanded a tariff be placed on imports of Canadian lumber.

The American lumber interests' case for a countervailing duty on lumber was that Canada was "subsidizing" timber production because the forest land was publicly owned and not privately owned as in the United States. Numerous investigations (including the most recent finding of the WTO) have shown that there is no subsidy involved. Despite these findings, U.S. lumber interests pressured the U.S. government into requiring Canada to impose an export duty on Canadian lumber. As a result, Canadian lumber is more expensive in the United States, reducing the income of Canadian lumber companies. Not only is this counter to all the trade agreements and to the WTO rules, but U.S. lumber interests are demanding even greater tariff protection from Canadian competition.

The trade aspects of these treaties and of the WTO are less important than are their investment, service and intellectual property rights provisions. These provisions extend the protection offered to intellectual property, including everything from Disney's "ownership" of Winnie the Pooh's image to Upjohn's patents on anti-AIDS drugs. They provide that health and education services, once opened to "for profit" multinational corporations, may not be returned to universal, "not for profit," public programs without payment of prohibitively large fees to compensate foreign owners for profits *in perpetuity* that they would have received from continued delivery of the service. They provide for similar payments to foreign firms to compensate for any losses or lost profits from new or existing environmental regulations that any company can convince a (pro-free trade) panel have not been proven necessary to correct a proven problem. Under this approach, if there is uncertainty about whether an industrial product might damage the environment, the government cannot regulate. This completely negates the precautionary principle that is the fundamental principle underlying protection of the environment. The agreements restrict governments from public investing in economic development where that investment competes with multinational enterprises. Indeed, they are so comprehensive in restricting what democratically elected governments can do to promote the economic and social welfare of their citizens that it is not an exaggeration to say that they threaten the very foundations of democratic government.[9]

The primary effects of the trade agreements and of the World Trade Organization (WTO) have been threefold. First has been the expansion of trade between the signatories but without benefit and at some cost to workers. Indeed, there is substantial evidence of "the race to the bottom" that labour and critics of the trade agreements had predicted. NAFTA has been used extensively, at least in the United States, to destroy or disarm unions. Second, the new trade rules have been used widely to overturn laws and regulations protecting the environment. Third, these agreements have had the effect of undermining the public sector and generally promoting economic deregulation. The rulings and decisions of a number of Canadian institutions promoting economic development and regulating resource exploitation have been challenged and overturned. Furthermore, they threaten a number of popular Canadian cultural and social programs, including Medicare and public education.

> ### 10.14 Softwood Lumber: "America's been Bushwhacked"
>
> The following is from a Globe and Mail editorial on the US government's decision to impose a 19.3-per-cent countervailing duty on nearly all Canadian softwood lumber imports, which account for approximately 35 per cent of U.S. softwood lumber consumption.
>
> Even ignoring the possibility of retaliation by Canada, the economic consequences of the Department of Commerce's move to reduce foreign competition for domestic softwood lumber producers are substantial. If the preliminary decision to impose this tariff stands, we estimate the following effects:
>
> * Softwood lumber prices in the U.S. will increase by between 6.9 percent and 8.7 percent;
> * New home construction costs will rise on average by $420 to $850;
> * This will cost American consumers $875 million to $1.35 billion annually;
> * The increased lumber prices will depress housing construction (housing starts) by 53,000 to 106,000 units;
> * U.S. gross domestic product will fall by 0.13 to 0.26 percent.
>
> ...If the 19.3 percent duty had been applied on April 1 of this year, U.S. GDP growth in the second quarter would have been 0.45 to 0.57 percent, rather than the 0.7 percent growth we did experience.
>
> –David Leband and Daowei Zhang, "America's been Bushwhacked, "Globe and Mail, August 18, 2001

The International Debt Crisis

During the 1970s a number of factors combined to create enormous pools of available credit in the financial institutions of North America, Europe and Japan.[10] One was the rise in commodity prices, particularly, but not exclusively, the price of oil. A second was the growth of multinational business, including large international financial institutions. A third was the imbalance in economic power between the developed and the underdeveloped world combined with the

10.15 NAFTA and Unions: The Effects of Plant Closing or Threat of Plant Closing on the Right of Workers to Organize

After Sprint Corporation closed its Hispanic marketing division in California in 1994 just days before a scheduled union representation vote, the Mexican Telephone Workers Union filed a complaint on behalf of the Communication Workers of America (CWA), under the provisions of the NAFTA labour side agreement. Kate Brofenbrenner of Cornell University's School of Industrial and Labor relations was asked to investigate the impact of NAFTA on union representation and bargaining rights covering the period 1993 through 1995. She found the following after collecting data on over 500 union organizing campaigns and 100 first contract negotiations.

- When faced with a union organizing drive the majority of private sector employers threatened to shut down operations and move them to Mexico. If the drive succeed many employers lived up to the threat.
- Rather than negotiate a first contract, 18 percent of employers threatened to close the plant, and 12 percent actually closed operations.
- Where the employer threatened to close the plant, workers were far less willing to vote for a union.
- The threats to close the plant were usually coupled with other bullying tactics, including firing workers, keeping them under electronic surveillance and changes in wages and benefits.

The study concluded that NAFTA had created a climate that has emboldened employers to more aggressively threaten to close, or actually close their plants to avoid unionization.

–Kate Bronfenbrenner, "The Effects of Plant Closing or Threat of Plant Closing on the Right of Workers to Oraganize" Report to the Labor Secretariat of the North American Commission for Labor Cooperation, 1997 [Full Report can be viewed on http://www.ilr.cornell.edu]

stagnation of the Western industrial economies. The banks, including the major Canadian ones, aggressively sought profitable outlets for these funds, preferably outside North America. They found willing borrowers not only in the Third World but also among some of the smaller countries of Eastern Europe including Poland, Hungary, Romania and Yugoslavia.

Resource-rich Third World countries borrowed heavily on the strength of their resources in an attempt to accelerate development, and resource-poor Third World countries borrowed to stave off starvation. The Eastern European countries borrowed to attempt to improve flagging growth and with the expectation of producing commodities that could be sold to Western markets.

The average real interest rate—the interest rate minus the inflation rate—in the United States was –0.4 percent over the decade of the seventies. Then international monetarism raised its ugly head. Interest rates were driven up and economic growth slowed in the developed world. Demand for Third World and Eastern European exports fell and protectionism re-emerged, particularly in the United States and the European Economic Community (now the European Union). Resource prices tumbled, Third World exports stagnated and interest rates on loans escalated, leaving the developing countries unable to pay the interest—never mind the principal—on the debts. Banks in North America and Europe were forced to loan these countries money just to pay back the interest due. Loans thus got bigger and bigger with little prospect of repayment (a process that has become known as "Brazil-ing" a loan after the country that pioneered the process). This, of course, created a debt crisis for the Third and Second (Communist) worlds and was instrumental in the collapse of the economies of Eastern Europe and the disintegration of the Soviet Union.

One result has been the resurgence of hyper-inflation in a number of countries, including Argentina and some of the former Communist countries. In effect, these countries had to resort to printing money to meet debt obligations, thereby inflating the money supply beyond control. A similar debt problem and resort to printing money was the cause of the post-First World War inflation in Germany that was instrumental in the decline of democracy and the rise of fascism in that country.

But the debt crisis not only threatened the debtor countries. There was also a debt crisis in North America. It was a crisis for the lender banks because these "bad" loans threatened the stability of the financial systems in the developed economies of North American and Europe. The North American banks responded in two ways. One was to cut their losses and sell title to the loans for whatever they could get. Indeed a market in high-risk loans, particularly to South America, developed. Banks sold their bonds to other buyers, sometimes to what are

---

10.16 What Do Dolphins, Sea Turtles and Canadian Children have in Common?

Very simply, they are all endangered because of recent "free trade" agreements, in particular NAFTA and the WTO. All three involved appeals to the WTO or NAFTA by countries or corporations against environmental regulations in the United States or Canada that had the effect of restricting trade. In all three cases, trade triumphed over the environment. In the 1990s the Canadian government banned the importation of MMT, a manganese-based fuel additive. The product is used to improve gasoline performance, but is linked to injury to the human nervous system, and is a particular threat to children. In response the U.S. multinational, Ethyl Corporation

> ...immediately filed a claim under NAFTA for $350 million in damages for lost profits. The Canadian Liberal government, in what must be one of the most gutless moves in recent history, gave in and agreed to rescind the MMT ban, pay Ethyl in excess of $19 million, and take the unprecedented step of issuing a statement that MMT was neither an environmental nor a health risk.
>
> Thus, the first case to invoke the powerful enforcement rules of NAFTA resulted in a stunning victory for a U.S.–based transnational corporation unhappy with Canadian environmental regulation.

–Steven Shrybman, *The World Trade Organization* (Ottawa: CCPA and Lorimer, 1999), pp. 132–133 [The Dolphin and Sea Turtle cases are also recounted in Steven Shrybman, *The World Trade Organization*, pp. 22–24 and pp. 66–68.]

Indeed, Canada's capitulation sent a message to other U.S.–based corporations who have since challenged other Canadian environmental laws and regulations.

---

know as "vulture buyers," sometimes back to the governments that had issued the bonds, for as little as 24 percent of their value. Why would anyone wish to buy such risky loans? First, some buyers (the "vultures") were speculating on what they thought the embattled countries would be able and willing to pay off. More importantly, some companies in these debt-ridden countries, including the multinationals, which had access to "hard currency" (such as the American dollar, the German Mark or the Japanese Yen), wanted to invest in these countries. They would convert their hard currency into the local, domestic currency at the official exchange rate and then buy the discounted bonds using that domestic currency at one-quarter their face value, thereby earning a large premium equal to the discount on the debts purchased. The debt was still payable, but in local currency, which the foreign company wanted for local investment in any case.

At the same time, North American banks were forced to accumulate reserves against the possibility that part or all of these problematic debts will never be repaid. In Canada this meant that the major banks had to put many billions of

10.17 *UPS Latest U.S. Firm to Sue Federal Government under* NAFTA

10.17 *UPS Latest U.S. Firm to Sue Federal Government under* NAFTA

United Parcel Services of America Inc. (UPS) recently sued the Chretien government for $230 million under the terms of NAFTA, charging that Ottawa has failed to stop Canada Post from subsidizing its courier services, including Xpress Post, Priority Post and Purolator. UPS officials claim that this violates the competition terms of NAFTA.

If the NAFTA dispute panel hearing this complaint agrees with UPS, it will not only award the American firm the damages it seeks, but it will also force Canada Post either to divest its 96% ownership of Purolator, convert its courier services to a completely separate company, or get out of the courier business altogether.

NAFTA's competition section (chapter 15) states that governments must ensure, "through regulatory control," that government monopolies do not engage "in anticompetitive practices in a non-monopolized market," including "cross-subsidization or predatory conduct."

–CCPA *Monitor*, July/August 2000

dollars into reserves. Utilizing their market powers, the banks moved to restore their profits by passing the cost of their imprudent loans on to the Canadian consumer through high user charges. In the United States the external debt crisis has been compounded by a domestic debt crisis among the savings and loan associations where risky lending on real estate led to bad debts estimated in excess of U.S.$100 billion. The ultimate cost to the American taxpayer as a result of the government's bailout has been estimated to be as high as U.S.$500 billion or more.

A number of plans for an international rescue operation using the International Monetary Fund (IMF) and the World Bank (WB) have been proposed, most of which would involve the transfer of bad debts from the private banks to governments and the cancellation of some of the debt for the most-indebted nations, providing they adopt IMF dictated policies of structural adjustment. However, little has yet been achieved to obviate the crisis or relieve the debt load from the poorer countries. A number of the poorest have been forced to implement structural adjustment programs thereby transferring the burden of the debt to their citizens.[11] The record of the IMF and the WB in spreading poverty and de-developing Third World countries in support of global finance has become an international scandal and has been a primary cause for various movements to abolish them as they have ceased doing what they were established to do.

Globalism: What is it and is it a Threat?

In summary, globalism is the process of worldwide integration of economies through trade in goods and services, capital markets and, ultimately, cultures. It is promoted by most of the international and regional economic agencies and trade and investment agreements that have come into prominence in the postwar period (see Glossary at the end of this chapter). It has also been defined as the internationalization of unregulated market capitalism. Many argue that it is made possible by the decline and collapse of the Soviet Union.

The argument for globalism is the same one used by business, economists and the governments of the leading industrial countries to promote and institute international trade agreements. The core of their argument is that free markets for goods, services and capital are more efficient than regulated ones. Free markets increase efficiency, which translates into higher rates of economic growth, higher standards of living for all countries and greater economic opportunities for all citizens, both in the developing South as well as the industrialized North.

This argument is based on classical trade theory from the early nineteenth century. There are a number of assumptions underlying this theory that do not hold in the real world. Furthermore, the theory would also call for the free movement of labour as well as goods, services and capital. But few, if any, of the business elite who champion the free flow of capital, are willing to see labour move freely across national borders (though this is now provided for within the European Union). It is interesting, for instance, that one of the arguments used by the American government to mobilize support for the passage of NAFTA was that increased American investment in Mexico would help keep Mexican migrants from coming to the United States.

In any case, the argument that globalism and the freeing of markets will improve incomes and rates of growth is not supported by what has happened. A major World Bank study shows that growth rates world-wide have fallen in the last few decades of globalism while the number of those in poverty in the Third World has mushroomed.

In Canada and the United States, real wages have stagnated during the last two decades of globalization while inequality has grown to obscene levels.

> ### 10.18 The Third World Debt Crisis
>
> The Third World debt crisis occurred during the 1980s when over two dozen countries, led by Mexico in 1982, announced that they were unable to maintain their scheduled payments of principal and interest to international bankers. These payments, repayable in American dollars, were for loans taken out in the 1970s. During the 1970s there had been major price shocks in both food and oil. Many of the Third World countries were forced to borrow to pay for the higher prices. At the same time the international banks were flush with money deposited by the OPEC countries, who were the beneficiaries (and cause) of skyrocketing oil prices. The banks aggressively sought out borrowers among Third World countries and offered them loans at low, but floating, interest rates. That is, the original interest rates were low but they were free to rise if, and when, prevailing international interest rates rose.
>
> In the early 1980s that happened. "Tight money" (monetarist) policies in the U.S. and Britain forced interest rates up to extremely high levels (they were over twenty percent in Canada at one point) and drove the developed world's economies into a deep recession. The Third World was caught in a double bind. It now had to pay much higher interest charges on its debts and at the same time, the recession reduced demand for its exports by which it earned the U.S. dollars to pay its scheduled interest and principal payments. In fact, most of the Third World countries were simply unable to do so, creating the crisis of the 1980s.
>
> For a more detailed discussion, see Chris Barrett, "Debt Crises in the Third World," *Encyclopedia of Political Economy*, P.A. O'Hara, ed. (London: Routledge, 1999), pp. 183–185.

The rates of growth in both Canada and the U.S. have been paltry compared to those of national income and wages in the 1950s and 1960s, in the "preglobalization" period. In Canada, the pro-business and "free market" policies in the 1980s and 1990s did little to increase economic growth or to close the productivity gap between Canada and the United States. Indeed, the FTA and NAFTA, and the neoliberal policies of privatization, deregulation, government downsizing and economic policy passivity were counterproductive.[12] There is little to support a positive evaluation of the growing internationalization of capital on the Canadian economy—or on the rest of the world—unless you are a capitalist, a financier or a banker.

If there is little or no evidence of any benefit from globalism, does it pose any threats to Canadian workers and average citizens? The answer is yes. The first is

10.19 Structural Adjustment Programs, the IMF and the World Bank

Here's how International Monetary Fund (IMF)/World Bank structural adjustment programs (reflecting U.S. Treasury policies now known as the "Washington Consensus") increase poverty around the world:

Privatization—Structural adjustment policies call for the sell-off of government-owned enterprises to private owners, often foreign investors. Privatization is typically associated with layoffs and pay cuts for workers in the privatized enterprises.

Cuts in government spending—Reductions in government spending frequently reduce the services available to the poor, including health and education services (though the IMF and World Bank now say they preserve health and education spending).

Imposition of user fees—Many IMF and World Bank loans call for the imposition of "user fees"—charges for the use of government-provided services like schools, health clinics and clean drinking water. For very poor people, even modest charges may result in the denial of access to services.

Promotion of exports—Under structural adjustment programs, countries undertake a variety of measures to promote exports, at the expense of production for domestic needs. In the rural sector, the export orientation is often associated with the displacement of poor people who grow food for their own consumption, as their land is taken over by large plantations growing crops for foreign markets.

Higher interest rates—Higher interest rates exert a recessionary effect on national economies, leading to higher rates of joblessness. Small businesses, often operated by women, find it more difficult to gain access to affordable credit and often are unable to survive.

Trade liberalization—The elimination of tariff protections for industries in developing countries often leads to mass layoffs. In Mozambique, for example, the IMF and World Bank ordered the removal of an export tax on cashew nuts. The result: 10,000 adults, mostly women, lost their jobs in cashew nut-processing factories. Most of the processing work shifted to India, where child laborers shell the nuts at home.

—www.50years.org (fact sheet)

to "good" jobs. The recession following the passage of the FTA resulted in the permanent loss of hundreds of thousands of manufacturing jobs, many of them to low-wage areas in Mexico and, perhaps surprisingly to some, to the southern U.S., right-to-work (that is, anti-union), low-wage states. Though the subsequent recovery—partial as it may be—has created new jobs, they are almost all in the low-wage secondary, service market. It is this that accounts for stagnant or falling average male wages in Canada over the last decade.

The second threat is to the environment. We have already noted the use of the WTO and NAFTA to attack environmental regulation. A third threat is to public social programs, in particular Medicare and education, cultural programs, and many public utilities including Canada Post and the various provincial public electricity companies. The increased protection of intellectual property in these trade agreements also threatens to increase drug and information costs, eroding our standard of living and possibly contributing to the collapse of the Medicare system.

But the most important threat of the current trend in globalization is to democracy itself. We already have had an official of the Trilateral Commission arguing that there is too much democracy in the world for the good of business. He writes: "Our analysis suggests ... [that] some of the problems of governance in the Untied States today stem from an excess of democracy."[13] The effect of the WTO, NAFTA, and all the other agreements and treaties is to restrict democratic governments world-wide from bringing in legislation that citizens want to improve their economic, environmental and social security. It is a case of enshrining private property rights in what has been called an international constitution for capital, at the expense of the democratic and social rights of individual citizens and nations.

Notes

1. It should be recognized, however, that there are some barriers to completely free trade in goods and services between provinces within Canada. In many cases, for instance, professionals (doctors, lawyers, engineers) cannot sell their services from one province to another without first being certified by the professional association in both provinces.

2. The term "tilt to the secondary labour market" was first used by Michael Piore ["Introduction," *Unemployment and Inflation,* Michael Piore, ed., (White Plains, NY: M.E. Sharpe, 1979), p. xxii] in reference to structural changes in the American economy due to techno-

logical change and shifts in demand, but it is equally relevant to structural changes due to shifting trade patterns induced by recent commercial agreements and globalization.

3. For some effects of the restructuring of American industry, see Bertrand Bellon and Jorge Niosi, *The Decline of the American Economy* (Montreal: Black Rose, 1988).

4. One of the first major studies of the impact of multinational companies on the Canadian economy was Kari Levitt, *Silent Surrender: The Multinational Corporation in Canada* (Toronto: Macmillan, 1970).

5. Canada's export dependence and structural vulnerability is detailed in a number of essays in Daniel Drache and Meric Gertler, eds., *The New Era of Global Competition* (Montreal: McGill-Queen's University Press, 1991).

6. The Auto Pact Agreement with the United States has also been a victim of the new trade regime. It was struck down by the WTO in 2001.

7. Duncan Cameron, *The Free Trade Deal* (Toronto: Lorimer, 1988); Jesse Vorst and Jim Silver, eds., *Why No Free Trade?* (Winnipeg: Society for Socialist Studies, 1988).

8. The NAFTA agreement incorporating Mexico does provide for agricultural provisions that are somewhat different between the three parties.

9. For just a few of the Canadian studies evaluating the negative impact on democracy

---

10.20 Delinking of Wages to Productivity

The dismal performance of real wages in Canada during the 1990s is in part due to the "delinking" of wage growth from productivity growth. This was the result of downward competitive pressures from the United States and Mexico where weakened unions and falling labour market standards have allowed employers to claim virtually all the growth in productivity during the past decade.

Contrary to the assumption of neo-classical economists that wages reflect relative productivity, it was argued that in the U.S. and, even more dramatically, in Mexico, productivity and wages had become delinked....

With the option of relocation to a lower wage, lower labour standards jurisdiction with little or no loss of quality or productivity, employers will be placed in a position to successfully push workers for wage concessions and to better resist unionization.

Percentage Growth in Hourly Wages and Labour Productivity in Manufacturing

| Productivity | | Real Hourly Wages | |
	Canada	U.S.	Canada	U.S.
Average 1981-1988	2.3	3.1	0.4	0.7
Average 1989-1995	2.0	2.6	0.2	0.1

–Andrew Jackson, "Impact of the Canada–U.S. Free Trade Agreement (FTA) and the North American Free Trade Agreement (NAFTA) on Canadian Labour Markets," in Bruce Campbell, *Pulling Apart* (Ottawa: CCPA, 2000), pp. 114–115

of the trade agreements and the WTO see Bruce Campbell, et al., *Pulling Apart: The Deterioration of Employment and Income in North America Under Free Trade* (Ottawa: CCPA, 1999).

10. Tom Naylor, "The Crisis of Debt," *Dominion of Debt* (Montreal: Black Rose, 1985); Naylor, *Hot Money and the Politics of Debt* (Toronto: McClelland and Stewart, 1987).

11. See Michael Chossudovsky, *The Globalization of Poverty* (Penang, Malaysia: Third World Network, 1997).

12. Andrew Jackson and David Robinson, *Falling Behind: The State of Working Canada, 2000* (Ottawa: CCPA, 2000), pp. 16–18.

13. Quoted by Murray Dobbin in *The Myth of the Good Corporate Citizen* (Toronto: Stoddard, 1998), p. 162.

Glossary—International Economic Institutions and Treaties: A "Rogues' Gallery"

IMF (International Monetary Fund): The IMF was established in the 1944 Bretton Woods Agreements along with the World Bank. Its original purpose was to provide short-term funding to countries to prevent trade-related currency crises and, thus, to encourage international trade. In recent decades after the United States unilaterally abandoned the gold exchange standard in 1971, the IMF has adopted a new role, that of international economic policeman using long-term loans to force implementation of neoliberal economic policies on any nation that requires loans to prevent or contain currency crises. (See "Washington Consensus.")

WB (World Bank or the International Bank for Reconstruction and Development): The World Bank was also established in 1944 to provide long-term loans to finance post-war reconstruction and the development of third world economies. As with the IMF, in recent decades the WB has changed its role. It makes its loans conditional on recipient countries adopting neoliberal economic policies outlined in the "Washington Consensus." According to a previous vice-president of the WB, these conditions placed on borrowing countries are producing increased poverty and de-development in Third World economies defeating the original intent of the WB.

WTO (World Trade Organization): The WTO succeeded GATT in 1995 as the ultimate overseer of international trade and investment. Its prime purpose is to reduce or eliminate tariffs and non-tariff barriers to trade in goods and services; to create and protect intellectual property rights internationally; and to provide constitutional protection for multinational capital. (See GATS, TRIPS, TRIMS, and MAI.)

GATT (General Agreement on Tariffs and Trade): This was the original trade treaty that came out of the Bretton Woods meetings in 1944. This multilateral agreement was signed in 1947 with the main intention of reducing barriers to trade. It was subsumed in the WTO in 1995.

FTA (Canada–United States Free Trade Agreement): This was the initial agreement between Canada and the United States that came into effect in 1989. Though called a "free trade" agreement and does provide for reduction in trade barriers, the majority of the agreement provided for integration of regulations and standards, deregulation of capital markets and the provision of increased rights for multinational investors.

NAFTA (North America Free Trade Agreement): NAFTA extended the FTA both geographically to include Mexico, and in terms of provisions and coverage to include the infamous investor rights to sue governments arising out of newly created investor property rights (chapter 11 of NAFTA). It came into effect in 1994.

FTAA (Free Trade Agreement of the Americas): The FTAA is the proposed extension of NAFTA to the whole of the western hemisphere (excluding Cuba) despite the devastating effects NAFTA has had on government efforts in all three countries covered by the agreement on the environment.

MAI (Multilateral Agreement on Investment): The MAI was a secret agreement under negotiation by members of the OECD to establishing rights for global corporations and restricting governments' rights to control corporate behavior or regulate capital and currency flows and speculation. When the agreement was exposed in 1998, opposition was so intense that the MAI was abandoned by the OECD. Many of the MAI provisions have been proposed for inclusion in the WTO, a factor that lead to the demonstrations against the WTO in Seattle in 2000. However, these provisions are still on the agenda for the WTO when it meets for its next round of expansion.

GATS (General Agreement on Trade in Services): A sub-agreement of the WTO restricting regulations on the trade in services. Currently under negotiation, the U.S. in particular is pressing for the extension of coverage to health, education, cultural industries and water.

TRIMS (Trade Related Investment Measures): Also a sub-agreement within the WTO, it contains "only the bare bones of the investment agreement subsequently given full expression in the now-abandoned MAI." [Shrybman, *The World Trade Organization*, p. 15.] Current negotiations, however, are aimed at incorporating the MAI agenda into an augmented TRIMS within the WTO.

TRIPS (Trade Related Intellectual Property Rights): An important sub-agreement of the WTO compels member countries to adopt and enforce U.S.-style patent protection regimes. It makes U.S. and European patents enforceable through trade sanctions. It was under this agreement that the pharmaceutical companies tried to prevent South Africa from producing generic anti-AIDS drugs to combat the AIDS epidemic sweeping southern Africa. World revulsion at the attempts by the U.S. and the pharmaceutical companies to enforce its patents through the WTO led the pharmaceutical companies to drop their lawsuits.

OECD (Organization of Economic Co-operation and Development): An organization of 29 developed industrial countries in Western Europe, North America and Japan designed as a business-oriented "think-tank" promoting the economic interests of the richer nations.

Source: Shrybman, A *Citizen's Guide to the World Trade Organization* (Ottawa: CCPA and Lorimer, 1999); and Working Group on the WTO/MAI, A *Citizen's Guide to the World Trade Organization* (New York: Apex, 1999)

There Is An Alternative—Democracy

Since its early days, economics has had the reputation, probably deservedly, of being the "dismal science." And perhaps anyone reading the previous ten chapters might well be convinced that political economy's forecast for the future of human material welfare, at least for the majority of working people, is equally dismal. Margaret Thatcher, the architect of Britain's reactionary policies in the 1980s, declared "there is no alternative," to the onslaught of legislative measures privatizing and deregulating public utilities, cutting public services, selling off publicly owned assets and generally undermining the whole infrastructure of the democratic state. And governments across the Western world, and even more so among the former communist countries, have adopted a vicious neoliberal agenda that has undermined the basis of liberal democracy and the level of economic welfare and material security for the vast majority of citizens. Under attack are the health systems, the education systems, the pension systems, the unemployment insurance systems, family income supports, collective bargaining, employment security and collective labour rights. Almost the entire fabric of social and income security and the supporting democratic institutions are being eroded, most aggressively in Canada by the rightward racing Liberal Party. But is there no alternative?

Fortunately, for Canadians and workers around the world, there is an alternative. Reforming our system and bringing back democratic values will not be easy. But it is not impossible if one understands the basic political economy of Canada and is willing to challenge the power elite that is manipulating the political system for its private benefit.

This must all sound very rhetorical and theoretical to the average worker who must labour daily to put bread on the family table and a roof over its head. They might well ask, "So what? And what can I

> ### 11.1 The Fraser Institute on Taxes and Income Distribution
>
> Joel Emes, a senior research economist at the Fraser Institute and co-author of *Tax Facts 12*, said ... that the average tax burden—or the share of income eaten up by taxes—is now at its lowest since 1996....
>
> However ... taxation is still a relatively heavy burden on Canadians and argues it is especially unfair to high-income earners....
>
> The tax report also suggests that if the tax system is unfair, as some critics claim, it is unfair to upper-income Canadians.
>
> The 30% of families with the highest incomes—those earning $63,209 or more—earned 59.4% of total Canadian incomes but paid 65.7% of all taxes, the institute said.
>
> The 30% with the lowest incomes earned 8.1% of all incomes and paid 4.3% of all taxes.
>
> –Eric Beauchesne, "Taxes dip—but still devour 47.5% of income," *National Post*, June 13, 2001, pp. 1, 8.
>
> Neither the *National Post* article nor the Fraser Institute's report say the Canadian tax system remains mildly progressive, meaning that those with the ability to pay, pay more—which is exactly what a tax system designed to develop equity in society is supposed to do.

do about it anyway?" Let us ask ourselves what are the threats, the problems, the increasing day-to-day pressures that are grinding us down. What are the causes? What *can* be done about it?

The Neoliberal Threat to Democracy and Economic Security

Simplistic economic theory is being used to push an ideological agenda that is not supported by more sophisticated economic theory or by economic facts. Take, for instance, so called "free trade" and, more particularly, treaties like the Canada–U.S. Free Trade Agreement, the North American Free Trade Agreement, and the projected Free Trade Agreement of the Americas. Why are these treaties and agreements so dangerous and why should they be resisted?

In the first place, they have very little to do with trade. Yes, they reduce the average level of tariffs on imports thereby reducing consumer costs for imports, but they do this at the cost of jobs for Canadians. Yes, they lower costs to foreigners of our exports, thereby increasing exports and creating jobs. But do the increased jobs and income generated from exports equal the decreased jobs and income lost to imports? The empirical answer is no, both for Canada and the United States. Hundreds of thousands of jobs were lost to both Canada and the United States while workers' wages stagnated after the passage of NAFTA. The jobs went to Mexican workers, according to academic studies, but the Mexican workers' wages have fallen 40 percent, after accounting for inflation, since NAFTA was implemented. The money went to the executives and managers of the multinational corporations whose incomes soared to levels unheard of and unjustified by any legitimate economic theory.

I have issued a challenge on the Internet and elsewhere asking any economist to give one example where free trade has helped a poor or lesser developed country become developed and increase its standard of living. After many years of offering this challenge I have never had one single economist give one example of where "free trade" did not benefit the rich at the expense of the poor or the developed at the expense of the developing countries.[1] The most recent studies of the World Bank and others have further supported the contention that free trade has hurt the poorer at the expense of the richer nations—what was called in the nineteenth century, "free trade imperialism."

These so-called trade deals are pri-

> ### 11.2 Globalization and Economic Development
>
> Globalization and the policies of its most powerful advocates, the International Monetary Fund and the World Bank, have come under increasing criticism in recent years. In the United States, the median real wage is about the same today as it was 27 years ago....
>
> However, throughout the growing debate, it has generally been assumed that globalization has helped spur economic growth throughout most of the world. Even critics of globalization, and of the IMF and World Bank, have generally accepted this assumption....
>
> The official data from the last two decades (1980–2000) tell a different story. Economic growth has slowed dramatically, especially in the less developed countries, as compared with the previous two decades.... For the overwhelming majority of the world, especially in less developed countries, the last two decades of increasing globalization have seen a considerable slowing of economic growth.
>
> –Mark Weisbrot, Robert Naiman and Joyce Kim, "The Emperor Has No Growth: Declining Economic Growth Rates in the Era of Globalization," *Center for Economic and Policy Research*, September 2000, pp. 2,4 (Full paper at www.cepr.net)

marily oriented at putting corporations, employers and capitalists above and beyond the control of democratic states. They place corporations above the law, giving them supra-national status beyond the power of nation states to control and regulate their behaviour. The threat to labour and the environment is not only hypothetical, it is real and documented in the study quoted previously on the use of NAFTA to destroy U.S. unionism (see chapter 10, box 10.15); and by the results of numerous decisions of NAFTA and the WTO striking down environmental legislation in Canada, the United States and Mexico (see chapter 10, box 10.16).

Multinational, corporate capital must be brought back under the control of democratic governments. This does not

---

11.3 Where There's Smoke?

Carla Hills, the U.S. Trade Representative who oversaw the NAFTA negotiations for Bush 1 and now heads her own trade-consulting firm, was among the very first to play this game of bump-and-run intimidation. Her corporate clients include big tobacco—R.J. Reynolds and Philip Morris. Sixteen months after leaving office, Hills dispatched Julius Katz, her former chief deputy at USTR, to warn Ottawa to back off its proposed law to require plain packaging for cigarettes. If it didn't, Katz said, Canada would have to compensate his clients under NAFTA and the new legal doctrine he and Hills had helped create. "No U.S. multinational tobacco manufacturer or its lobbyists are going to dictate health policy in this country," the Canadian health minister vowed. Canada backed off, nevertheless.

–William Greider, "The Right and U.S. Trade Law: Invalidating the 20th Century," *The Nation*, October 15, 2001 (http://thenation.com)

---

necessarily mean repeal of existing trade agreements and withdrawal from international trade organizations. It does mean, however, that we must be willing to withdraw from NAFTA and the WTO if other governments are unwilling to bring international corporations back under control by introducing measures to promote *fair trade*. The short-run costs of withdrawing from international treaties and agreements would be substantial. But the long-run costs of not withdrawing if other governments refuse to compromise may well be catastrophic.

What do we mean by "fair trade" rather than "free trade"? Obviously it is not fair trade in agricultural products when the United States and the EU massively subsidize their domestic agricultural industries at the cost of billions and billions of taxpayer dollars so they can undercut agriculture in developing countries. It is not fair trade to demand that underdeveloped countries remove all their tariffs and quotas while we maintain ours on textiles, steel and other domestically sensitive industries and subsidize research and development in patent protected technology. This is particularly unfair when we then sell at monopoly prices to the poor countries in exchange for primary commodities that they are required to sell to us at competitive prices. An example of fair (or managed) trade that worked to both countries' advantage (but which has since been outlawed by the WTO) was the Canada–U.S. Autopact. This provided for rationalization of the industry and "free-trade" (i.e., no customs duties or tariffs) in the automobile industry but provided certain job and investment guarantees for the smaller country, Canada, in exchange for eliminating duties and tariffs. The overall principle was that one car would be produced in Canada for every car sold in Canada. That meant that Canada would specialize in certain models for the entire North American market, and the U.S. would specialize in others, providing that, after shipping models back and forth over the border, net sales in Canada equalled net production in Canada.

11.4 Metalclad

When the small central Mexican town of Guadalcazar refused to allow the U.S.–based Metalclad Corporation to build a landfill site for toxic waste near its community, the company lodged a complaint under the North American Free Trade Agreement. The town's alleged "offence" was really their fear that the landfill would pollute their drinking water. When a majority of local townspeople turned out to protest the Metalclad proposal, their town council denied the building permit. Metalclad claimed that the town's decision to refuse them a building permit interfered with their right to earn profits. They demanded that the Mexican government be forced to pay them for the profits they could have earned. The panel agreed and awarded Metalclad damages of $16.7 million (U.S.).

See Linda McQuaig, *All You Can Eat: Greed, Lust and the New Capitalism* (Toronto: Penguin, 2001), pp. 3–5

The Autopact is just one model of fair trade type agreements. The Soviet Union had an arrangement with Cuba to exchange crude oil for sugar at a price for sugar that reflected its real cost of production rather than at the world free market price. This was fair because the market price was artificially depressed by government subsidies of beet and cane sugar both in North America and Europe, and by many Third World countries desperate for foreign exchange. The same distortion of world prices is now plaguing many coffee-producing countries. Raw bean prices have declined to unsupportable levels by new production (aided and supported by the World Bank and the IMF) in such countries as Vietnam, while because of the monopoly power of the multinational coffee companies, retail prices in developed markets have remained high. A few cooperatives and non-governmental organizations have organized a "fair trade" coffee brand that helps a few farmers in the Third World. These cooperatives are virtually impotent against the power of the food multinationals and the retail chains that dominate the retail market in developed countries. Any real fair trade initiative must involve bilateral and multilateral agreements with developing countries—and between developed countries—that guarantee market access and cost-of-production prices without resort to protective duties and tariffs.

One measure in NAFTA that needs be repealed and excluded from any future trade agreements is Chapter 11. This section permits corporations to sue governments for damages should any legislation or regulation threaten the profits, *or expected profits*, of a multinational corporation. The Ethyl Corporation used this section to force Canada to remove its ban on the importation of the gasoline additive, MMT. Metalclad Corporation used it to penalize a poor Mexican municipality for banning a toxic dump on an ecologically sensitive site within the municipality. Even the United States is having second thoughts about this section since Canadian corporations are using it to try to overturn environmental laws in some American states.

The attempt to extend the trade and capital agreements to also cover public and social services and culture must be resisted. Canadian governments will do this only if they are under strong political pressure from the public. It is important that public services and culture not be commodified for a number of reasons. Perhaps the most important is that it would bring an end to Medicare and our public education system by effectively privatizing these systems under American corporate control. Anyone familiar with the disaster that is the American health insurance system with its runaway costs, or with the deterioration of its public school system, will understand immediately the need to protect the Canadian system. In the case of culture, failure to protect and nurture Canadian music, broadcasting, theatre, publishing, film, magazines and all other manifestations of the domestic cultural industry will mean its virtual demise under the incoming tide of the huge American cultural industry.

The meltdown of the Asian economies in 1997, the collapse of the Mexican peso in 1995, the more recent Russian, Brazilian, Argentinean and Turkish financial crises and crashes, the collapse of Long Term Capital Management (an enormous international financial derivatives trader, the collapse of which almost brought a financial crisis to the whole world economy)—all within the last half decade, should have served as a warning to governments

> ### 11.5 GATS and the Threat to Democracy
>
> What is GATS?
> The General Agreement on Trade in Services is a multilateral framework agreement that restricts government actions affecting services through legally enforceable constraints backed up by trade sanctions. The GATS is one of the numerous agreements that were adopted in 1994 as part of the newly established World Trade Organization system and that apply to all WTO members....
>
> The agreement is not confined to cross-border trade, but intrudes into many domestic policy areas, including the environment, culture, natural resources, health care, education and social services.... The GATS played a pivotal role in several recent WTO cases, where its broad working was interpreted forcefully. The rulings in these cases show that the "services" agreement can be used to challenge an almost unlimited range of government regulatory measures [including education and health services].
>
> –Scott Sinclair, "New WTO negotiations on services (GATS) threaten democracy," CCPA Monitor, October 2000

that deregulated financial markets pose a continuing threat of economic disaster. In recent years, the amount of money traded on international markets has risen to one hundred times the amount of goods and services. Exchange rates no longer represent trade flows but rather the speculation in the global financial casino.

Many economists and financial traders have recognized that unregulated speculation poses an economic threat to the international economy—Keynes commented on the danger as early as 1935. More recently, Nobel Prize winner James Tobin proposed dampening the destabilizing speculation by placing a small tax on international financial trades. American economist Paul Davidson has argued for much more extensive measures to regulate international capital flows and completely reform the international financial system. Economics Nobel Laureate Joseph Stiglitz has most recently suggested the complete abolition of the IMF. The New Democratic Party was able to get the federal parliament to pass unanimously a resolution favouring the Tobin Tax but the Liberal government, while expressing initial support, has abandoned it in the face of American opposition.

There are other areas where Canada needs to act or where Canadian sovereignty needs to be protected from multinational corporate takeover. It is extremely important that we reverse the privatization and deregulation of public enterprises, services and utilities, and other infrastructure industries such as air transport. Privatization and deregulation have been sold to the public on the grounds that private, deregulated firms are more efficient.

For utilities the evidence is clear. Publicly owned corporations are at least as efficient as the best private corporations and more efficient than most of their private counterparts. In Britain, the government has had to effectively "re-

11.6 The Tobin Tax

The Tobin tax on financial transactions has been proposed as a way to reduce currency speculation, without affecting real investment. In arguing for the tax, economist James Tobin has written that the tax is aimed as discouraging short-term speculative investments. In these cases, speculators buy foreign currencies and sell them again, often in a matter of a few days. Real investors on the other hand, make investments that will last for years. Here he describes why the tax would discourage speculative investment, but not affect real investment:

The exchange transactions tax [would be] the same amount for every transaction. So it automatically, in the simplest possible manner, discriminates between short- and long-run round trips. Suppose the exchange tax is 0.5% for each transaction. If you're going to move from Toronto to New York in order to exploit an interest rate differential and you come back within the same week, that costs you 1% for the round trip. If the advantage is only a few basis points of difference in short-run interest rates on an annual basis, the tax will erase the gain.

On the other hand, let's say you want to make a transaction because you're going to make a serious real capital investment—building a physical capital facility, plant or equipment in another country, another currency. When you're going to repatriate the money—let's say, in ten years from now—so small a tax is not going to make the slightest bit of difference to your calculation of the advantages of making that investment in the first place.

–James Tobin, "How an international transactions tax would work," CCPA Monitor, October 1995, pp. 8–9

nationalize" the rail system because the privatized companies not only went bankrupt but the accident rate rose to unacceptable levels due to poor maintenance of the roadbed. Perhaps the most high profile cases in North America have been the disasters of deregulated electricity in California and Alberta. In California, deregulation of the electricity industry led in 2000–01 to brownouts and blackouts, price hikes that at peak times reached 1,000 percent, corporate bankruptcies and government bailouts in the billions of dollars.[2] The only stable utilities in the state were those owned by municipal governments. In Alberta the situation was not quite as chaotic as in California. Even so, huge increases in the cost of electricity led to government subsidies of consumers, the shutdown of businesses and price instability.[3] New Zealand, the first to experiment with deregulation and privatization of electricity, also experienced repeated blackouts and brownouts and, after a decade, has still not recovered. These experiences should be sufficient to turn any consumer or elector off deregulation and on to public ownership.

In Canada and the United States, deregulation led (after a brief period of increased competition) to a series of airline bankruptcies and a major decrease in the number of airlines, and increased airfares. Because of the competition-enforced reorganization of routes into "hub and spokes" systems that funnelled traffic through a number of major centres, customers experienced decreased service in the form of longer travelling times. It has reached such a level in the United States that the Bush administration is talking about taking ownership positions in the airlines to bail them out of their economic miseries that long preceded the 2001 terrorist tragedies. At the time this is being written, one major American airline has already declared bankruptcy, two are reportedly on the verge of seeking a form of "protected bankruptcy" and only one of the majors is profitable. Canada has also moved to "de-privatize" airport security, given the poor record of private firms in protecting the safety of air passengers both before and after the terrorist attacks of September 11, 2001. And every Canadian is aware of the woes of the industry and of Canadian passengers following privatization of Air Canada and deregulation of the industry and the subsequent collapse of Canadian Airlines.

As the water crises in Walkerton, North Battleford and numerous other communities from Newfoundland and Labrador to the West Coast clearly attest, fresh, unpolluted bulk water is becoming increasingly scarce in North America. In these cases, *e. coli* and other contaminants have led to mass illness, even death, or at the least, to "boil-water" advisories. In all cases, the cause of the contamination was a combination of lack of regulation of water quality (or in Walkerton's case, deregulation of water quality control) and lack of environment regulation of industry, including agriculture.[4] To bring water into a privatized, continental market would be clearly detrimental to Canadian consumers (privatized water systems in Latin America resulted in price increases of over 100 percent that put unpolluted water out of the income range of average working families[5]). Given Britain's experience, privatization of municipal water systems would also result in a deterioration in the quality of the water supply.

Sweden, Denmark and Norway showed that the destruction of the social safety net is not a necessity of "globalization." Most independent studies find that the European economic tribulations—slow growth and unemployment—can be attributed not to unionization, strong safety nets for workers and protection of the social wage (the welfare state). Rather they are the result of restrictive monetary and fiscal policies mandated by the European Central Bank and the Maastrict treaty promoting European economic integration. What has become more and more clear is that those countries which have centralized bargaining between unions, employers and governments, not only over wages but also over the social safety net, the budget, public investment and economic objectives, have been much more successful in achieving economic goals and raising the quality of life than those who have promoted deunionization, labour market "flexibility" and deregulation of markets. Austria and Slovenia are two small countries with "social contracts," centrally negotiated agreements between labour, business and government covering income and social wage policies. As a result, they have been more successful in controlling unemployment

---

11.7 High European Unemployment: Labour Market Institutions or Macroeconomic Policies?

The principal findings [of this study] are that macroeconomic policy variables consistently and robustly matter for the evolution of a country's unemployment rates, and that macroeconomic policy affects unemployment rates in the manner expected. High interest rates and slow growth raise unemployment, as does a slowdown in export growth. With regard to the microeconomic labor market variables the evidence is more problematic.... These findings lead to the conclusion that high unemployment in Western Europe is principally the result of self-inflicted dysfunctional macroeconomic policy. European policy makers adopted a course of disinflation, high real interest rates, and slower growth that raised unemployment. Moreover, they all adopted this course at the same time, thereby generating a wave of trade based cross-country spill-overs that generated a continent wide macroeconomic funk and further raised unemployment.

–Thomas Palley, "The Role of Institutions and Policies in Creating High European Unemployment: The Evidence," Working Paper 336, Levy Institute, August 2001, p. 2, www.levy.org/docs/wrkpap/papers/336.html

and inflation. This has been found to be generally true for the industrialized nations as a whole. "If properly paired, co-ordination of wage bargaining and union wage coverage can actually lower unemployment. If both of these institutions were maximally implemented, then the unemployment rate would be reduced by 0.6% points."[6]

Unions Matter

In a recent book comparing the Canadian and American labour markets, prominent American labour economists David Card and Richard Freeman concluded that unions and Canada's social institutions really do matter to the economic welfare of Canadians.

Labour market institutions have resulted in less income inequality and poverty in Canada than in the US. The United States chose to give relatively free play to market forces during the 1980s, whereas Canada pursued a more activist strategy of providing broader social safety nets and labour regulations that were more favourable to trade unionism. The American policies generated substantial employment growth, but did little to mitigate the redistribution of income towards higher income workers and families. Canada's programs produced comparable employment growth, but also eased the forces that tended to promote inequality and poverty. Subtle differences in unemployment compensation, unionization, immigration policies and income maintenance programs have significantly affected the levels of poverty, unemployment and income inequality in the two countries."[7]

European studies have shown that high levels of union membership, strong employment security measures and high wages and benefits have produced much higher levels of worker welfare, less poverty and inequality, and a higher quality of working life. This has been done *without adversely affecting employment and economic growth*. This is quite contrary to the neoliberal rhetoric that blames labour market rigidity for the poor economic performance in Europe in recent years.

This means that there is an alternative, an alternative that must be fought for and won by workers, their unions and their political allies. It is important that workers and their unions reach out to the unorganized and bring them into union ranks. It means also reaching out to our ethnic minorities and Aboriginal peoples. But it is an alternative that cannot be won simply with industrial organization. In the end, it can only be won by political action, not just in the legislatures, but also on the streets, in the media and wherever Canadians and their politicians gather to meet, to de-

---

11.8 Swedish Social Democracy and Globalism

[Despite global integration] no attempt has been made to completely or radically overhaul Swedish social policy or to dismantle Sweden's welfare state. Nor, given the dominant values, more unified nature of the state, and continuing strength of the Swedish labour movement, is this very likely in the foreseeable future. Despite some quite significant rollbacks, the nation still possesses all the hallmarks of a relatively generous and comprehensive welfare state. In short, it remains a welfare leader. In addition, it still has lower rates of poverty and inequality and a notably larger middle class than are found in either Canada or the United States—or in most other capitalist nations, for that matter.

–Gregg Olsen, *The Politics of the Welfare State: Canada, Sweden, and the United States* (Don Mills, Ont.: Oxford University Press, 2002), pp. 167–168

bate and to discuss our future as a nation. For one thing, it will take political action to change the labour laws that now discriminate against labour and restrict the right and ability to organize, particularly for those in the growing ranks of the service occupations.

Labour must ally itself with all those other groups—non-governmental organizations, environmentalists, health activists—all those who seek an alternative to the destructive path on which we are currently headed. It must also ally itself with like-minded groups in other countries, particularly those in Latin and South America where workers are oppressed and where union leaders are routinely murdered, jail or "disappeared," including Mexico, Columbia, Bolivia, Nicaragua and Guatemala.

Up to now I have not talked much about political parties and policies, subjects that dominate media discussions of economics and economic policy. There are two reasons why I have tended to gloss over the topic. First, among the political parties in Canada, even less in the United States or Britain, there is no essential difference in the understanding of the political economy of contemporary capitalism among the political parties. Second, the form of liberal democracy that prevails in the Western industrial world is unable, or unwilling, to come to grips with the fundamental issue of contemporary political economy, that of the distribution of economic and political power between capital and the mass of the working population.

The collapse of the Soviet system has effectively reduced the world from a bi-polar to a uni-polar system, that is, instead of two competing ideological systems, we now have only one, and one that has aggressively imposed its views on all that have resisted its embrace. No political parties have taken that message more to heart than many of the social democratic and labour parties of Western Europe and Canada. Having lost the competitive challenge from their left, they have become converts to "efficient," or perhaps more charitably, a "softer, gentler" neoliberalism. Perhaps the best example of this is the British Labour Party under Tony Blair.

Social democratic parties, by and large, have accepted the neoliberal, capital-dominated political economy. They are restricting their political demands to haggling over the price of that acceptance. In the case of the British Labour Party, the price has been extremely low. In the case of Canada's New Democratic Party, the price is perhaps more moderate, while in the case of the Swedish Social Democratic Labour Party, the price demanded for acceptance is quite high.

The problem is that parliamentary social democratic parties in liberal democracies have little leverage and little bargaining power, particularly in the Anglo-American electoral system where the "first past the post" are the sole winners. Dissenting and alternative views are effectively shut out of the political debate, particularly since control of the media and what is reported rests with big business and their political allies. If and when such parties achieve parliamentary power, they do not have access to the levers of economic power, the levers that control investment, employment, production and distribution. If they attempt to use legislative levers to regulate economic activity, they are faced with capital flight—in effect a "capital strike." Moreover, the creation of the trade agreements and the international financial institutions have reduced the political sovereignty of national governments replacing nation-state-rooted liberal democracy with capital-controlled bureaucracies of technocrats trained to implement the neoliberal economic orthodoxy. If progressive political parties are not willing to challenge these non-democratic control institutions, they will effectively be stymied in achieving democratic reform.

Again, this is not to say there *is* no alternative nor, as the Swedish experience has demonstrated, that social democratic parties cannot claim better returns from the economic system in terms of income distribution and social benefits if they have the solid backing of unions and the working people. What it does say, however, is that electoral politics is not enough. It must be backed not only by unions, but also by worker and citizen organization and participation in decision-making at the workplace, in the community, in the schools, in the media— wherever the decisions are taken that determine the socioeconomic shape of our society. That is the alternative.

A Democratic Agenda

The first criteria for any progressive agenda must be for the extension of democratic decision-making—that is, a reversal of the trend of taking decision-making out of the realm of the public, political institutions and restricting it to private, market institutions. To use Karl Polanyi's language, we must "re-embed" the economy in society rather than make society the handmaiden of the market. This means we must resist and turn back *capitalist* globalization without restricting trade that will benefit North and South, rich nations and poor nations—"fair trade," not "free trade." This also implies re-regulation of international capital movements in order to stabilize international money markets.[8]

The democratization criteria also means that labour must not only step up its organizational efforts to bring more workers under the "rule of law" of a collective agreement, but also to bring more democracy to the workplace. Workers must become more involved in decision-making at all levels—at the shop or office floor, at the department or firm level, and at the corporate or government department or agency level. This means a whole rethinking of workplace participation.

Democratization of the economy and of decision-making will be difficult, if not impossible, if we do not join forces with workers in other countries, particularly those close to Canada and who are, or potentially will be, integrated into an hemispheric competitive labour pool through extension of market integration by NAFTA or the FTAA. In the end, however, the most powerful tool we have at our command is the recognition that—quite contrary to the proclamations of Margaret Thatcher and the neoliberals—there is an alternative. It is time to stop being on the defensive and go on the offensive, under the banner of democracy.

Notes

1. This is the theme of a recent and widely praised book by University of Cambridge economist Ha-Joon Chang, *Kicking Away the Ladder—Development Strategy in Historical Perspective* (London: Anthem Press, 2002).
2. The problem was compounded by the deregulation of the activities of companies such as Enron, an energy trader and active participant in the California market. Subse-

quently, it has been revealed that the bankruptcy of Enron (at the expense of its shareholders and, in particular, its employees) was caused by all sorts of shady deals and accounting irregularities, a number of them associated with the California energy deregulation scam.

3. See "Hoax: How Deregulation Let the Power Industry Steal $71 Billion from California," U.S. Foundation for Taxpayer and Consumer Rights, www.consumerwatchdog.org.

4. The fish kills in Nova Scotia in the summer of 2002, which scientists believe resulted from the runoff of fertilizers, pesticides and herbicides from potato fields due to unusually heavy rains, is an additional case in point.

5. A prime example was in Bolivia where, under IMF pressure, a municipal water system was sold to the American multinational Bechtel. When the company doubled the price of water, many in the poorer communities could not afford water from the private system and were forced to get their drinking water from nearby ditches and polluted ponds. As a result the people rioted and forced the government to "re-nationalize" the water system and Bechtel to leave. Bechtel has since filed legal action against Bolivia under the WTO for compensation for lost profits.

6. Thomas Palley, "The Role of Institutions and Policies in Creating High European Unemployment: The Evidence," Working Paper 336, Levy Institute, August 2001, p. 8, www.levy.org/docs/wrkpap/papers/336.html

7. See David Card and Richard Freeman, *Small Differences that Matter* (Chicago: University of Chicago Press, 1993)

8. It should be noted that regulation of international financial flows is a prerequisite of controlling "hot money" flows; that is, flows of money to "launder" and hide the profits of drug syndicates and organized crime, and also to restrict the flows of money financing terrorism. These flows are not insignificant in exacerbating international financial instability. However, this is an issue beyond the scope of this book.

References

Akyeampong, Ernest, "Work Absences: New Data, New Insights," *Perspectives*, Spring 1998 (Statistics Canada no. 75-001-XPE)

Anderson, Sarah, and John Cavanagh, "The Top 200: Key Findings," *CCPA Monitor*, March 2001

Anielski, Mark, "The Genuine Progress Indicator – A Principled Approach to Economics," *Pembina Institute,*(www.piad.ab.ca/green/gpi.htm)

Averitt, Robert, *The Dual Economy* (New York: Norton, 1968)

Bakker, Isa, "Canada's Social Wage in an Open Economy," in Daniel Drache and Meric Gertler, eds., *The New Era of Global Competition* (Montreal and Kingston: McGill-Queen's University Press, 1991)

Bank of Canada, *Banking and Financial Statistics*, September 2001

Barnet, Richard, and Ronald Muller, *Global Reach* (New York: Simon and Schuster, 1974)

Barrett, Chris, "Debt Crises in the Third World," in P.A. O'Hara ,ed., *Encyclopedia of Political Economy* (London: Routledge, 1999)

Bazelon, David, "What is Property?" in David Mermelstein, ed., *Economics: Mainstream Readings and Radical Critiques* (New York: Random House, 1970)

Beauchesne, Eric, "Taxes dip – but still devour 47.5% of income," *National Post*, June 13, 2001

Bellan, Ruben, *The Unnecessary Evil* (Toronto: McClelland and Stewart, 1986)

Bellon, Bertrand, and Jorge Niosi, *The Decline of the American Economy* (Montreal: Black Rose, 1988)

Berggren, Christian, *Alternatives to Lean Production* (Ithaca, N.Y.: Cornell University Press, 1993)

Blau, Francine, Marianne Ferber and Anne Winkler, *The Economics of Women, Men, and Work* (Upper Saddle River, NJ: Prentice-Hall, 2002)

Bliss, Michael, *A Living Profit* (Toronto: McClelland and Stewart, 1974)

Bowles, Samuel, and Richard Edwards, *Understanding Capitalism* (New York: Harper and Row, 1985)

Bradwin, Edmund, *The Bunkhouse Man* (Toronto: University of Toronto Press, 1972)

Braverman, Harry, *Labor and Monopoly Capital* (New York: Monthly Review Press, 1974)

Bronfenbrenner, Kate, "The Effects of Plant Closing or Threat of Plant Closing on the Right of Workers to Organize" Report to the Labor Secretariat of the North American Commission for Labor Cooperation, 1997 (www.ilr.cornell.edu)

Butler, Gavan, "Fiscal Crisis Of The State," *Encyclopedia of Political Economy,* in P.A. O'Hara, ed., *Encyclopedia of Political Economy* (London: Routledge, 1999)

Cameron, Duncan, *The Free Trade Deal* (Toronto: Lorimer, 1988)

Campbell, Bruce, Maria Teresa Guitierrez Laces, Andrew Jackson, Mehrene Larudel and Matthew Sanger, *Pulling Apart: The Deterioration of Employment and Income in North America Under Free Trade* (Ottawa: Canadian Centre for Policy Alternatives, 1999)

CCPA Monitor, "How the corporate agenda was legislated by Liberal and Tory governments, 1980–1997," *CCPA Monitor*, November 1997

Canadian Labour Congress, "Sweatshop Alert," http://www.clc-ctc.ca/publications/mag_archive/ sweatshop_alert_e.pdf

Canadian Encyclopedia, The, Second edition, "Potlatch," (Edmonton: Hurtig, 1988)

Card, David, and Richard Freeman, *Small Differences that Matter* (Chicago: University of Chicago Press, 1993)

Chandler, Alfred, *The Visible Hand: The Managerial Revolution in American Business* (Cambridge, MA: Harvard University Press, 1977)

Chang, Ha-Joon, *Kicking Away the Ladder – Development Strategy in Historical Perspective* (London: Anthem Press, 2002)

Cherry, Robert, Christine D'Onofirio, Cigdem Kurdas, Thomas Michl, Fred Moseley and Michele Napels, eds., *The Imperiled Economy, Book I: Macroeconomics from a Left Perspective* (New York: Union for Radical Political Economics, 1987)

Chossudovsky, Michael, *The Globalization of Poverty* (Penang, Malaysia: Third World Network, 1997)

Chuchman, George, "Regulation, Competition and Privatization in the Electric Utility Industries," Unpublished paper (Department of Economics, University of Manitoba, 1995)

Clark, S., and M. Stephenson, "Housework as Real Work" in K. Lundy and B. Warme, eds., *Work in the Canadian Context* (Toronto: Butterworths, 1981)

Clarke, Tony, "Silent Coup: Confronting the Big Business Takeover Of Canada," *CCPA Monitor*, July/August 1997

Clement, Wallace, *The Canadian Corporate Elite.* (Toronto: McClelland and Stewart, 1975)

Clement, Wallace, and Glen Williams, "Introduction," in Wallace Clement and Glen Williams eds., *The New Canadian Political Economy* (Kingston: McGill-Queen's, 1989)

Cook, Malcolm, and Peter Cribbett, "Transfer Pricing," in Philip O'Hara, ed., *Encyclopedia of Political Economy* (Routledge: 1999, p. 1167)

Costanza, Robert, Herman Daly and Joy Bartholomew, *An Introduction to Ecological Economics* (Boca Raton, Florida: St. Lucie Press, 1997)

Cozier, Barry, "Wage and Price Dynamics in Canada," Bank of Canada Research Department Working Paper, November (Bank of Canada, Ottawa) 1991

Daly, Herman, *Toward a Steady-State Economy* (San Francisco: Freeman, 1973)

Dobbin, Murray, *The Myth of the Good Corporate Citizen* (Toronto: Stoddard, 1998)

Doeringer, Peter, and Michael Piore, *Internal Labor Markets and Manpower Analysis*, 2nd edition (New York: M.E. Sharpe, 1985)

Drache, Daniel, and Harry Glasbeek, *The Changing Workplace* (Toronto: Lorimer, 1992)

Drache, Daniel, and Meric Gertler, eds., *The New Era of Global Competition* (Montreal: McGill-Queen's Universities Press, 1991)

Dunlop, John, "Wage Contours," in Michael Piore, ed., *Unemployment and Inflation* (White Plains, NY: M.E. Sharpe, 1979)

Edwards, Richard, *Contested Terrain* (New York Basic Books, 1979)

Freeman, Richard, "The College Labor Market," in Richard Freeman, *Labor Markets in Action* (Cambridge, Mass.: Harvard University Press, 1989)

Galbraith, John Kenneth, *The New Industrial State* (Boston: Houghton Mifflin, 1967)

———, *Money: Whence it Came and Where it Went* (Boston: Houghton Mifflin, 1975)

Gonick, Cy, *The Great Economic Debate* (Toronto: Lorimer, 1987)

———, *Inflation or Depression* (Toronto: Lorimer, 1975)

Gordon, David, Richard Edwards and Michael Reich, *Segmented Work, Divided Workers* (Cambridge: Cambridge University Press, 1982)

Gordon, David, Thomas Weisskopf and Samuel Bowles, "Power, Accumulation and Crisis: The Rise and Demise of the Postwar Social Structure of Accumulation" in Robert Cherry et al., eds., *The Imperiled Economy* (New York: Union for Radical Political Economics, 1987)

Grant, Hugh, and Frank Strain, "'The Power of the Sack': The Cost of Job Loss in Canada, 1953–1985," *Labour/Le Travail*, 25 (Spring) 1990

Greider, William, "The Right and US Trade Law: Invalidating the 20th Century," *The Nation*,

October 15, 2001 (www.thenation.com)

Harvey, John, "Bretton Woods System," in Philip O'Hara, ed., *Encyclopedia of Political Economy* (London: Routledge, 1999)

Heilbroner, Robert, *The Worldly Philosophers* (New York; Simon and Schuster, 1972)

Henwood, Doug, *Wall Street: How It Works and for Whom* (New York: Verso, 1997)

Heron, Craig, and Robert Storey eds., *On the Job* (Montreal: McGill-Queen's University Press, 1985)

Human Resources and Development Canada (HRDC), Departmental Performance Report (Ottawa: HRDC, 2001)

Jackson, Andrew, and David Robinson, *Falling Behind: The State of Working Canada, 2000* (Ottawa: Canadian Centre for Policy Alternatives, 2000)

Jackson, Andrew, "Impact of the Canada-US Free Trade Agreement (FTA) and the North American Free Trade Agreement (NAFTA) on Canadian Labour Markets," in Bruce Campbell et al., eds., *Pulling Apart* (Ottawa: Canadian Centre for Policy Alternatives, 2000)

Jacobs, Michael, *The Green Economy* (Vancouver: UBC Press, 1993)

Jain, Harish, "Employment and Pay Discrimination in Canada," in John Anderson and Morley Gunderson, eds., *Union-Management Relations in Canada* (Don Mills: Addison-Wesley, 1982)

Kealey, Gregory, ed., *Canada Investigates Industrialism: The Royal Commission on the Relations of Labour and Capital 1889* (Toronto: University of Toronto Press, 1973)

Kerr, Clark, "The Balkanization of Labour Markets," in Lloyd Reynolds et al., eds., *Readings in Labor Economics and Labour Relations*, Fifth edition (Englewood Cliffs, NJ: Prentice Hall, 1991)

Keynes, J.M., *The General Theory of Employment, Interest and Money* (London: Mcmillan, 1961 (c. 1936)

Kierans, Eric, and Walter Stewart, *Wrong End of the Rainbow* (Don Mills: Collins, 1988)

Klein, Seth, "Loss of Professions to U.S. Exaggerated," *CCPA Monitor*, March 1999

Kotz, David, "Radical Theories of Inflation"; and Part 5: "Macroeconomic Policy," in Robert Cherry et al., eds., *The Imperiled Economy* (New York: Union for Radical Political Economics, 1987)

Krahn, Harvey, and Graham Lowe, *Work, Industry and Canadian Society,* 3rd edition (Toronto: Nelson, 1996)

Krugman, Paul, "California screaming," *New York Times*, December 10, 2000

Kuttner, Robert, "Markets are Fundamentally Amoral," *CCPA Monitor*, June 1997

Kwoka, John. "Pricing in the Electric Power Industry: The Influence of Ownership, Competition, and Integration," Paper presented at the American Economic Association Meetings, Boston, 1993

Lamontagne, Maurice, *Business Cycles in Canada* (Toronto: James Lorimer Ltd. in association with the Canadian Institute for Economic Policy, 1984)

Leband, David, and Daowei Zhang, "America's Been Bushwhacked," *Globe and Mail*, August 18, 2001

Lee, Marc, "Business Takeovers Boon to Investors, but not Consumers," *CCPA Monitor*, February 2000

Levitt, Kari, *Silent Surrender: The Multinational Corporation in Canada* (Toronto: Macmillan, 1970)

Littler, Craig, *The Development of the Labour Process in Capitalist Societies* (London: Heinemann, 1982)

Livernash, Ronald, "Job Clusters" in Michael Piore, ed., *Unemployment and Inflation* (White Plains, NY: M. E. Sharpe, 1979)

Livingstone, David, *The Education-Jobs Gap* (Toronto: Garamond, 1999)

Lowe, Graham, and Harvey Krahn eds., *Work in Canada* (Scarborough: Nelson, 1993)

Lowe, Graham, *Women in the Administrative Revolution* (Toronto: University of Toronto Press, 1987)

MacLeod, Greg, *From Mondragon to America* (Sydney, NS: University College of Cape Breton, 1997)

McMillan, Alan, *Native Peoples and Cultures of Canada* (Vancouver: Douglas and McIntyre, 1995)

McQuaig, Linda, *All You Can Eat: Greed, Lust and the New Capitalism* (Toronto: Penguin, 2001)

National Farmers' Union, "Submission to the Senate Standing Committee on Agriculture and Forestry," *CCPA Monitor,* May 2000

Naylor, Tom, *Dominion of Debt* (Montreal: Black Rose, 1985)

———, *Hot Money and the Politics of Debt* (Toronto: McClelland and Stewart, 1987)

Nickerson, Mike, "Measuring Well-Being in Canada," *CCPA Monitor,* April 2000

Niosi, Jorge, *Canadian Capitalism: A Study of Power in the Canadian Business Establishment* (Toronto: Lorimer, 1981)

Olsen, Gregg, *The Politics of the Welfare State: Canada, Sweden, and the United States* (Don Mills, ON: Oxford University Press, 2002)

Organization for Economic Cooperation and Development (OECD), Economic Outlook, June 1999

Palley, Thomas, "The Role of Institutions and Policies in Creating High European Unemployment: The Evidence," Working Paper 336, Levy Institute, August 2001, (www.levy.org/docs/wrkpap/papers/336.html)

Panitch, Leo, and Donald Swartz, *The Assault on Trade Union Freedoms* (Toronto: Garamond, 1993)

Phillips, Paul, and Bogomil Ferfila, "The Legacy of Socialist Self-Management: Worker Ownership and Worker Participation in Management in Slovenia," *Socialist Studies Bulletin,* 61 (July-September), 2000

———, *The Rise and Fall of the Third Way: Yugoslavia 1945–1991* (Halifax: Fernwood, 1992)

Phillips, Paul, and Erin Phillips, *Women and Work* (Toronto: Lorimer, 2000)

Piore, Michael, "Introduction," in Michael Piore, ed., *Unemployment and Inflation,* (White Plains, NY: M.E. Sharpe, 1979)

Polanyi-Levitt, Kari, "Some Books Refuse to Go Away", *Signalling LEFT,* vol. 2 # 2, (June 2000) p. 12

Polanyi, Karl, *The Great Transformation* (Boston: Beacon, 1944)

Redefining Progress, *The Genuine Progress Indicator,* 1998 Update

Reiter, Ester, "Life in a Fast-Food Factory," in Craig Heron and Robert Storey, eds., *On the Job* (Kingston and Montreal: McGill-Queens University Press, 1986)

Rinehart, James, *The Tyranny of Work,* 3rd edition (Toronto: Harcourt Brace, 1996)

Ross, Arthur, "Orbits of Coercive Comparison," in Michael Piore, ed., *Unemployment and Inflation* (White Plains, NY: M.E. Sharpe, 1979)

Ross, David, and Peter Usher, *From the Roots Up* (Toronto: Lorimer, 1987)

Samuelson, Robert, "The Fed: Another myth on its way out?" *Newsweek,* October 22, 2001

Shrybman, Steven, *A Citizen's Guide to the World Trade Organization* (Ottawa: Canadian Centre For Policy Alternatives and Lorimer, 1999)

Stanford, Jim, *Paper Boom* (Ottawa and Toronto: Canadian Centre for Policy Alternatives and Lorimer, 1999)

Statistics Canada, "Households' Unpaid Work: Measurement and Valuation" (catalogue13-603-E, no. 3) (Ottawa: Statistics Canada, 1994)

———. *Survey of Labour and Income Dynamics* (Ottawa: Statistics Canada, 1994)

———. *Employment, Earnings and Hours,* (catalogue SC 72-002) (Ottawa: Statistics Canada, January 1998)

————. *Labour Force Historical Review* (catalogue 71-F0004XCB) (Ottawa: Statistics Canada, 2001)

————. *National Income and Expenditure Accounts* (catalogue SC 13-001-XPB) (Ottawa: Statistics Canada, 2001)

————. *Historical Statistics* (Ottawa: Statistics Canada, 2001)

————. *Cansim* (Ottawa: Statistics Canada, 2002)

Struthers, James, *No Fault of Their Own* (Toronto: University of Toronto Press, 1983)

Taylor, S., "Foreign Ownership and Control in Canada," *Canadian Economic Observer* (Ottawa, Statistics Canada, June 2001)

Tobin, James, "How an international transactions tax would work," *CCPA Monitor*, October 1995

Thurow, Lester, "A Job Competition Model," in Michael Piore, ed., *Unemployment and Inflation* (White Plains, NY: M. E. Sharpe, 1979)

Urquhart, M.C., and K.A.H. Buckley, eds., *Historical Statistics of Canada* (Cambridge, UK: Cambridge University Press, 1965)

U.S. Foundation for Taxpayer and Consumer Rights, "Hoax: … How Deregulation Let the Power Industry Steal $71 Billion from California," (www.consumerwatchdog.org/utilities/rp/rp002169.pdf)

Vanek, Jaroslav, *The Participatory Economy* (Ithaca: Cornell University Press, 1971)

Vickery, William, "Fifteen Fatal Fallacies of Financial Fundamentalism: A Disquisition on Demand Side Economics," (www.columbia.edu/dlc/wp/econ/vickrey.html)

Vorst, Jesse, and Jim Silver, eds., *Why No Free Trade?* (Winnipeg: Society for Socialist Studies, 1988)

Walkom, Tomas, "'Free Trade' Pacts Are Really All About Making Governments Subservient To Business," *CCPA Monitor*, July/August 2001

Waring, Marilyn, *Three Masquerades: Essays on Equality, Work and Hu(man) Rights* (Toronto: University of Toronto Press, 1996)

Weisbrot, Mark, Robert Naiman and Joyce Kim, "The Emperor Has No Growth: Declining Economic Growth Rates in the Era of Globalization," Center for Economic and Policy Research, September 2000 (www.cepr.net/IMF/TheEmporerHasNoGrowth.htm)

Werther, William, Keith Davis, Hermann Schwind and Hari Das, *Canadian Human Resource Management*, 3rd edition (Toronto: McGraw-Hill Ryerson, 1990)

Wolfe, David, "The Rise and Demise of the Keynesian Era in Canada: Economic Policy, 1930-1982" in Michael Cross and Gregory Kealey, eds., *Modern Canada* (Toronto: McClelland and Stewart, 1984)

Working Group on the WTO/MAI, *A Citizen's Guide to the World Trade Organization* (New York: Apex, 1999)

Yalnizyan, Armine, *The Growing Gap* (Toronto, Centre for Social Justice, 1998)

About the Author

Paul Phillips was born in Hong Kong to Canadian schoolteachers teaching in the Orient, though he grew up on the west coast of B.C., in Vancouver, Nanaimo and Victoria. His first two years of university were taken at Victoria College, now the University of Victoria. He completed his B.A. (Honours) and M.A. in Economics at the University of Saskatchewan and went on to complete a Ph.D. in Labour Economics and Labour Relations at the London School of Economics (1967). Much of the material of his thesis was incorporated into his first book, *No Power Greater: A Century of Labour in British Columbia* (1967). He returned to British Columbia from London to teach at the Unversity of British Columbia and the University of Victoria for two years before leaving academic life to become Research Director of the B.C. Federation of Labour (1966–68). He returned to teaching in 1968 at Simon Fraser University before accepting a permanent position at the University of Manitoba in 1969 where he has been since.

At Manitoba, Paul Phillips has been involved not only with advising and assisting government (Chair, Milk Prices Review Board; Research Director and Executive Secretary, Manitoba Economic Development Advisory Board; Research Director, Manitoba Labour Management Legislative Review Commission; member of the Provincial Panel of Labour Arbitrators, among other posts), he was also involved in establishing the University of Manitoba Labour Studies Program (of which, on several occasions, he has served as Program Co-ordinator) and the Global Political Economy Program. He has also been active for many years on the executive of the Society for Socialist Studies.

Paul Phillips has published numerous books, including several editions of economics principles texts, but is perhaps best known for two Canadian political economy studies: *Regional Disparities* and *Women and Work* (with Erin Phillips). He has also co-authored a number of books on Yugoslavia and Slovenia with his colleague Professor Bogomil Ferfila. In addition to his primary appointment at the University of Manitoba, he is currently also Professor of American Studies at the University of Ljubljana in Slovenia (where he also teaches labour economics) and Adjunct Professor of History at the Okanagan University College in British Columbia.

Index